REFORMING

THE WHOLE WO

Reforming the Catholic Tradition: The Whole Word for Whole Church

Proceedings of the 6th Annual Convivium Irenicum

Presented May 30 – June 2, 2018

Edited by Joseph Minich

ISBN: 1-949716-93-7

ISBN-13: 978-1-949716-93-1

Front cover image taken from Job Adriaenszoon Berckheyde (1630–93), *Interior of the St Bavo Church at Haarlem* (Gemäldegalerie Alte Meister, Dresden, Germany).

Cover design by Rachel Rosales, Orange Peal Design.

"And he gave the apostles, the prophets, the evangelists, the shepherds and teachers, to equip the saints for the work of ministry, for building up the body of Christ, until we all attain to the unity of the faith and of the knowledge of the Son of God, to mature manhood, to the measure of the stature of the fullness of Christ, so that we may no longer be children, tossed to and fro by the waves and carried about by every wind of doctrine, by human cunning, by craftiness in deceitful schemes. Rather, speaking the truth in love, we are to grow up in every way into him who is the head, into Christ, from whom the whole body, joined and held together by every joint with which it is equipped, when each part is working properly, makes the body grow so that it builds itself up in love."

—Ephesians 4:11-16

LIST OF CONTRIBUTORS

Rev. Dr. Christopher Dorn currently resides in Holland, Michigan. He serves as chair of Christians Uniting in Song and Prayer, an ecumenical fellowship in Holland dedicated to promoting and practicing worship that embodies sound liturgical principles. He serves as pastor of First Presbyterian Church in Ionia, Michigan and preaches occasionally at Redeemer Presbyterian Church in Holland.

Steven Duby (Ph.D, University of St. Andrews) is Associate Professor of Theology at Grand Canyon University. He is author of *Divine Simplicity: A Dogmatic Account* (Bloomsbury) and the forthcoming volume *God in Himself: Scripture, Metaphysics, and the Task of Christian Theology* (IVP Academic). He and his wife, Jodi, live in Arizona with their four children.

Andre Gazal (Ph.D, Trinity Evangelical Divinity School) teaches church history for North Greenville University, Trinity International University, and Nicolet Bible Institute, and serves as the Assistant Project Editor for the *Reformation Commentary on Scripture* (IVP Academic). He is the author of *Scripture and the Royal Supremacy in Tudor England: The Use of Old Testament Historical Narrative,* and *Believers' Baptism in Cromwellian Ireland: Thomas Patient and his Doctrine of Baptism,* as well as co-editor of *Defending the Faith: John Jewel and the Elizabethan Church.*

David Haines (Ph.D, Université Laval) lives with his wife and their 4 children in Québec. David is Associate Professor of Philosophy and Religion at VIU, Associate Professor of Ethics at SEMBEQ, and has taught history of Christian Apologetics at FTE-Acadia. He is also the founding president of Association Axiome, an association of French Evangelical scholars, and the Christian Philosophy Apologetics Center. His academic research focuses on ancient and medieval metaphysics, C.S. Lewis, Thomism, and natural theology.

Bradford Littlejohn (Ph.D, University of Edinburgh) is a scholar and writer in the fields of political theology, Christian ethics, and Reformation history. He is the President of the Davenant Institute and also serves as Headmaster of Loudoun Classical School in Purcellville, VA, and recently served as Visiting Assistant Professor of Political Theory at Patrick Henry College. He is the author of several books, including *The Peril and Promise of Christian Liberty: Richard Hooker, the Puritans, and Protestant Political Theology*.

Joseph Minich (Ph.D, The University of Texas at Dallas) is Editor-in-Chief of The Davenant Press and author of *Enduring Divine Absence*. He lives in Garland, Texas, with his wife and children.

Iain Provan is the Marshall Sheppard Professor of Biblical Studies at Regent College Vancouver. He is the author of several books, including *The Reformation and the Right Reading of Scripture* (Baylor University Press, 2017).

Gregory Soderberg is the Academic Dean at LAMP Seminary RDU, in Raleigh and a Proctor for the BibleMesh Institute. He is completing a Ph.D in historical theology at the Free University of Amsterdam.

CONTENTS

INTRODUCTION

Joseph Minich, The Davenant Institute

IN HIS *Deconstructing Evangelicalism*, D. G. Hart argues that the label "evangelical" is so elastic that it is useless for solidifying any theological or ecclesiastical identity. And indeed, it has not been uncommon in the last decade to watch theologian after theologian problematize or obsess about labels—evangelical or otherwise. Undoubtedly, some would connect the identity crisis of evangelicalism specifically to the identity crisis of Protestantism more broadly. The proliferations of thousands upon thousands of denominations in the West, and the rootlessness of much of its practices and doctrines, have been the background content of "catholicity" movements from the Mercersburg movement in the middle of the nineteenth century, to the "Reformed catholicities" of the twenty-first—each claiming the label "catholicity" in its own distinctive way. Some see it as a supplementation to their Reformed identity, some see the former as the modification of the latter, and others conflate the two altogether. Between these two moments have been similarly motivated projects far outside Reformed circles—in the paleo-orthodoxy of Thomas Oden, the attempted recovery of ancient practices in the emerging church movement, or (perhaps most obviously) the number of persons who have converted from evangelicalism to Roman Catholicism, Eastern Orthodoxy, Jewish Messianic Christianity, Anglo-Catholicism, and so forth.

It is important to note, however, that these questions of identity (and authority) are not raised in an existential or cultural vacuum. Indeed, there is a rough parallel between the entire conversation about "Reformed catholicity," and the current conversation and controversy over what it means to be "American" or "Western." Roughly the same fault lines exist between those who want to go back to the Founding Fathers, to a particular interpretation of the Constitution, or to the founding sources of Western thought. These discourses can even go together. Not a few conversions to the Roman Catholic Church have been attended by the corresponding hunch that it is in the see of Rome (or Constantinople) that we can find a mechanism for the preservation of Western values in general, or American values in particular—especially in light of the failure of other American-identity "recovery" projects. The cobelligerencies on this score are fascinating to behold.

And in each of these debates, there are legitimate questions to be asked, and important lines of inquiry to follow. There is some value in speaking about the democracy of the dead. There is wisdom in a kind of deference to the opinions of ancestors whose vantage point and sense of the world was often much larger than our own. Indeed, many have pointed out that the Reformers often rhetorically justified their project by pointing to Rome as the innovator and themselves as simply trying to preserve the simple Christian faith and attendant practices.

However, the repetition of this claim can cover a multitude of historical and strategic sins. While it is true that Rome could be condemned for innovations, the Reformers were also acutely aware that many of the traditions they condemned were very old, and had been part of Christendom for close to a millennium. To this extent, therefore, there is no way and no reason to deradicalize the Reformation. The call for Reform irreducibly implied that the institutional church could be wrong, and be severely wrong, for a very long time. Tradition could be wrong. One's fathers could be wrong. The vast majority of Christendom could be wrong, and wrong in awful and long-lasting ways.

We are still adjusting to the cultural shock of this claim and its aftereffects—a claim that stands in as much tension with the Roman see as with the instincts of much traditional human culture. Whatever else the Reformers taught, and whatever else they emphasized, no realistic reading of their message could but require the church to recast the extent and limits of its authority. Many have sought to disconnect the Reformation from the fallout that occurred in the Enlightenment, but the organic connection between the two moments must be admitted. The "universal acid" of their catastrophic claim had the capacity to eat through "authorities" of a more general than a merely ecclesiastical sort. Though largely a dialectical rather than a linear development, the crisis of authority showed up in philosophy (the reliability of the senses and reason), in theology (the historical and factual reliability of the texts), in politics (the rights of kings and governments), and so forth.

Exhibit A of this effect has, of course, been the situation in the United States of America since its inception. Denomination after denomination, disintegrated tradition after disintegrated tradition, has rendered America—for all practical purposes—an unhappy home for "tradition" in general. Some of this is cultural, and some of it is the simple manifestation of its geographic expanse, the diversity of its inhabitants (from its inception), and the constitutional refusal to prevent difference from flourishing. But in this context, the theological and cultural free-for-all has increasingly rendered its inhabits despairing of an identity (a conundrum that accounts for all sorts of movements in American culture).

Before evaluating this phenomenon, it is worth highlighting it as a simple fact. However we respond to it, the above nevertheless describes the situation in which we find ourselves. And even if we take the above-mentioned strategies, these are but Band-Aids on forces that are (at least apparently) far more powerful and prevalent than any of our suggested antidotes in Reformed confessionalism, Roman Catholicity, or the dawn of a future united church. And, as I have already stated, bound up with such strategies are usually prognostications and therapies with respect to the destiny of the West more generally.

But there is a different response to offer. What if this situation is not a problem to be overcome, but an opportunity for a kind of growth that can only come from the very consumption of heritage that feels like a crisis to us? And note that no "return to our roots" can ever recover the past. To choose one's theological or cultural roots can never be the same thing as simply *having* them. And what can be obscured in that motion, therefore, is that we exist in an irreducible state of unmoored and unhinged agency in respect of the most fundamental questions of truth and life. We are forced to be ecclesiastically and culturally free, and no free conversion to Rome, or sentiment about our confessions, can erase this.

Indeed, our one and only option (even if retrospectively redescribed) is to *make choices* about what seems most prudent to us given what we can see and know from our own vantage point. And it is precisely in the irreducibility of this choice that Reformed catholicity can be an aid. The Reformed synthesis is cryptically and seminally captured in Luther's speech at Worms—a manifesto of the Protestant movement, itself the surrogate of anything that we retroactively project upon and preserve in the "West." To wit, common to man are God's two books of Scripture and reason. And we ultimately must submit and subject our conscience to these alone. Indeed, reason is the most "universal" (i.e., catholic) tool of all. The project of the Enlightenment, on this score, was not defective for its pretension to universality, but for its particular conflations of the particular with the universal and vice versa. But what we see in the Reformation, and in the Protestant tradition that followed it, was an "in principle" openness to revision, to maturity, to growth in grace (perhaps paralleled in the openness of all modern constitutions to "amendment"). If the Reformation was a legitimate moment, then the church must always be open to new understanding. And for this reason, the Reformed churches rarely received even the ecumenical creeds as inerrant in themselves, but because they consciously agreed with the consensual exegesis they represented. But "receiving" the creeds is a far cry from simply assuming them. It is not that the doctrine is different, but one's relationship to it most certainly is—just as the child's relationship to food is different than that of the preparer of the meal.

And this can sound scary. Letting the buck stop at "Scripture" and "reason" sure sounds like a recipe for disaster. And indeed, anti-Protestant polemicists and shamefaced Protestants make much of this concern. But again, this simply is the situation of Christendom, and it does not change simply because one decides to treat a particular creed or church as infallible. One makes that choice, hopefully, as a free and responsible individual. Moreover, the only appeals one has to persuade others to do the same are, ironically, Scripture and reason. Scary or not, this is our situation. Reformed catholicity, then, is simply to put in discursive and programmatic terms what we already find ourselves doing when we're doing anything useful. We *all* behave like Protestants now, and radically so.

But what I want to claim here is that the Reformed solution was not merely an unfortunate accommodation to tumultuous times, but the solidification of a vital project that began in the early church and which was the only game in town for a proper orientation to the modern world that followed it. In truth, the only path through the thicket of modernity is to be found in self-possessed responsibility toward the future. What the Reformers left us with was not only a body of doctrine, but a pattern of thinking (in the largest Renaissance sense of this term) and of exegesis. Whatever the controversy, the relentless push of the Protestant project was to understand the Scriptures more and to understand reality more. It is in this intersection that God speaks, and the unity of the church and of society was to be found through that common frame of reference rather than outside of it. To stand in this project today is not merely to agree with our Protestant fathers on each point of doctrine, but to courageously remain in a project that pushes at the boundaries of our knowledge and wisdom.

It is obvious, then, that what I describe here as "Reformed catholicity" has little in common with those versions of it that think of Protestantism as requiring principled supplementation from other traditions. What those proposals miss is that the principle of maturity and supplementation is already built into the project's first principles. As such, what we require is not some Protestantism "plus" package, but rather to recover and absorb the wisdom of our Protestant fathers themselves who thought with extreme care about the principles of theological and cultural maturity. And interestingly, there is a parallel here with discourse about the fate of the West generally. Many think of it as requiring principled supplementation with foreign elements. But as Remi Brague (*Eccentric Culture*) has demonstrated, whatever can be reasonably described as the "West" has always had (even "external") supplementation and maturation built into its DNA.

In any case, of course, part of Protestant discourse involves sophisticated accounts of tradition as a mediate authority. While the books of God's revelation remain our ultimate authority, the tradition of the church and the large community of interpreters (exegetes, scientists, politicians, parents, etc.) are involved in a collective project. The reason we should respect the fathers, listen to other traditions, and so forth is not because they are even functionally of the same authority as God's revelation itself, but because it would be stupid not to. Just as no physicist or mathematician should ignore the work of his or her predecessors, so no exegete or theologian or parent or sociologist should ignore the enormous amount of work that has gone before them. The threshold of persuasion against a distinctive point of the Lutheran or Reformed faith might be only so high. The threshold of persuasion over against a doctrine of the ecumenical creeds is extraordinarily high for precisely this reason. But unless we believe in justification by perfect doctrine alone (rather than in a gospel and a God who transcend our discourse about them), then this need worry us no more than it does in other relatively fixed disciplines and discourses. Mathematicians, after all, do not fret over the possible falsification of the Pythagorean theorem, even if they do not think Pythagoras was divinely inspired.

Still, one might be concerned that no amount of strategic deference to our fathers could prevent the chaos of identity in these times. But why should this be the goal? Once again, there is no "solution" that will fully get rid of this challenge and no forthcoming Sanhedrin of reality that will download its declarations into our collective consciousness. Whining about our lack of such a resource, or propping up a parody of one, is simply to avoid the calling that is right in front of our faces. Moreover, it is to reject the far more interesting project that we seek to carry out faithfully *coram deo.*

What is this project? Like Adam in the Garden, we are to bring order to the wilderness. We are to bring whatever wisdom we can muster to bear upon the small piece of the jungle in which we find ourselves. The Protestant project pushes us outside of this comfort zone. Rather than retreating to an enclave that we can perfectly predict, we are rather to be mature, to trust God, to understand and receive the benefits of our ancestors' labor, and to push forward into a confusing future with both the Bible and the world before us. And doing this wisely (once again) involves some deference to authorities past and present, as well as particular postures of character and heart that render one open to truth and repentance. Moreover, and most importantly, this means that the maintenance and proliferation of the Protestant faith is a proliferation that comes from a place of self-possessed persuasion rather than team spirit. We speak the truth of Christ and of His world not because this is our chosen community, but because (perhaps via our community) we are persuaded—truly persuaded—that this is the reality in which all humans commonly dwell. And from that vantage point, we can speak to our neighbors with the dignity, ethos, and poise that helps to persuade other men.

And it is this project of a "culture of persuasion" that remains the genius of the Protestantism and of whatever we want to preserve of the West more generally. A culture of persuasion is a culture that demands responsible ownership of the world, and the cultivation of spaces where men can engage and help craft one another. The task of "Reformed catholicity," then, is the task of persuading other men (via Scripture and reason) that Protestant first principles are the project in which they ought to be engaged—or indeed, in which they are rightfully engaged—whether they like it or not. It is the task of pursuing the truth in wisdom. The creeds and confessions are not accidental or discardable to this pursuit, but are received and perpetuated precisely as that of which we are persuaded.

What the Protestant project afforded each Christian was a greater theological, rhetorical, and cultural capacity to self-possess the riches of their own faith and involvement in its expression in this world. Whether or not the Reformers would have liked the modern world, the discourse in which they engaged was uniquely suited to helping us navigate it. Our modern crisis of identity, of course, is not merely due to the influence of Reformation ideas, but the entirely history of modern globalization and trade, the proliferation of modern technologies, and so on. And what has disintegrated in the massive rupture of modernity is any plausibility of outsourcing our ecclesiastical and cultural responsibility to surrogate believers and reasoners (whether church, confession, or community). This has led to all varieties of Pharisaism. Rather, the Christian man lives before God and with his neighbor. And responding to both, he internalizes wisdom and brings it to bear on his small piece of the world. What the modern order affords us, arguably, is not merely a threat to what ought to be the goals of the Christian faith but, rather, a major opportunity for ordinary believers (all priests) to take a more prominent role in the task of dominion. The chaos is a simple fact. But the ordering effect of wisdom is up to all of us (each in our own way).

Arguably, then, the Protestant project is just the human project writ small. Consequently, its challenges and its tools are as wide as the human race and its resources. And if the particular articles of the Protestant faith are indeed correspondent to the Scriptures and to the world, then we should not fear that they lack innate persuasive gravitas. Precisely to the extent that we point persons back to the Scriptures and to reality, we will point them to the law and the gospel as summarized in our doctrine. Only it will not exist as the nomenclature of a team member, but rather as the vital and orienting truth that just *is* reality for them. Our situation is no tragedy. It is a vital moment for us to cultivate the church and the world.

The articles of this volume each aid us in the pursuit of this project in their own way. The first two essays, in particular, help us to properly define "catholicity." Brad Littlejohn tackles a fundamental incoherence in many modern proposals for catholicity or ecumenism: their rejection of the

Protestant doctrine of the invisible church and insistence that we must prioritize visible forms of unity. Such proposals, which have in recent years found their way from the mainline ecumenical movement into Reformed and evangelical discourse, tend to equivocate constantly on what exactly is meant by visible unity, and whether it relates to the *esse* or the *bene esse* of the church. Clarity on such matters is essential, for if formal structures of visible unity are prioritized as essential to the one, holy, catholic church, we will be hard pressed to long avoid embracing an exclusivist sectarianism—whether that of the separatist cult or that of the Roman church. An authentic catholicity that is able to articulate and witness to the unity of the scattered and sometimes divided members of Christ's body, Littlejohn argues, actually *requires* the doctrine of the invisible church. In other words, we can't actually hold on to the "catholicity" part of "Reformed catholicity" unless we also hold on to the "Reformed" part. Following Littlejohn, Andre Gazal's essay explores the manner in which Bishop John Jewel (1522–1571), the first major apologist of the Elizabethan church, attempted to redefine catholicity in order to vindicate England's Protestant national church as "truly catholic" by reappropriating the Vincentian Canon and the Cyprianic conception of the episcopate. Another central feature of Jewel's enterprise was his transfer of "catholic authority" from general councils to regional and national synods.

The three following essays detail the relationship between Reformed catholicity in relation to the doctrines of God and Scripture more specifically. Steven Duby engages recent discussions among Roman Catholic, Eastern Orthodox and Protestant theologians, in which the topic of the so-called 'analogy of being' has played a significant role. Often Protestant theology, in the wake of Karl Barth, is portrayed as having little room for an analogical relationship between (sinful) creatures and God the Creator. In some circles this has yielded an assumption that a consistently Protestant approach to human knowledge of God will reject the project of natural theology and hold that human beings can know God only on the basis of God's grace given in Christ and the act of faith. Contrary to this, Duby argues that a Reformed Protestant approach to human knowledge of God does in fact have room for an 'analogy of being' and can, in constructive dialogue with medieval and contemporary Roman Catholic theologians, pursue a truly catholic vision of the knowledge of God available by nature. Following this, Iain Provan challenges the prominent claim within some recent discussion of Protestantism and catholicity that much Protestant exegesis of Scripture has been lamentably out of step with the glorious tradition of patristic Scripture-reading, which in turn has commonly been represented as grounded in apostolic authority. Provan argues, however, that the magisterial Reformers were in fact correct in their judgments about the unwarranted and dangerous nature of much pre-Reformation exegesis, and that these judgments themselves were grounded in patristic perspectives (i.e., in tradition). Protestants should not, therefore, welcome contemporary initiatives aimed at resurrecting such "spiritual" readings of Scripture. Finally, David Haines addresses the question of how can we "infallibly" determine which doctrines are necessary for a person to be considered orthodox if the only authority for Protestant theology is the Bible, as interpreted by the individual reader? Any approach to solving "the Protestant problem," he argues, must be multifaceted. For example, one must reconsider the doctrine of *sola scriptura* and the notion of individual interpretation; the interaction between the individual and the interpretative community; the role of Christian doctors and of the Holy Spirit; how we should understand theological authority, truth, infallibility, certainty, consistent hermeneutics, and so forth. Part of the solution to the Protestant problem is, Haines proposes, found in the role of natural knowledge in biblical interpretation. He argues that natural knowledge of man, God, and the universe is necessary for biblical interpretation, and is a key element in a well-rounded solution to the Protestant problem.

The final two essays address matters of liturgy. Christopher Dorn surveys the impact of the twentieth-century liturgical and ecumenical renewal movements on the conception of worship in the Reformed and Presbyterian churches in North America and then attempts to answer the question why this impact did not entirely succeed in reaching into the twenty-first century. Following this, Gregory Soderberg traces appeals to "catholicity" in various branches of the Scottish Reformed and English Protestant traditions. He contrasts some contemporary voices arguing for more frequent communion with authors who argued for more frequent communion in the English and Scottish churches in the 1700s and 1800s. By comparing and contrasting some of the similarities and discontinuities of communion frequency debates in the past, he provides theological and historical resources for those who are navigating issues of communion frequency in the present.

I: IS CHRIST DIVIDED? WHY REFORMED CATHOLICITY NEEDS REFORMED ECCLESIOLOGY

Bradford Littlejohn, The Davenant Institute

I. THE MODERN ECUMENICAL IMPERATIVE

IF THERE is one thing that everyone writing on ecclesiology in the twenty-first century can agree on, it seems to be this: the church today is fragmented by divisions; the body of Christ has been torn into pieces at war with one another. The fact of our problem seems often to be taken for granted, and the only debate is over the solution: whether Protestants should renounce their intrinsic sectarianism and take refuge in the one true undivided church of Rome or Constantinople, or hope that the Catholics and Orthodox will rejoin us someday in an undefined "Church of the Future"; whether we should work for an ecumenism built on common creed, common worship, common mission, or all of the above.[1]

Most ecumenically minded theologians also seem remarkably agreed on one prime culprit for our persistent divisions: an unhealthy preoccupa-

[1] This essay draws upon material previously published in my article "Believing in the Church: Why Ecumenism Needs the Invisibility of the Church," *Religions* 10, no. 2 (2019), https://doi.org/10.3390/rel10020104 (accessed April 30, 2019), and, to a lesser extent, "The Search for Visible Catholicity and the Danger of Boundary-Drawing: Lessons from John Nevin and Richard Hooker," in *Marking the Church: Essays in Ecclesiology*, ed. Greg Peters (Eugene, OR: Pickwick, 2016).

tion with the "invisible church." Ola Tjørhom, for instance, asserts in his 2004 *Visible Church—Visible Unity* that ecumenism has been hampered by a kind of Protestantism in "which the church is understood as essentially invisible. As a consequence of this misinterpretation, the church tends to emerge as a kind of *societas platonica*, or as a mere idea that has no 'body.' … When the church is described as fundamentally invisible, there will be no room for the concept of visible church unity."[2] More recently, Harald Hegstad begins his *The Real Church: An Ecclesiology of the Visible* by rejecting outright the visible/invisible church distinction as incoherent, lacking biblical support, and making the church here and now "something unreal in relation to theological ideas about the church."[3] Instead, he insists that the church should instead be seen "from an *eschatological* perspective. From the perspective of faith, the church is understood in light of its future as a sign and anticipation of that fellowship between God and humans which will be brought about by the forthcoming kingdom of God."[4] The reader might well ask whether a future eschatological reality is visible, as such, now—and if not, then doesn't that mean it is *invisible*?

However, evangelical theologian Peter Leithart has made similar moves in his 2016 book *The End of Protestantism: Pursuing Unity in a Fragmented Church*, stating that "an invisible unity is not a biblical unity," that "Paul expected—demanded—that the church's unity be visible in table fellowship, in loyalties and allegiances," and that "the unity of the church is not an invisible reality that renders visible things irrelevant. It is a *future* reality that gives present actions their orientation and meaning."[5] In recent follow-up articles, Leithart has acknowledged that "there *are* invisible dimensions of the church,"[6] but questioned whether there is any theologically appropriate sense in which we can speak of "the invisible church," especially when it comes to the question of church unity. The only result of such language, he

---

[2] Ola Tjørhom, *Visible Church—Visible Unity: Ecumenical Ecclesiology and the "The Great Tradition of the Church"* (Collegeville, MN: Liturgical Press, 2004), 77.

[3] Harald Hegstad, *The Real Church: An Ecclesiology of the Visible* (Eugene, OR: Pickwick, 2013), 2.

[4] Hegstad, *Real Church*, 2.

[5] Peter J. Leithart, *The End of Protestantism: Pursuing Unity in a Fragmented Church* (Grand Rapids, MI: Brazos, 2016), 20, 19.

[6] Peter J. Leithart, "Attaining Unity: A Response to Mike Allen," Theopolis Institute, June 13, 2017, accessed April 30, 2019, https://theopolisinstitute.com/attaining-unity-a-reply-to-mike-allen/.

thinks, can be a complacency and escapism: "If we think the church is an invisible community of true believers, then we might be tempted to avoid the mess of membership in a real community. If we pound a wedge between the 'church-as-she-appears' and the 'church-as-she-truly-is,' we mistake the very nature of redemption."[7]

Similar charges recur in much modern ecumenical writing.[8] John Webster summarizes, "The consensus of much recent ecclesiology has been…[that] no ecclesiology can be adequate which does not give primacy to the church's *visibility*."[9]

Since most modern ecclesiologists seem agreed that the church is deeply divided, and that any appeal to its invisible unity will simply compound the problem, we should not be surprised to also find a consensus that ecumenism must prioritize the search for visible forms of unity. Leithart puts it crisply: "If the church is a visible reality, its unity must be visible.… The church's present unity is visible, or it isn't ecclesiastical unity."[10] John Paul II's crucial encyclical, *Ut Unum Sint*, agrees: "The ultimate goal of the ecumenical movement is to re-establish full visible unity among all the baptized."[11] More generally, Veli-Matti Kärkkäinen writes, "With the exception of most Free churches, almost all other Christian churches cur-

---

[7] Peter J. Leithart, "The One City of God," Theopolis Institute, February 21, 2019, accessed April 30, 2019, https://theopolisinstitute.com/article/the-one-city-of-god.

[8] For instance, Eduardus Van der Borght, "The Unity of the Church in the Reformed Tradition: An Introduction," in *The Unity of the Church: A Theological State of the Art and Beyond*, ed. Eduardus Van der Borght (Leiden: Brill, 2010), 1; J. H. (Amie) van Wyk, "'Is Christ Divided?'—An Analysis of the Theological Justification of a Church Schism," in *The Unity of the Church*, ed. Van der Borght (Leiden: Brill, 2010), 62, 65.

[9] John Webster, "On Evangelical Ecclesiology," *Ecclesiology* 1, no. 1 (2004): 24.

[10] Leithart, "One City of God."

[11] John Paul II, *Ut Unum Sint: On Commitment to Ecumenism* (Rome: The Vatican, 1995), §77. John Webster, in "The Goals of Ecumenism," in *Paths to Unity: Explorations in Ecumenical Method*, ed. Paul Avis (London: Church House, 2004), 1–28, and "*Ut Unum Sint:* Some Cross-Bench Anglican Reflections," in *Ecumenism Today: The Universal Church in the 21st Century*, ed. Francesca Aran Murphy and Christopher Asprey (Aldershot, UK: Ashgate, 2008), 29–44, critically surveys the prominence of the language of "full visible unity" in modern Anglican–Roman Catholic dialogue; for a broader survey of recent models of ecumenism, see Lukas Vischer, Ulrich Luz, and Christian Link, *Unity of the Church in the New Testament and Today* (Grand Rapids, MI: Eerdmans, 2008), 19–27.

rently regard visible unity as the desired goal of ecumenism."[12]

On one level, it is difficult to disagree with these aims. Who would not love to see a true visible unity of the Christian church realized in history? However, the recent ecumenical consensus has been more passionate than precise. In what sense is the church actually divided? Certainly, plenty of empirical divisions suggest themselves, but ecclesiology is (or at least used to be!) a subdiscipline of theology, not of sociology.[13] How should we assess the unity and division of the church from a theological standpoint? Answering this question, of course, requires that we also give a theological account of *what the church is*, which will, I argue, necessitate a recurrence to the category of the invisible church. Moreover, we must ask more carefully just what is envisioned by the ideal of "full visible unity." There are several different kinds of visible unity that might be imagined, and it matters a great deal which we prioritize. In the following section, I will briefly address each of these points, before turning to argue that the reactionary catholicity of much modern ecclesiology actually tends to generate the very sectarianism that it decries. A more promising path toward practical catholicity, I will conclude, can be found via a thoughtful refocusing of the doctrine of the invisible church.

II. CLARIFYING THE ISSUES

The Invisible Unity of the Church

The New Testament church, like the church of our own day, was no stranger to divisions. Early in 1 Corinthians, Paul famously admonishes the Corinthian church:

> I appeal to you, brothers, by the name of our Lord Jesus Christ, that all of you agree, and that there be no divisions among you, but that you be united in the same mind and the same judgment. For it has been reported to me by Chloe's people that there is quarreling among you, my brothers. What I mean is that each one of you says, "I fol-

---

[12] Veli-Matti Kärkkäinen, *An Introduction to Ecclesiology: Ecumenical, Historical, and Global Perspectives* (Downers Grove: IVP Academic, 2002), 84.

[13] Pace Leithart in "Attaining Unity."

> low Paul," or "I follow Apollos," or "I follow Cephas," or "I follow Christ." Is Christ divided? Was Paul crucified for you? Or were you baptized in the name of Paul? (1 Cor. 1:10–13)

The final questions, however, are obviously rhetorical, with the obvious answer, "May it never be!" Whatever divisions might empirically exist among the members of the church, they are telling a lie about the true body of Christ. If this were not clear from context, it is made clear toward the end of the epistle. In chapter 12, Paul says,

> For just as the body is one and has many members, and all the members of the body, though many, are one body, so it is with Christ. For in one Spirit we were all baptized into one body—Jews or Greeks, slaves or free—and all were made to drink of one Spirit. For the body does not consist of one member but of many. If the foot should say, "Because I am not a hand, I do not belong to the body," that would not make it any less a part of the body. And if the ear should say, "Because I am not an eye, I do not belong to the body," that would not make it any less a part of the body.... Now you are the body of Christ and individually members of it. (1 Cor. 12:12–16, 27)

We *are*—indicative fact—all members of one body, however much we might try to deny that fact. Paul makes similar statements in Ephesians 4, asserting emphatically that "there is one body and one Spirit," united to one head, Christ. Any discussion of church unity must begin with the *fact* of the church's unity, not with the fact of its division. On this basis, we may then ask what the empirical divisions within the life of the church do and do not mean, instead of assuming that we already know this and can rush forward to the business of providing solutions.

Now, the very fact that these theological statements about the church conflict so starkly with our empirical observations should give us pause about dismissing so quickly the doctrine of the invisible church. Something very fundamental about the church must be invisible if Paul can make statements about the church that fly in the face of visible appearances. And indeed, the Christian church has always acknowledged that, in a very important sense, the church is an object of faith, not sight; otherwise why should we need to confess in the Nicene Creed, "We believe in one, holy, catholic, and apostolic church," right alongside our confession of faith in other unseen truths?

The church lives not of itself, or by the actions of its human members, but by the power of the Word of God and the action of the Spirit. Otherwise, the church would not be *the church*, but merely another religious association or social club. As Christoph Schwöbel puts it, "The Church is *creatura verbi divini*: the creature of the divine Word. The church is constituted by God's action and not by any human action. It is not an association of people who have a shared taste for religion or the creation of some kind of human community spirit."[14] Of course the church thereby created does take shape as a visible community of worship and witness—but it can only become visible *as the church* because of its prior (and continuing) invisibility. This is why the Reformed tradition insists that the church's essence derives from its true members, that properly speaking, the church simply is the whole body of those mystically united to Christ their Lord, though their identity remains partially hidden in this life.[15]

---

[14] Christoph Schwöbel, "The Creature of the Word: Recovering the Ecclesiology of the Reformers," in *On Being the Church: Essays on the Christian Community*, ed. Colin E. Gunton and Daniel W. Hardy (Edinburgh: T&T Clark, 1989), 122.

[15] See, for instance, Henk van den Belt, Riemer Faber, Andreas Beck, and William den Boer, eds., *Synopsis Purioris Theologiae: Latin Text and English Translation*, vol. 2 (Leiden: Brill, 2016), 559, 573–75: "In general the meaning of the word is defined as the meeting of those whom God in His grace calls out from the state of nature into the supernatural state of children of God, in order to show his glorious mercy…The invisible church is called the multitude of elect believers who, whether they are in specific meetings or in all the churches and places throughout the world, are conspicuous to the eyes of God. And so it is called 'invisible' because its inner, essential form, namely its true faith and holiness, are not seen by mortal people.… Along with Scripture we give to this multitude of believers the name *ecclesia* because by God's Word and Spirit they have been called out of the world to faith and holiness, and because they have a genuine and inner communion and fellowship with Christ and all true believers. And therefore throughout the Scriptures it is called by names of the sort that effectively denote this inner fellowship and communion with Christ and all the saints.… And to this Church, too, properly belong all the salutary and spiritual promises that are made to the Church of God everywhere in Scripture; both the hypocrites and the unrighteous are excluded from these promises."

Also, Gulielmus Bucananus, in Heinrich Heppe, *Reformed Dogmatics* (London: Allen & Unwin, 1950), 660: "What it says in the Creed is understood not of this or that one Church, but of the Catholic Church, i.e. of the whole body of the Church, at whatever time it ever existed on earth. And since it consists of the godly and elect who have once existed from the foundation of the world, exist now and are to exist till the end of the world, all gathered together, whom no man can ever see

Not only must we be willing to predicate invisibility of the church, but we must especially be willing to speak of the invisibility of *church unity*, precisely the point on which so many modern ecumenists protest. Obviously, the individual members of the church are visible; they are human beings, after all, and have bodies.[16] But the thing that knits these members together into one body—the "one Lord" of Ephesians 4:5, the head that gives life to the whole body, their union with the Head—is invisible. As Richard Hooker says: "Only with our minds can we conceive of this body, containing a huge multitude, a real body and yet invisible, because the nature of its union is utterly beyond our sense experience."[17] And just as the thing that holds them together as one thing is invisible, so is that which separates them from everything else.

We cannot say the church has visible and invisible aspects in simply the same way that an iceberg does—the human beings who make it up are visible above the surface, and Christ who gives it life is hidden—or even in the way that we might speak of a human body as visible and the animating force that gives it life as invisible. The church is a unity, but a composite unity, made up of many individuals, and *which* individuals share live-giving union with Christ remains unknown to us. We may illustrate with an odd—but hopefully illuminating—analogy. Consider a cluster of dandelions. Dozens of dandelions might appear aboveground but turn out to be a single organism, sharing a common root structure. But the fact that their bond of unity remains hidden means that at the same time so does their boundary of separation—there may be other dandelions in close proximity that are not, in fact, part of the same organism, but there is no way we can discern this from above. The analogy fails, of course, at the point when we note that those who are not truly of Christ's church are not members of another church, but members of no church at all. But the point remains that when we look out upon the multitude of professing Christians, we know that some are united to Christ, and thus are the church, and some are not.

---

with his eyes, assuredly the Church is believed in and not seen." The compilation of quotes in Heppe, pp. 557–61, are all very helpful in this regard.

[16] Although of course, since the church is a reality that spans history, only a small fraction of its members are visible on earth at any given time.

[17] Richard Hooker, *The Word of God and the Words of Man: Books II–III of Hooker's* Laws; *A Modernization*, ed. Bradford Littlejohn, Bradley Belschner, and Brian Marr (Moscow, ID: Davenant Press, 2018), 47.

Not knowing which are which, we are admonished by Hooker and other Protestant theologians to not try too hard to guess, but to extend a judgment of charity, treating all those who profess Christ as members of His visible church.[18] However, we should not shy away from the fact that this does give us in some sense two churches: one body of individuals who are indeed the church, and another larger body, including all these but also many more, that is a *corpus permixtum* of believers and unbelievers. This confession of the church's invisibility is thus a standing rebuke to any misguided attempt to identify visible historical guarantees of where the church is and isn't, as we shall see in the case studies below.

Five Forms of Visible Unity

Having hopefully established this too-neglected basic ontological point—that to identify the elements of a thing's *unity* is thereby to identify the elements of its *being* and the elements that *separate it* from all that is not it—let us consider again the calls for visible unity. There are, it seems to me, five distinct kinds of visible unity that might be envisioned and sought:

> 1. *Confessional unity*: a situation in which all Christians around the world profess the same body of truths, or at least the same body of fundamental doctrines, jointly acknowledging that the remaining points of difference are secondary or tertiary
>
> 2. *Liturgical unity*: a situation in which churches, while not liturgically identical, at least exhibit a common practice of the core rites of Christian worship, and just as importantly, recognize one another's rites as valid
>
> 3. *Missional unity*: a situation in which churches clearly work together in pursuit of a common mission or goal, whether evangelistic or social
>
> 4. *Fraternal unity:* a situation in which the different members or communities of the church display brotherly love and charity toward one another, and recognize one another as brothers

[18] For a fuller discussion, see my *Richard Hooker: A Companion to His Life and Work* (Eugene, OR: Cascade, 2015), ch. 10.

5. *Institutional unity*: a situation in which some kind of shared structure of oversight and authority exists, which binds all churches together into a self-regulating or at least mutually regulating whole

Now, although each of these might be in some measure desirable goals for the church to pursue, what should we think of them as grounds for identifying what the church *is* (which is what we need if we are to give a fundamentally visible, rather than invisible, account of church unity)? The fourth, *fraternal unity*, is the one that we can be most sure will only ever be partially realized this side of the eschaton; it will always only be relatively more or less present, and hence a vague qualitative measure for assessing our progress toward visible unity. Moreover, it is somewhat parasitic on the other criteria, inasmuch as we can only know who our brothers are, and what kind of charity we owe, if we know which so-called Christians can actually be deemed part of the church. Similarly, the third, *missional unity*, is rather parasitic on (1) and perhaps (2), since we can only share a common mission inasmuch as we agree on the truths we are seeking to preach or the practices we are seeking to foster. Let us then turn to consider (1) and (2).

Since both criteria acknowledge that there can be some acceptable diversity, so long as there is unity on core beliefs or core worship elements, both immediately raise the question, By what standard do we distinguish core from periphery, primary from secondary? Inevitably, differences will arise on such questions, and even if, through the blood, tears, toil, and sweat of decades or centuries of ecumenical initiatives, a substantial consensus is reached, there will inevitably be some churches that refuse to accept it. Are they then to be considered churches? If so, we will not have visible unity. If not, on whose authority?

The question of institutional unity is thus unavoidable for the advocate of "full visible unity," however much we may wish to avoid it in an age when "institution" is something of a dirty word, for which the warmer and fuzzier "communion" is often substituted.[19] Thus the Meissen Declaration, one of the key documents of the modern ecumenical movement in the Church of England, defines as a key element of "full visible unity":

---

[19] See, for instance, Kärkkäinen, *Introduction to Ecclesiology*, 85–87, 95–102; Robert Jenson, "The Church and the Sacraments," in *The Cambridge Companion to Christian Doctrine*, ed. Colin Gunton (Cambridge: Cambridge University Press, 1997), 207–25.

> bonds of communion which enable the Church at every level to guard and interpret the apostolic faith, to take decisions, to teach authoritatively, to share goods and to bear effective witness in the world. The bonds of communion will possess personal, collegial and communal aspects.[20]

The wording here minimizes the disciplinary implications of this criterion, but there is no avoiding the fact that "guarding," "interpreting," "taking decisions," and certainly "teaching authoritatively" involve authorities, and ultimately authority structures—which is to say institutions by which those authorities are authorized, within which they function, and whose boundaries they guard. Indeed, some are less hesitant. In *Unity of the Church in the New Testament and Today*, Lukas Vischer and his coauthors assert: "The unity we are seeking exists only as a unity that can be seen and demonstrated, or it does not exist at all. It is institutional unity, or else it remains a phantom."[21] And in *The End of Protestantism*, Peter Leithart goes so far as to say:

> Guided by Scripture above all and by the Christian tradition, the [reunited future] church will issue binding judgments about which deviations are tolerable and which are intolerable. Some opinions and teachers will be judged a threat to the gospel itself, and impenitent teachers will be expelled from the church.... [T]he reunited church will have one advantage over the churches of today: expulsion from the reunited church will be plausibly seen as expulsion from *the church*. It will not be expulsion from one denomination that leaves the expelled with the option of going down the road to start his or her own denomination.[22]

Although Leithart is vague about the formal structures underlying these binding judgments, it has generally been assumed within Anglican and Roman Catholic ecumenical endeavors at least that these authority struc-

---

[20] The Church of England, The Meissen Agreement, 1991, §8, accessed November 30, 2018, https://www.churchofengland.org/sites/default/files/2017-11/meissen_english.pdf.

[21] Vischer, Luz and Link, *Unity of the Church*, 231.

[22] Leithart, *End of Protestantism*, 29–30.

tures must lie in the historic episcopate, and even that some form of papal primacy might need to be conceded as its point of integration.[23] Naturally such an account would require the exclusion of all those who do not accept these authority structures from the reunited church. The result, as Donald MacLeod shrewdly observes, is that while documents like *Ut Unum Sint* are framed in terms of a dialogue of mutual reconciliation, "it looks, however, as if the full price of any reconciliation must be paid by Protestants."[24]

We are thus brought back to the ontological point that whatever it is that makes something *one thing* is also that which holds it apart from everything else. We often recognize this clearly enough at the front end of the ecumenical task, observing that the very things that bind us together into distinct denominations or traditions are the things that clearly mark us off from other groups of Christians. But too often, as we gaze into the mists of the future with rose-tinted spectacles, we forget that the same must be true of the church of the future. To whatever extent our churches are visibly united, they will have the means to exclude all those outside their union, and once the church attains "full visible unity," this will entail an institutional church with the capacity to authoritatively define who is in the church and who is not.

This then raises the unsettling prospect that the terminus of ecumenism might be some kind of sectarianism—however large the sect may be. The quest to make the church *one* requires, on this account, adopting criteria whereby we can say, "This group of churches belongs to the one, holy, catholic, and apostolic church, and the rest of you do not." Those making such claims are usually careful to draw the criteria of ecclesial identity around their own traditions, or else, worrying that their traditions are deficient when it comes to the visible boundary markers, jump ship to other traditions, effectively unchurching those from which they began. Many find themselves beginning the ecumenical enterprise with a more capacious ac-

---

[23] See Charles Morerod, "The Ecumenical Meaning of the Petrine Ministry," in *Ecumenism Today: The Universal Church in the 21st Century*, ed. Francesca Aran Murphy and Christopher Asprey (Aldershot, UK: Ashgate, 2008), 121–38; Webster, "*Ut Unum Sint*"; Martin Davie, "Anglican Ecumenism: The Liberal Catholic Consensus and the Conservative Evangelical Challenge," in *Paths to Unity: Explorations in Ecumenical Method*, ed. Paul Avis (London: Church House, 2004), 29–51.

[24] Donald MacLeod, "The Basis of Christian Unity," in *Ecumenism Today: The Universal Church in the 21st Century*, ed. Francesca Aran Murphy and Christopher Asprey (Aldershot, UK: Ashgate, 2008), 77.

count of the being and form of the church, which paradoxically shrinks under the pressure of the ecumenical project—and often, I would argue, in precise proportion to their fear of sectarianism. To begin the ecumenical quest with a demand for visibility, and seek to create such visibility by human action, is to begin on un-Protestant premises, and thus naturally terminates in an un-Protestant and ultimately exclusive (rather than genuinely ecumenical) church. In what follows, I will seek to highlight this trajectory through three case studies: the sixteenth-century experience of English Separatism, the nineteenth-century experience of the American Mercersburg Theology, and the twenty-first-century experience of reactionary catholicity.

III. CASE STUDIES

English Separatism

The case of English Separatism is perhaps a curious one to consider here, since at first glance it seems to be the very opposite of an ecumenical endeavor. After all, it's right there in the name: Separatism. But it will not seem so odd once we remember the point just emphasized: the elements of a thing's unity are also the elements of its separation. At issue in English Separatism was the attempt to define where the church was, and where it wasn't. Although the resulting church may have been small and exclusive indeed, it was, according to the premises of the movement, an ecumenical or catholic church; it was the whole church united to its one Lord by one faith and one true baptism. It was, however, a fundamentally un-Protestant vision of the church, albeit one that arose naturally in response to tensions within Protestantism.

The Augsburg Confession of 1530 had established two marks of the church: "The Church is the congregation of saints, in which the Gospel is rightly taught and the Sacraments are rightly administered," but some over the next couple of decades, wanting to emphasize that just as true Christians must be characterized by godly life, so must the true church, added a third, "discipline," which initially had quite a broad sense, rather than simply designating excommunication and its precursors.[25]

[25] See P. D. L. Avis, "'The True Church' in Reformation Theology," *Scottish Journal of Theology* 30, no.4 (1977): 319–45; Jordan J. Ballor and W. Bradford Littlejohn, "European Calvinism: Church Discipline," in *European History Online* [EGO], ed.

Now, these were all fairly useful in giving you a decent idea of where the church *was* (although they obviously could not stand alone; they presupposed a Protestant understanding of what the Gospel and sacraments were): if you saw a minister faithfully expounding the text of Scripture, and administering baptism and the Lord's Supper, well then, you could assume that there was a manifestation of Christ's body—imperfect, perhaps, but in communion with the Head. But they weren't so good at telling you where the church *wasn't*.[26] How false did a church's preaching have to be before it could no longer count as part of the body of Christ? How distorted or rationalistic or superstitious did its sacramental practice have to be? How lax did its discipline have to be? In response to Catholic polemic and persecution, many Protestants in the latter half of the sixteenth century, particularly among the Reformed, increasingly deployed the *notae ecclesiae* to brand Rome as a wholly false church, and in the process, felt the need to lay increasing stress on the adverb "rightly." Some also tended to redefine "discipline" specifically in terms of a structure of church government, namely, presbyterianism, without which, it was suggested, a minister could not *rightly* preach or administer the sacraments. Such a sharp blade of division, wielded zealously, could quickly be turned upon other Protestants, as it was in Elizabethan England. The militant presbyterians suggested that the Church of England was not in fact a true church, despite its Protestant confession, due to the deficiencies in its preaching, sacraments, and discipline.[27] "We in England are so far off from having a church rightly reformed," fulminated the *Admonition to Parliament*, "according to the prescript of God's word, that as yet we are not come to the outward face of the same."[28]

For these presbyterians, sometimes called disciplinarians, their con-

---

Irene Dingel and Johannes Paulmann (Mainz, Germany: Institute of European History [IEG]: 2013), accessed November 30, 2018, http://www.ieg-ego.eu/en/threads/crossroads/religious-and-denominational-spaces/jordan-ballor-w-bradford-littlejohn-european-calvinism-church-discipline.

[26] Avis, "'True Church,'" 334: "The *notae ecclesiae* is a qualitative concept; theoretically one can say whether a certain ecclesial body possesses the marks or not. But in practice it was found to need supplementing by a quantitative one, such as Calvin's concept that Rome contained the *vestigia* of the church."

[27] See Avis, "'True Church," 337–39.

[28] John Field and Thomas Wilcox, *An Admonition to Parliament*, in *Puritan Manifestoes: A Study of the Origins of the Puritan Revolt*, ed. W.H. Frere and C.E. Douglas, eds. (London: Society for Promoting Christian Knowledge, 1907), 9.

cern with discipline was bound up with a concern that there be as little distinction as possible between the visible and invisible churches: the visible body of Christ should consist only of those who were true followers of Christ, and any who strayed should be pruned off by discipline.[29] In this they followed the trajectory established earlier by the Anabaptists, who had reacted against what they saw as the laxity of Luther's evangelical church by insisting on the necessity of both rebaptism and "the ban" to ensure that the visible church was the true church.[30] Although most English presbyterians equivocated and held back from quite following through on the implications of their charge that a church without proper discipline could not be a true church, others broke away into Separatism. Henry Barrow, one of the Separatist leaders, would write:

> The true planted and rightlie established Church of Christ is a companie of faithful people; separated from the unbelievers and heathen of the land [i.e., professing members of the Church of England]; gathered in the name of Christ, whome they trulie worship...joined together as members of one bodie; ordered and governed by such officers and lawes as Christ in his last will and testament hath thereunto ordeyned.[31]

The Separatists, in turn, by application of the same principles, divided and divided still further, particularly once transplanted into America, thus bequeathing to the United States its oft-lamented habit of sectarianism.[32]

---

[29] See Peter Lake, *Anglicans and Puritans? Presbyterianism and English Conformist Thought from Whitgift to Hooker* (London: Allen & Unwin, 1988), 31–41; W. Bradford Littlejohn, *The Peril and Promise of Christian Liberty: Richard Hooker, the Puritans, and Protestant Political Theology* (Grand Rapids, MI: Eerdmans, 2017), 99–102.

[30] See P. D. L. Avis, *The Church in the Theology of the Reformers* (London: Marshall, Morgan, and Scott, 1981), 51–61; Kenneth R. Davis, "No Discipline, No Church: An Anabaptist Contribution to the Reformed Theological Tradition," *Sixteenth Century Journal* 13, no. 4 (1982): 43–58.

[31] Quoted in Avis, *Church in the Theology of the Reformers*, 62.

[32] See Michael P. Winship, *Godly Republicanism: Puritans, Pilgrims, and a City on a Hill* (Cambridge, MA: Harvard University Press, 2012), for a chronicle of the Separatists' obsession with distinguishing true from false churches, and their influence on early America.

The Mercersburg Theology

Two of the most able and insistent later critics of American sectarianism were the German Reformed theologians Philip Schaff and John Williamson Nevin, who in the 1840s and 1850s decried the rampant individualism and division they saw in the wake of the Second Great Awakening and which they blamed on the sectarian root of "Puritanism." Upon arriving in America in 1844 from Germany, Schaff fulminated against the ecclesial chaos he found awaiting him on the shores of his new homeland in his *Principle of Protestantism*, in a passage too delightful not to quote at length:

> Any one who has, or fancies that he has, some inward experience and a ready tongue, may persuade himself that he is called to be a reformer; and so proceed at once, in his spiritual vanity and pride, to a revolutionary rupture with the historical life of the Church, to which he holds himself immeasurably superior. He builds himself of a night accordingly a new chapel in which now, for the first time since the age of the apostles, a pure congregation is to be formed; baptizes his followers with his own name, to which he thus secures an immortality, unenviable it is true, but such as is always flattering to the natural heart; rails and screams with full throat against all that refuse to do homage to his standard; and with all this though utterly unprepared to understand a single book, is not ashamed to appeal continually to the Scriptures, as having been sealed entirely, or in large part, to the understanding of eighteen centuries, and even to the view of our Reformers themselves, till now at last God has been pleased to kindle the true light in an obscure corner of the New World! Thus the deceived multitude, having no power to discern spirits, is converted not to Christ and his truth, but to the arbitrary fancies and baseless opinions of an individual, who is only of yesterday. Such *con*version is of a truth only *per*version; such *theo*logy, *neo*logy; such exposition of the Bible, wretched imposition. What is built is no Church, but a chapel, to whose erection Satan himself has made the most liberal contribution.[33]

---

[33] Philip Schaff, *The Principle of Protestantism*, vol. 1 of *Lancaster Series on the Mercersburg Theology* (Chambersburg, PA: German Reformed Church, 1845), reprint, ed. Bard

Schaff himself (in part due to his continued fidelity to the Reformed doctrine of the invisible church) was able in time to transform these fierce salvos into a constructive ecumenical agenda for America and ultimately for the world, culminating in his 1893 coordination of the Evangelical Alliance and the World Parliament of Religions, and his classic pamphlet *On the Reunion of Christendom.* His colleague Nevin, however, ultimately embarked on a more cynical path.

Beginning, like Schaff, with brilliant satire and polemic against the excesses of American sectarianism and religious fanaticism,[34] Nevin increasingly found himself drawn to characterize certain American Protestant churches as not merely unhealthy and ahistorical, but as cut off entirely from the historic life of the church:

> A Sect, on the other hand, stands in no such organic connection with the Church as a whole. It is the creature in full of private wilfulness and caprice, not the growth of the true Church life itself.... According to this distinction, Sects as such are always evil, and very man is bound to shun them, as he values his own salvation.[35]

Naturally, a claim of this sort required Nevin to furnish criteria of exactly what it did and didn't take to have an "organic connection with the Church as a whole." Unlike Schaff, Nevin became increasingly critical of the traditional Protestant distinction of the visible and invisible church and highlighted the need for visible bonds of church unity.[36] Although he began by stressing the importance of forms of credal orthodoxy and historic continuity, he increasingly recognized that institutional structures were needed to give such creeds teeth and to make them effective in maintaining the unity of the church. In the course of a detailed study of Cyprian, Nevin became increasingly enamored of the idea that the rule of faith was nothing without the episcopal ministry that carried it on and sustained it.

Thompson and George H. Bricker (Eugene, OR: Wipf and Stock, 2004), 149–50.

[34] His 1849 essays on "The Sect Spirit" remain classics of the genre.

[35] John Williamson Nevin, *Antichrist*, in *The Anxious Bench, Antichrist, and the Sermon Catholic Unity*, ed. Augustine Thompson (Eugene, OR: Wipf and Stock, 1999), 55.

[36] See W. Bradford Littlejohn, *The Mercersburg Theology and the Quest for Reformed Catholicity* (Eugene, OR: Pickwick, 2009), 66–76, for a summary, though one unduly biased in Nevin's favor.

Accordingly, after years of hand-wringing in which he considered converting to Rome, Nevin articulated his position in a paradoxical sermon entitled "The Christian Ministry," renewing his commitment to remain Protestant while articulating an un-Protestant understanding of the church:

> the Church [is] to be considered as starting in the Apostles, and extending itself out from them in the way of implicit submission to their embassy and proclamation. They were to stand between Christ and the world, to be his witnesses, his legates, the representatives of his authority, the mediators of his grace among men. They were to preach in his name, not merely a doctrine for the nations to hear, but a constitution to which they were required to surrender themselves, in order that they might be saved. The new organization was to be formed, and held together, by those who were thus authorized and empowered to carry into effect officially its conditions and terms.... The law of derivation is downwards and not upwards, from the few to the many, and not from the many to the few.[37]

In fact, he goes so far as to call the alternate view heresy. The only reason that such a view did not compel Nevin to convert to Rome or at least Anglo-Catholicism was Nevin's embrace of the Hegelian historicism that saw church history as a dialectical process of differentiation and reunification. This historical process meant that Nevin did not need to accept the conclusions of his premises and unite himself to any currently existing church of the past, but could sit contentedly on the sidelines awaiting the appearance of a "church of the future" that would somehow transcend the currently insurmountable boundaries of Protestant and Catholic, and bind the severed churches back into one body united by one common (presumably episcopal) ministry and juridical organization. In short, beginning as he does with an impassioned critique of the ahistorical exclusivism of the sect, Nevin seems to have concluded that the only remedy to the visible division it has produced is a historicist (which is not to say a historic*al*) embrace of an exclusive sect writ large, beyond whose authority there is no salvation.

---

[37] John Williamson Nevin, "The Christian Ministry," in *The Mercersburg Theology*, ed. J. H. Nichols (New York: Oxford University Press, 1966), 359; cf. also John Williamson Nevin, "Cyprian: Second Article," *Mercersburg Review* 4, no. 2 (1852): 361–62.

Contemporary Reactionary Catholicity

Although Nevin himself may have hung back from following through on his premises and converting to Roman Catholicism, given the stigma that involved in nineteenth-century America, an increasing number of Protestants since, tormented by the sectarianism of their tradition, have been more willing to jump ship. One poignant recent example with striking similarities to Nevin[38] is Ola Tjørhom, a Norwegian Lutheran who began writing his *Visible Church—Visible Unity* to outline the need for Protestants to recover visible forms of church unity only to despair of this possibility and convert to Rome upon completion of the book.[39]

Tjørhom, even more forcefully than Nevin, stresses the need for the church's unity to be visible: "Unity belongs inseparably and necessarily to the church's nature."[40] This leads Tjørhom to repeatedly downplay and marginalize the Protestant doctrine of the invisible church, reinterpreting its confessions to stress the visibility of the church.[41] Although Tjørhom's passion for visible unity is clear enough, his meaning is often elusive. He rejects the idea that "the Church as such is invisible" or that it is "fundamentally invisible" but without clarifying in what senses it may be said to be invisible. His account of visible unity downplays institutional language and focuses on sacramental language:

> One may even argue that structures are essential to both the Church as such and to the unity in faith that is at the core of its life. Yet ecclesial visibility should not be identified with the structural aspect.... In understanding the visibility of the Church, the constitutive means of grace offer a far more suitable point of departure. The key concern here is simply that the Church is just as empirically recognizable as the outward word and the visible sacraments that constitute it.[42]

---

[38] Geoffrey Wainwright, Foreword to Tjørhom, *Visible Church*, vii

[39] See Tjørhom, preface to *Visible Church.*

[40] Tjørhom, *Visible Church*, xvi.

[41] See particularly Tjørhom, *Visible Church*, 11–13, where he seeks to downplay the invisibility of the church in the Augsburg Confession, and p. 7, where he goes so far as to say, "The Reformers...were firmly committed to keep the episcopal order or polity of the Church."

[42] Tjørhom, *Visible Church*, 70–71.

Accordingly, Tjørhom, like many modern ecumenists, finds *communio* language appealing: "Since the sacramentally grounded and socially directed *communio* is basically visible, this concept also contributes to an affirmation of the fundamental visibility of the Church."[43] Nonetheless, like Nevin, the need to clarify the boundaries of this sacramental fellowship in "a world marked by militant division" means that Tjørhom must ultimately stress the importance of structure: "There will be a clear need for binding structures for authoritative teaching and decision-making. This will allow unified churches to speak with one voice.... Thus we are summoned to reaffirm our commitment to the goal of visible unity, or more precisely, to the goal of a visibly structured community."[44] It should hardly surprise us that Tjørhom found the ideal of a single "visibly structured community" thoroughly unrealizable within the terms of Protestantism, and thus embraced a church that has always claimed to provide such a community.

Another modern-day analogue of Nevin would seem to be Peter Leithart, who, although not abandoning Protestantism himself, has called for the "End of Protestantism." Like Mercersburg's attempted renewal movement, Leithart's call for Reformed catholicity is similarly framed first and foremost in terms of a reaction, a visceral rejection and lamentation of the divided state of the contemporary church. It is also guided throughout by a neo-Hegelian historicism that can accept divisions as a provisional good within the historical dialectic of the repeated rending and remaking of the church. But the weaknesses of Mercersburg's call for Reformed catholicity if anything loom even larger in Leithart's account.

Where Mercersburg seemed fuzzy at first on whether denominations were a problem or only sects—an ambiguity that Schaff resolved in the negative and Nevin, it would seem, in the positive—Leithart is explicit in his conflation of denominations with sects. Denominations, on his account, are ipso facto sins against the unity of the church:

> We can live with ourselves because we have created a system to salve our conscience and to deflect the Spirit's grief. We have found a way of being church that lets us be at peace with division. Denominationalism allows us to be friendly to one another while refusing to join one anoth-

43 Tjørhom, *Visible Church*, 70.

44 Tjørhom, *Visible Church*, 93.

> er.... Denominational churches do not dwell in, nor are they indwelt by, one another. Methodist churches dwell in other Methodist churches; Lutheran churches are indwelt by other Lutheran churches. In the nature of the case, being a Methodist church means *not* dwelling in a Lutheran church. Being a Methodist church means *not* exhibiting the unity of the Father and the Son.[45]

Lest this still seem a bit ambiguous, highlighting only an ethical failing in denominations' overly exclusive *attitudes* toward one another, Leithart later asserts, "In its *essence*, denominationalism falsifies central Christian truths about the church and her members.... Denominationalism *institutionalizes* division. So long as we are denominational Christians, we will not be one as the Father and Son are one."[46]

Of course, if "sect" is to be distinguished from "church," we need a clear definition of the latter. Whereas Nevin made a number of efforts toward a theological definition of the church, recurrently employing categories of "ideal" and "actual" that in some ways approximated, but historicized, the classic Protestant categories of "invisible" and "visible," Leithart is considerably more evasive, preferring a sociological account of the church to a theological account (although, in neo-Hegelian fashion, he rejects the distinction between these two disciplines), and questioning or rejecting the usefulness of the category "invisible church."[47] Throughout *The End of Protestantism*, we seek in vain for a theological account of *what the church is* that would explain why we must say that it is not presently united.

Finally, as we have already seen above, Leithart openly endorses the idea that visible church unity will require authoritative structures for determining who's in and who's out,[48] although like Nevin and unlike Tjørhom, he stops short of embracing the Roman magisterium and instead gestures vaguely toward the "church of the future," a church that will be defined by some kind of external institutional unity, just not on the pope's terms.[49]

---

45 Leithart, *End of Protestantism*, 3–4.

46 Leithart, *End of Protestantism*, 71–72, italics his.

47 Leithart, "Attaining Unity." Cf. also Leithart, "One City of God."

48 Leithart, *End of Protestantism*, 26, 27, 29, 30.

49 For Leithart's philosophy/theology of history, see ch. 8 of *The End of Protestantism*; for his sketch of the "church of the future," see ch. 3.

Lessons from These Case Studies

In fact, I would submit that any account of church unity that begins by stressing the necessity of a single "visibly structured community" that can claim to be *the church*, outside of which will be only "no-church," will tend to lead toward a basically Roman Catholic ecclesiology. The picture may be reproduced in miniature—as in the case of English Separatism or the sects that Nevin decried—or in an elusive futuristic form. But the basic claim will be the same: the true church must be distinguished from the false here and now in history, authoritative human structures must uphold that distinction, and all those outside the bounds of this communion will not be the church. Indeed, John Webster and others have charged that this is precisely the trajectory of much of the Anglican–Roman Catholic dialogue, and that even *Ut Unum Sint*, often hailed as the Catholic Church's most generous ecumenical gesture yet, ultimately fails to materially back down from the papacy's central claim: to be the authorized representative and guardian of the church's visibly structured community, who alone can determine the conditions of communion for other professing Christians.[50] Nor is the essentially Roman Catholic trajectory of this form of ecumenism confined to ecclesiology. Rather, I would argue that the logic of this quest for full visible unity is essentially Pelagian, or at least semi-Pelagian, endeavoring to create the unity of the church by human effort rather than resting gratefully in the unifying activity of God in Christ.

To point this out is not to engage in the outmoded pastime of Catholic-bashing, but simply to point out what should be obvious: that there are two radically different and fundamentally incommensurable ecclesiologies, whose clash created the Protestant Reformation, and that these are rooted in different accounts of divine grace and human action. To begin the ecumenical quest with a demand for visibility, and seek to create such visibility by human action, is to begin on un-Protestant premises, and thus naturally terminates in an un-Protestant and ultimately exclusive church.

When we assume that the presence of visible division is automatically problematic, we tacitly grant that the essence of the church lies in its visible forms. But what matters, from a Reformed standpoint, is not divisions per

[50] See Webster, "*Ut Unum Sint*"; Kenneth Padley, "Early Anglican Ecclesiology and Contemporary Ecumenism," *International Journal for the Study of the Christian Church* 9, no. 1 (2009): 3–16; McLeod, "Basis of Christian Unity."

se, but *what we make of* these divisions. The existence of two denominations can be unproblematic, if they both maintain orthodoxy, respect one another, and keep brotherly fellowship with one another. But as soon as one denomination concludes that the division is inexcusable, that the denominations must merge into a unified body, then it will be tempted to dismiss as schismatic anyone who refused to get on board with the reunion scheme. Many overhasty efforts to dissolve denominational boundaries have resulted in fresh schisms or deep wounds of mutual suspicion within Christian churches. There is nothing wrong with a multitude of denominations, but there is something wrong with the claim that "denominationalism institutionalizes division."

In the final section of this essay, I will argue that the only basis upon which we can in fact pursue catholicity is on the basis of a Reformed ecclesiology that refuses to concede genuine theological significance to the empirical and institutional divisions in the church.

IV. THE TASK OF WITNESS: MAKING UNITY VISIBLE

Justification and Sanctification

We have noted already the continuity between Reformation ecclesiology and soteriology—our confession of the church's dependence on God's gracious action is an extension of a broader confession of that God's prevenient grace precedes, makes possible, and is never absorbed into human action. Thus I would suggest that our ecclesiology can also learn from Reformation soteriology's distinction of justification and sanctification. Richard Hooker summarizes the distinction crisply:

> There is a glorifying righteousness of men in the world to come: and there is a justifying and a sanctifying righteousness here. The righteousness, wherewith we shall be clothed in the world to come, is both perfect and inherent. That whereby here we are justified is perfect, but not inherent. That whereby we are sanctified, inherent, but not perfect.[51]

---

[51] Richard Hooker, *A Learned Discourse of Justification, Workes, and How the Foundation of Faith Is Overthrowne*, in *The Folger Library Edition of Richard Hooker: V. Tractates and Sermons*, ed. Laetitia Yeandle and Egil Grislis (Cambridge, MA: Belknap, 1990), 109.

In the grace of justification, the believer lives eccentrically, her life hidden in Christ, resting upon the perfect and complete righteousness that is found only in Christ. Just so, the church lives not of herself, but in her Head, Christ, her perfect life contained invisibly in Him. In the grace of sanctification, Christ by His Spirit empowers those who live in Him to live like Him, or to at least make some small beginning in that direction; righteousness thus becomes inherent in them—always imperfect, yet a genuine manifestation of the reality of which Christ is the firstfruits. Just so, the church, through the power of the Spirit, is enabled bit by bit, haltingly and inconsistently, to visibly manifest her hidden identity, so that the unity and holiness that she has perfectly in Christ come to exist imperfectly but really in her external structures and common life. Finally, at the consummation the believer looks forward to glorification, in which the perfect but extrinsic righteousness of justification and the imperfect but inherent righteousness of sanctification come together and the life of Christ is fully manifest in the perfected believer. Similarly, the church looks forward to the eschaton when, purged of her corruptions and false professors, and fully united in faith and love, she becomes fully and truly one holy bride of Christ for all eyes to see.

With a Reformed ecclesiology as our starting point, we must remember that it is not the church's task to *make itself united*, but simply to witness to its union. The church *is* one in Christ, the cornerstone on whom the whole building is built, the vine from which all the branches give life, the bridegroom who has bound Himself to each of us.[52] Nothing we do can actually destroy this unity. But we can fail to manifest it as we are commanded to. "Signs must resemble the things they signify,"[53] as Richard Hooker said about the church's worship, and the same must be said of the visible church as a whole, which serves as a sign of Christ's body in the world. In pursuing the unity of the church, we aim to make the church appear, as much as possible within the limitations of its temporal form,[54] as an

I have modernized spelling and punctuation in this quotation from Hooker and the one that follows.

[52] Eph. 2:20–22; John 15:1–7; Eph. 5:25–32.

[53] Richard Hooker, *Of the Laws of Ecclesiastical Polity, Book V*, in *The Folger Library Edition of Richard Hooker: V. Tractates and Sermons*, ed. W. Speed Hill (Cambridge, MA: Belknap, 1977), V.6.1 (p. 33).

[54] This qualifier is an important one, for not all lack of unity is disunity. To take the

image of the eschatological city it will one day be.

This framework gives us a basis for genuinely seeking to make the invisible reality visible—thus the legitimacy of a quest for visible unity—while also warning us against a confusion of our present work with Christ's final glorifying work, and against unrealistic expectations for what we can make visible here and now. As Schaff notes, "The reunion of Christendom presupposes the original union which has been marred and obstructed, but never entirely destroyed."[55] And this is true, he goes on, not merely because of the hidden unity in Christ that persists, but because of the significant forms of empirical unity that remain, most notably in shared core doctrines and ethical commitments.

Revisiting the Five Forms of Unity

With these cautions in mind, let us reconsider the five potential forms of unity within the context of the imperative to witness to the church's hidden unity in Christ—institutional unity, liturgical unity, confessional unity, missional unity, and fraternal unity. Each of these, it should be noted, pertain to the outward form of the church.

From a Reformed standpoint, institutional unity is suspect as a goal of our ecumenical strivings. After all, such unity is in no sense a feature of the church as the hidden body of Christ or even of the eschatological New Jerusalem, where there will be no mediating hierarchy, laws, or disciplinary structures. The institutional form of the church is part of its outward and temporal garb, and the juridical authority needed to police the boundaries of any institution is seated firmly in the temporal kingdom of law. In this realm, local variation and regional administration are the norm, and we should be no quicker to embrace one-world church government than one-world civil government. As Schaff notes, firmly rejecting the Roman demand for "organic or corporate union of all the churches under one government," "Christ promised one *flock* under one shepherd, but not one

most obvious example, linguistic, cultural, and geographic barriers suggest the ongoing value of distinct organizational structures within the global church. By extension, a strong case could be made that many of the differences that have given rise to different denominations are not marks of division that demand to be overcome.

[55] Philip Schaff, *The Reunion of Christendom: A Paper Prepared for the Parliament of Religions and the National Conference of the Evangelical Alliance held in Chicago, September and October 1893* (New York: Charles Scribner's Sons, 1893), 2.

fold.... Christ's flock is one, but there are many folds."[56] Where many institutions jostle for position in the same geographical space, however, as typifies our modern condition, this may pose a problem, and to the extent that institutional disunity is undermining the other forms of unity, then it may be something we should seek to overcome. For instance, if two denominations who follow the same confession are jealously squabbling and competing for members, then perhaps we should campaign for a merger. But conversely, if a Lutheran and a Reformed denomination were cheerfully working alongside one another while acknowledging their differences, those differences are certainly worth sorting through over the long haul of history, but we need not wring our hands in angst about the institutional separation *as such*. It all depends on how well confessional unity, missional unity, and fraternal unity govern these relations.

Liturgical unity would seem to fall under the same heading, though here the imperative for "signs to resemble the things they are signified" suggests some imperative toward unity. After all, our picture of the New Jerusalem in Revelation is a scene of worship,[57] and our liturgies today ought to serve as dim reflections—adapted for our current condition—of the eschatological worship we will one day enjoy together. To this extent, I think we can say that there are *some* worship practices that fall outside the pale, and we must unite in excluding those. Conversely, there are obviously certain core features of Christian worship and practice that we are bound in obedience to our Lord to maintain—the two sacraments, prayer, songs of praise, and the reading and preaching of the Word, at the very least. But Scripture provides nothing approaching a detailed blueprint for these, so the forms they take are largely prudential, and have varied enormously through time and space; indeed, there is no reason to suppose that they will not continue to vary in heaven, as appropriate expressions of praise from different tongues and tribes and nations. Certainly it might strengthen the church's life together and its mission to cultivate more common practice on many disputed points (e.g., the charismatic gifts and the frequency of the Eucharist), but we must not mistake these forms as the ground or even the primary signs of the church's unity.

Confessional unity looms much larger. If ecumenism is a matter of the church's sanctification, and if we are justified by faith, then, it would

---

[56] Schaff, *Reunion of Christendom*, 15.

[57] Rev. 4; 21:1–22:5.

seem, the faith of the church must be foundational, preceding the ecumenical task as a *sine qua non*. And yet, the "one faith" that does ground the church's unity must not be complexified beyond the faith that justifies, which we all know can be very lacking in doctrinal sophistication, and yet still pleasing to the Lord. In going beyond this basic confession of Christian faith, and hammering out more extensive areas of shared doctrine, we certainly aid the sanctification of the church, but must not confuse this with the definition of its essence. Indeed, we must be honest with ourselves that theology is very hard work, and many of our theological divisions are not so much the result of sin as of simple human frailty and finitude. God will always surpass our understanding and as we struggle to articulate Him rightly, we should not be surprised to find ongoing confessional diversity on some points. With the sanctification of the church rather than its definition in mind, we can approach questions of confessional unity more pragmatically, in tandem with concerns for missional unity.

The church's mission includes many tasks, from catechizing and preaching to serving the needy and reconciling the divided. An individual church will require more confessional unity for its Sunday school teachers than its members, and more for its elders and deacons than for its Sunday school teachers. Two denominations trying to decide whether to join in a campaign to fight sex trafficking shouldn't need to agree on much beyond the basics; if they're joining in an evangelistic mission work, they will probably want to establish somewhat fuller unity of faith; and if they're creating a Sunday school curriculum, considerably more. In short, the confessional unity that we must seek depends on the particular mission at hand. This is not to deny, of course, that our overarching goal should be for all Christians to be of one mind in all matters pertaining to the truth. This, however, is not the sort of thing that can be rushed or engineered, nor is it a goal we should expect to achieve this side of the eschaton. As Schaff notes in *The Reunion of Christendom*, "Doctrinal differences will be the most difficult to adjust. When two dogmas flatly contradict one another, the one denying what the other asserts, one or the other, or both, must be wrong. Truth excludes error and admits of no compromise."[58] In the meantime, we must

[58] Schaff, *Reunion of Christendom*, 12. Schaff, however, does insist that every denomination should "cheerfully recognize the excellencies and merits of the other branches of Christ's kingdom. No sect has the monopoly of truth. The part is not the whole; the body consists of many members, and all are necessary to one anoth-

work to carefully distinguish between essentials and nonessentials, anchor our agreement on essentials, and patiently work our way outward through secondary and tertiary matters, united in charity even when divided in mind.

This leads, of course, to the final and especially crucial type of unity: fraternal unity. Indeed, it is striking that when the Scriptures do call us to be of one mind, they seem to be concerned more with mutual love than with doctrinal uniformity:

> Complete my joy by being of the same mind, having the same love, being in full accord and of one mind. Do nothing from selfish ambition or conceit, but in humility count others more significant than yourselves. Let each of you look not only to his own interests, but also to the interests of others. Have this mind among yourselves, which is yours in Christ Jesus. (Phil. 2:2–5)

Perhaps none of the five kinds of unity highlights the distance between the church's justification and its sanctification so much as fraternal unity, the love that binds believers together. Nothing is so important for us to cultivate, and yet nothing so often, or so thoroughly, eludes us. In lamenting the pettiness and hatred that divides us, we must never be driven to the point of despair, since Christ promises to hold us together despite our attempts to pull apart. Neither should we fall prey to the postmodern feel-good idea of tolerance, and think that charity precludes judgment and discrimination. Christians are called to stand fast against sin and error, doing so with all charity and forbearance, but without wavering. Those who call on us to

---

er" and also that "truth is many-sided and all-sided, and is reflected in different colors" (12). Cf. Leithart, *End of Protestantism*, 27: "Pastors and theologians of the future church will draw on the *whole* tradition of biblical commentary and theology, all the tradition's wealth of pastoral wisdom and liturgical beauty, as they go about their work. Former Lutherans will discover fresh insights in the writings of former Mennonites and Calvinists; former Baptists will study encyclicals from Rome with appreciation; former Methodists will deepen their insight into the liturgy by studying Eastern Christian writers. Everyone will accept the whole of the tradition.… Churches will unite around the early creeds and will continue to use the treasures of the great confessions of the Reformation, of Trent and the Catholic Catechism, and of the hundreds of creeds and confessions that the global South will produce between now and then. Confessions, however, will cease to serve as wedges to pry one set of Christians from another. Confessions will be used for edification rather than as a set of shibboleths for excluding those who mispronounce."

embrace in visible unity those who by word and deed spurn the cross of Christ are making an idol of visible unity, a classic two-kingdoms confusion. On the other hand, we should remember that since Christian unity can be manifested in the civil and cultural sphere just as much as in the institutional church, both falling within the temporal kingdom, we should not downplay such displays of unity as irrelevant or insignificant. When Presbyterians and Baptists and Methodists unite in running soup kitchens or counseling ministries, and do so consciously as brothers and sisters in Christ, we should not think that this unity somehow "doesn't count" just because they remain distinct denominations.

Thus we find that in *The Reunion of Christendom*, Schaff concludes his survey of the possibilities for reunion by exhorting Christians to just these kinds of "moral unity." First, he says, we need "the cultivation of an irenic and evangelical-catholic spirit in the personal intercourse with our fellow-Christians of other denominations. We must meet them on common rather than on disputed ground, and assume that they are as honest and earnest as we in the pursuit of truth." Second, he notes, "cooperation in Christian and philanthropic work draws men together and promotes their mutual confidence and regard." Third, he calls for cooperation among missionaries of different denominations in the task of evangelism. And fourth, he notes, "the study of church history…[is] an important means of correcting sectarian prejudices and increasing mutual appreciation."[59]

A truly Reformed catholicity, then, learns to value all the outward tokens of the church's unity in their proper place, but precisely because of its calm confidence in the much deeper, richer, and life-giving original unity from which all these flow, refuses to make an idol out of these outward signs. Thus a Reformed catholicity enables a patient, incremental pursuit of ecclesiastical reunion and harmony, walking by faith, rather than by sight, and refuses to be frightened into pursuing half-baked schemes for engineering reunion in the present, or to despair over the present appearance of disunity in Christ's body.

---

[59] Schaff, *Reunion of Christendom*, 38–39.

BIBLIOGRAPHY

Avis, P.D.L. *The Church in the Theology of the Reformers*. London: Marshall, Morgan, and Scott, 1981.

———. "'The True Church' in Reformation Theology." *Scottish Journal of Theology* 30, no.4 (1977): 319–45.

Ballor, Jordan J. and W. Bradford Littlejohn. "European Calvinism: Church Discipline." In *European History Online* [EGO], edited by Irene Dingel and Johannes Paulmann. Mainz, Germany: Institute of European History [IEG]: 2013.

Davie, Martin. "Anglican Ecumenism: The Liberal Catholic Consensus and the Conservative Evangelical Challenge." In *Paths to Unity: Explorations in Ecumenical Method*, edited by Paul Avis, 29–51. London: Church House, 2004.

Davis, Kenneth R. "No Discipline, No Church: An Anabaptist Contribution to the Reformed Theological Tradition." *Sixteenth Century Journal* 13, no. 4 (1982): 43–58.

Field, John and Thomas Wilcox. *An Admonition to Parliament*, in *Puritan Manifestoes: A Study of the Origins of the Puritan Revolt.* Edited by W.H. Frere and C.E. Douglas. London: Society for Promoting Christian Knowledge, 1907.

Hegstad, Harald. *The Real Church: An Ecclesiology of the Visible.* Eugene, OR: Pickwick, 2013.

Heppe, Heinrich. *Reformed Dogmatics.* London: Allen & Unwin, 1950.

Hooker, Richard. *A Learned Discourse of Justification, Workes, and How the Foundation of Faith Is Overthrowne*, in *The Folger Library Edition of Richard Hooker: V. Tractates and Sermons.* Edited by Laetitia Yeandle and Egil Grislis. Cambridge, MA: Belknap, 1990.

———. *Of the Laws of Ecclesiastical Polity, Book V*. In *The Folger Library Edition of Richard Hooker: V. Tractates and Sermons.* Edited by W. Speed Hill. Cambridge, MA: Belknap, 1977.

———. *The Word of God and the Words of Man: Books II–III of Hooker's* Laws; *A*

Modernization. Edited by Bradford Littlejohn, Bradley Belschner, and Brian Marr. Moscow, ID: Davenant Press, 2018.

Jenson, Robert. "The Church and the Sacraments." In *The Cambridge Companion to Christian Doctrine*, edited by Colin Gunton, 207–25. Cambridge: Cambridge University Press, 1997.

John Paul II. *Ut Unum Sint: On Commitment to Ecumenism*. Rome: The Vatican, 1995.

Kärkkäinen, Veli-Matti. *An Introduction to Ecclesiology: Ecumenical, Historical, and Global Perspectives*. Downers Grove, IL: IVP Academic, 2002.

Lake, Peter. *Anglicans and Puritans? Presbyterianism and English Conformist Thought from Whitgift to Hooker*. London: Allen & Unwin, 1988.

Leithart, Peter J. "Attaining Unity: A Response to Mike Allen." Theopolis Institute. June 13, 2017.

——. *The End of Protestantism: Pursuing Unity in a Fragmented Church*. Grand Rapids, MI: Brazos, 2016.

——. "The One City of God." Theopolis Institute. February 21, 2019.

Littlejohn, W. Bradford. "Believing in the Church: Why Ecumenism Needs the Invisibility of the Church." *Religions* 10, no. 2 (2019):1–14.

——. *Richard Hooker: A Companion to His Life and Work*. Eugene, OR: Cascade, 2015.

——. *The Mercersburg Theology and the Quest for Reformed Catholicity*. Eugene, OR: Pickwick, 2009.

——. *The Peril and Promise of Christian Liberty: Richard Hooker, the Puritans, and Protestant Political Theology*. Grand Rapids, MI: Eerdmans, 2017.

——. "The Search for Visible Catholicity and the Danger of Boundary-Drawing: Lessons from John Nevin and Richard Hooker." In *Marking the Church: Essays in Ecclesiology*, edited by Greg Peters, 122–37. Eugene, OR: Pickwick, 2016.

MacLeod, Donald. "The Basis of Christian Unity." In *Ecumenism Today: The Universal Church in the 21st Century*, edited by Francesca Aran Murphy and Christopher Asprey, 107–120. Aldershot, UK: Ashgate, 2008.

Morerod, Charles. "The Ecumenical Meaning of the Petrine Ministry." In

Ecumenism Today: The Universal Church in the 21st Century, edited by Francesca Aran Murphy and Christopher Asprey, 121–38. Aldershot, UK: Ashgate, 2008.

Nevin, John Williamson. *Antichrist*. In *The Anxious Bench, Antichrist, and the Sermon Catholic Unity*. Edited by Augustine Thompson. Eugene, OR: Wipf and Stock, 1999.

———. "Cyprian: Second Article." *Mercersburg Review* 4, no. 2 (1852): 335–87.

———. "The Christian Ministry." In *The Mercersburg Theology*, edited by J. H. Nichols, 349–71. New York: Oxford University Press, 1966.

Padley, Kenneth. "Early Anglican Ecclesiology and Contemporary Ecumenism." *International Journal for the Study of the Christian Church* 9, no. 1 (2009): 3–16.

Schaff, Philip. *The Principle of Protestantism*, vol. 1 of *Lancaster Series on the Mercersburg Theology*. Chambersburg, PA: German Reformed Church, 1845. Reprinted by Bard Thompson and George H. Bricker. Eugene, OR: Wipf and Stock, 2004.

———. *The Reunion of Christendom: A Paper Prepared for the Parliament of Religions and the National Conference of the Evangelical Alliance held in Chicago, September and October 1893*. New York: Charles Scribner's Sons, 1893.

Schwöbel, Christoph. "The Creature of the Word: Recovering the Ecclesiology of the Reformers." In *On Being the Church: Essays on the Christian Community*, edited by Colin E. Gunton and Daniel W. Hardy, 110–155. Edinburgh: T&T Clark, 1989.

The Church of England. The Meissen Agreement. 1991.

Tjørhom, Ola. *Visible Church—Visible Unity: Ecumenical Ecclesiology and the "The Great Tradition of the Church."* With a foreword by Geoffrey Wainwright. Collegeville, MN: Liturgical Press, 2004.

Van den Belt, Henk, Riemer Faber, Andreas Beck, and William den Boer, eds. *Synopsis Purioris Theologiae: Latin Text and English Translation*, vol. 2. Leiden: Brill, 2016.

Van der Borght, Eduardus. "The Unity of the Church in the Reformed Tradition: An Introduction." In *The Unity of the Church: A Theological State of the Art and Beyond*, edited by Eduardus Van der Borght, 1–15.

Leiden: Brill, 2010.

Van Wyk, J. H. (Amie). "'Is Christ Divided?'—An Analysis of the Theological Justification of a Church Schism." In *The Unity of the Church*, edited by Van der Borght, 51–67. Leiden: Brill, 2010.

Vischer, Lukas, Ulrich Luz, and Christian Link. *Unity of the Church in the New Testament and Today*. Grand Rapids, MI: Eerdmans, 2008.

Webster, John. "On Evangelical Ecclesiology." *Ecclesiology* 1, no. 1 (2004): 9–35.

———. "The Goals of Ecumenism." In *Paths to Unity: Explorations in Ecumenical Method*, edited by Paul Avis, 1–28. London: Church House, 2004.

———. "*Ut Unum Sint:* Some Cross-Bench Anglican Reflections." *Ecumenism Today: The Universal Church in the 21st Century*, edited by Francesca Aran Murphy and Christopher Asprey, 29–44. Aldershot, UK: Ashgate, 2008.

Winship, Michael P. *Godly Republicanism: Puritans, Pilgrims, and a City on a Hill.* Cambridge, MA: Harvard University Press, 2012.

II:
REFORMING CATHOLICITY IN TUDOR ENGLAND: JOHN JEWEL'S DOCTRINE OF THE UNIVERSAL CHURCH

Andre Gazal, North Greenville University

WHEN Elizabeth I's Parliament declared in 1559 that the Church of England was a national Protestant Church, it did not abandon for that church the claim of catholicity. Rome, however, was not about to grant her that claim, insisting that by refusing to send delegates to the last session of the Council of Trent (1562), the Church of England had forsaken the "One, Holy, Catholic, and Apostolic Church." Such a charge had not merely theological but political implications, making the realm vulnerable to possible invasion by powerful states loyal to Rome, such as France and Spain. In the face of these threats, England's government sought to provide a response that would vindicate the catholic identity of its national church while justifying its rejection of the Council of Trent. This difficult task fell to John Jewel (1522–1571), bishop of Salisbury, resulting in an enduring classic of English Protestantism, the *Apology of the Church of England.*

First published in Latin in 1562 as *Apologia Ecclesiae Anglicanae*, the *Apology* defended before an international audience the orthodoxy of the Church of England's doctrine and practice—and its catholicity. To make the case, Jewel defined "catholicity" in a way that legitimated England's Protestant national church and its separation from Rome. Jewel would elaborate these arguments over the following years in the course of his polemical exchange with his Roman opponent, Thomas Harding (1516–1572).

This chapter will show that Jewel's reconciliation of England's claims to both catholicity and independence rested on three main arguments: a reappropriation of the Vincentian Canon, a recovery of Cyprian's view of the episcopate, and a revised conciliarism that emphasized the role of regional and national synods, rather than general councils like Trent. However, before examining these particular components of Jewel's doctrine of catholicity, we will first consider the bishop's definition of the church in part 2 of the *Apology*.

JEWEL'S DEFINITIONS OF THE CHURCH AND CATHOLICITY

Part 2 of the *Apology of the Church of England* is a statement of faith expounding in some detail the various doctrines professed by the English national church. Notably, the longest article in this section focuses on the church. Jewel begins by defining the church thus:

> We believe that there is one church of God, and that the same is not shut up (as in times past among the Jews) into some one corner or kingdom, but that is catholic and universal and dispersed throughout the whole world. So that there is no nation which can truly complain that they be shut forth and may not be one of the church and people of God. And that this church is the kingdom, the body, and the spouse of Christ; and that Christ alone is the prince of this kingdom; that Christ alone is the head of this body; and that Christ alone is the bridegroom of this spouse.[1]

Contrasting the church with Old Testament Israel, Jewel insists that it is not confined to one country, or particular part of the world. Rather, it encompasses every country where Christ is named. Furthermore, the church is the kingdom of which Christ alone is head and prince. From the outset, this definition of the church wrests from the Church of Rome its exclusive claim to catholicity. Rather, truly "catholic" church consists of churches throughout the world, including those of the East that are not in communion with Rome; the Church of Rome is, therefore, merely one of many local or regional churches that comprise the one Catholic Church.

---

[1] John Jewel, *Apology of the Church of England*, trans. Ann Bacon, ed. John Booty (New York: Church Publishing, 2002), 24.

The distinction between the "Catholic" Church and the Roman Church originates neither with Jewel nor with any of the other reformers. It was first employed in the ecclesiological discussions of the medieval canonists, especially Huguccio (d. 1210), who admittedly granted that the term *Romana ecclesia* could refer to either, depending on context.[2] In taking up this distinction, Jewel not only shows familiarity with this tradition, but he utilizes it to establish a catholicity that sharply distinguishes between the "Catholic Church," the entire *congregatio fidelium*, and the Roman Church, a local or regional church, without ever using the term *Romana ecclesia* for the universal church. The patristic grounds for this distinction, to which Jewel repeatedly refers, is Jerome's axiom that the world is greater than a city, the very statement Huguccio commented upon when making the same distinction.[3] Having distinguished the Catholic Church from the Roman Church, thereby removing the latter's absolute claim to the name "Catholic," Jewel proceeds to define catholicity.

Jewel expands upon his conception of catholicity in his *Defence of the Apology*, in which he responds to Harding's criticism of his definition of the church in the *Apology*. Jewel begins by defending the antiquity of Protestant doctrine and practice: "We reform our churches now according to the pattern and sampler of Christ's and his apostles' first institution."[4] For Jewel, the antiquity of a doctrine or practice is determined by its traceability to the Scriptures. In other words, the bishop views antiquity as a criterion that is includes biblical warrant. When Jewel applies this understanding of antiquity to the two churches, he maintains that the Church of Rome is the product of corrupt innovation.[5]

After discussing the nature of antiquity, Jewel unpacks the traditional criteria for determining catholicity given by Vincent of Lerins's (d. 445) *Commonitory*. Therein, Vincent defines catholic belief as that which has been believed "everywhere, always, and by all."[6] Disputing with Harding con-

---

[2] Brian Tierney, *Foundations of the Conciliar Theory: The Contribution of the Medieval Canonists from Gratian to the Great Schism* (Cambridge: Cambridge University Press, 1968), 41.

[3] For example, see Jewel, *Apology*, 107; Tierney, *Foundations of the Conciliar Theory*, 41.

[4] John Jewel, *The Works of John Jewel*, ed. John Ayre, 4 vols. (Cambridge: Cambridge University Press, 1845–1850), 3:267.

[5] Jewel, *Works*, 3:267.

[6] Jewel, *Works*, 3:267; Vincent of Lerins, *Commonitory*, ch. 2.6.

cerning the meaning of the Vincentian Canon, Jewel contends that Vincent did not posit these criteria without qualification. The ancient writer added the qualification, "Whereas the churches were not corrupted,"[7] referring to that period of church history ranging from the New Testament to the first four general councils (Nicaea I, Constantinople I, Ephesus, and Chalcedon).[8] If antiquity, and hence the other two marks of catholicity (universality and consent), are not understood within the specifically defined boundaries of the early church as just described, then certainly no Christian doctrine can be said to have been truly Catholic.[9] When correctly understood in historical context, as Jewel alleges, the Vincentian Canon directly invalidates the Roman Church's claim to catholicity. Applied to the then-present doctrines and practices of the Roman Church, the Vincentian Canon demonstrates their recent vintage, and worse, conflict with the theological parameters set by the ancient church.[10]

Although Jewel only explicitly references the Vincentian Canon in this section of the *Defence*, he cites it in part 5 of the *Apology* and applies it throughout to specific doctrines and practices. These include papal supremacy and the elements of the communion liturgy, showing that they were unknown in the early church and even flagrantly transgress its creedal boundaries.

To his understanding of the Vincentian Canon and application of it on behalf of the Church of England and against the Church of Rome, Jewel added criteria for orthodoxy that vindicate the Church of England and impeach the Church of Rome: the Scriptures, the first four ecumenical councils, the writings of the church fathers, and example of the primitive church. In utilizing these criteria, Jewel makes the church's first six hundred years normative for interpreting Scripture, defining doctrine, and instituting ecclesiastical practice. Jewel's definition of orthodoxy arises from his understanding of *sola Scriptura*: the church's final authority is Scripture as interpreted by the fathers and applied by the early church. This did not imply the latter two were equal to Scripture, but that they were consciously

---

[7] Jewel, *Works*, 3:267.

[8] It should be noted that Vincent himself states that the "General Councils" are the means by which the consensus of antiquity is expressed. See Vincent of Lerins, *Commonitory*, ch. 3.

[9] Jewel, *Works*, 3:367–68.

[10] Jewel, *Works*, 3:368.

subordinate to Scripture and sought faithfully to teach and practice it.[11] Although Gary Jenkins has characterized the criteria advanced by Jewel as largely arbitrary, intended to demolish the Catholic consensus resting upon ecclesiastical tradition,[12] it is more likely that the bishop of Salisbury's definition of orthodoxy depended upon existing ecclesiastical tradition.[13] Given that Jewel stresses Vincent of Lerins's own emphasis on the period of the general councils, and the councils themselves, as the source of catholicity and orthodoxy, it is plausible that he simply restates and applies the Vincentian Canon. This, of course, yields the same polemical results: confirmation of the Church of England's doctrine, and therefore Protestant doctrine, as firmly established in antiquity, and Rome's as an innovative contradiction and therefore heretical. Furthermore, it is worth noting that later Anglican interpretations of orthodoxy followed Jewel's interpretation of the Vincentian Canon.[14]

Among the three marks of catholicity comprising the Vincentian Canon, Jewel considers antiquity the chief mark. While the number of people believing the faith has varied, and continues to vary—as has the faith's geographical reach—it is the faith itself whose content has been defined and determined in antiquity that remains constant, and therefore serves as the principal basis of catholicity: "The catholic church of God standeth not in the multitude of persons, but in weight of truth. Otherwise Christ Himself and his apostles had not been catholic: for his flock was very little; and the catholic or universal consent of the world stood against it."[15] The essence of catholicity, then, is the unalterable constancy of the ancient faith. Thus having posited and applied the Vincentian Canon in order to establish

---

[11] Andre A. Gazal, *Scripture and Royal Supremacy in Tudor England: The Use of Old Testament Narrative* (Lewiston, NY: Edwin Mellen), ch. 4.

[12] Gary W. Jenkins, *John Jewel and the English National Church: The Dilemmas of an Erastian Reformer* (Burlington, VT: Ashgate, 2006), 73.

[13] Heiko Oberman, "'*Quo Vadis, Petre*': Tradition from Irenaeus to *Humani Generis*," in *Dawn of the Reformation Essays in Late Medieval and Early Reformation Thought* (Grand Rapids, MI: Eerdmans, 1992), 269–96; see also Andre A. Gazal, "'A Crime So Heinous': The Concept of Heresy in John Jewel's *Apology of the Church of England*" (paper presented at the Defending the Faith Conference, Salisbury, UK, September 17, 2014), 5.

[14] See Thomas G. Guarino, *Vincent of Lerins and the Development of Christian Doctrine* (Grand Rapids, MI: Baker, 2013).

[15] Jewel, *Works*, 3:268.

the foundation of the Protestant Church of England's catholicity, Jewel proceeds to buttress it further by reappropriating the Cyprianic view of the episcopate.

REAPPROPRIATING THE CYPRIANIC DOCTRINE OF THE EPISCOPATE

Following his definition of the church in part 2 of the *Apology*, Jewel discusses the orders of the church. Jewel acknowledges three: deacons, priests, and bishops, "to whom is committed the office to instruct the people and the whole charge and setting forth of religion."[16] Following this, Jewel immediately attacks the doctrine of papal supremacy:

> We say that there neither is nor can be any one man which may have the whole superiority in this universal state; for that Christ is ever present to assist his church and needeth not any man to supply his room as his only heir to all his substance; and that there can be no mortal creature which is able to comprehend or conceive in his mind the universal church, that is, to wit, all parts of the world, much less able to put them in order and to govern them rightly and duly.[17]

The one, true head of the church is continually present with it and therefore is infinitely capable of providing for his people. Because he is omnipotent as well as omnipresent, Christ has no need of assistance by a mere human being; nor *could* any man govern the entire Catholic Church—that is Christ's function as the head, and he alone is able to fulfill it. Jewel relates Christ's divine attributes to his governance of the universal church in order to highlight, by contrast, the absurdity of the pope's claims as earthly head of the Catholic Church. For Jewel, Christ's divine attributes, by which he governs the church, constitute the principal argument against the doctrine of papal supremacy.

Yet, in order to destroy the doctrine of papal supremacy, Jewel must neutralize its foundational doctrine of papal primacy, the superiority of the

[16] Jewel, *Apology*, 24.

[17] Jewel, *Apology*, 24.

pope to all other bishops. To accomplish this, Jewel argues for the recovery of a truly catholic conception of the episcopacy as defined by the ancient bishop Cyprian (200–258).

Immediately after making his Christological argument, Jewel quotes Cyprian's *De Unitate Ecclesiae* regarding the authority of the apostles: "For all of the apostles were of like power among themselves, and the rest were the same as Peter was."[18] Moreover, Jewel cites the words of Christ to this effect, interpreting them in the same manner as Cyprian: "It was said indifferently to them all, 'Feed ye'; indifferently to them all, 'Go into the whole world'; indifferently to them all, 'Teach ye the gospel.'"[19] Thus, Jewel observes with, he thinks, Cyprian that the commission to proclaim the gospel and the accompanying authority to do so are given equally to all the apostles by Christ Himself. Furthermore, Jewel quotes Cyprian specifically with respect to the episcopate: "There is but one bishopric, and a piece thereof is perfectly and wholly holden of every particular bishop."[20] There is one episcopate, and all bishops equally share in it. Jewel goes on to cite Jerome's *Epistle to Euagrius*, in which he declared: "All bishops, wheresoever they be, be they at Rome, be they at Eugubium, be they at Constantinople, be they at Rhegium, be of all like preeminence and of like priesthood."[21] Afterward, he quotes Augustine's *City of God*, in which he, wrote the bishop, "was the name of labor, and not of honor."[22] Jewel observes the ancient bishop of Hippo did not believe one was a bishop who desired preeminence over others.[23] Jewel then highlights instances in which bishops resisted attempts by their peers to usurp primacy, the most famous of which was Gregory the Great's rebuke of the patriarch of Constantinople, John the Faster, who wanted to claim for himself the title of "Ecumenical Patriarch."[24]

Jewel gives a detailed explanation of Cyprian's conception of the episcopate in the *Defence*. The bishop of Salisbury claims Cyprian understood the purpose of the episcopate as preserving unity and orderly government in the church, the purpose Paul himself declares in Ephesians 4:

---

[18] Jewel, *Apology*, 24; see also Cyprian, *De Unitate Ecclesiae*, ch. 4.

[19] Jewel, *Apology*, 24.

[20] Jewel, *Apology*, 25; see also Cyprian, *De Unitate Ecclesiae*, ch.5.

[21] Jewel, *Apology*, 24–25; see also Jerome, *Epistola ad Euagrium*.

[22] Jewel, *Apology*, 25; see also Augustine, *De Civitate Dei*, Bk. XIX. ch. 19.

[23] Jewel, *Apology*, 25.

[24] Jewel, *Apology*, 25.

> But for the unity and quiet government of the church of God, St. Paul saith: "Christ ascending above all the heavens hath given (not one universal pope to the rule the whole, but) some apostles, some prophets, some evangelists, some pastors, some doctors for the perfecting of the saints, for the work of ministry, for the building up of the body of Christ; that may all come into the unity of faith, and of knowledge of the Son of God." By these means God thought it sufficient to preserve his church in unity, and never made mention of one universal pope.[25]

Although Paul does not mention bishops explicitly in this passage, the principle that Jewel stresses in his interpretation of Paul is that unity of truth and stability of ecclesiastical government are preserved by plurality. The ascended Christ provided numerous apostles and pastors, the latter of whom receive their ministry of doctrine from the apostles and who themselves are also bishops.

At this point, it is important to note that Jewel did not hold to a *iure divino* view of episcopacy, but rather believed the office of bishop to have developed early during the New Testament period. Over time, it became an esteemed and venerable office in the primitive church. Elsewhere, Jewel ascribes to bishops the same essential authority as priests in general, namely, the preaching and teaching of the Word and the pastoral responsibilities incumbent upon it.[26] This accounts for the equivalence Jewel sees between bishops in England and the chief Protestant ecclesiastical figures on the Continent, including Theodore Beza in Geneva and Heinrich Bullinger and Peter Martyr Vermigli in Zurich. Thus, in his reappropriation of the Cyprianic episcopate, Jewel does not emphasize the office so much as the deposit of truth with which leaders of the church—whether called bishops, priests, pastors, elders, or the like—are entrusted. Therefore, Jewel conceives of the "Catholic Church" as consisting of national churches with sundry polities (Lutheran and Reformed) whose common and hence unifying possession is the body of biblical truth expounded and applied by the early church.

In the *Defence*, Jewel comments further upon the second citation of Cyprian's *De Unitate Ecclesiae*, given initially in the *Apology*: "There is but one

---

[25] Jewel, *Works*, 3:283–84.

[26] Jewel, *Apology*, 26–29.

bishopric, and a piece thereof is perfectly and wholly holden of every particular bishop."[27] Jewel stresses the protection and preservation of the truth by the plural episcopate, quoting from Cyprian's letters: "Therefore are there many bishops in the church, that if one fall into heresy, the rest may help."[28] All bishops, being entrusted with the same truth by Christ and the apostles, hold one another accountable in the same truth, rebuking one another necessarily if any should deviate from it. In connection with Cyprian's understanding, Jewel gives as examples Paul's confrontation of Peter in Galatians and Irenaeus's open criticism of Pope Victor.[29]

Next in the *Defence*, Jewel elaborates on his citation of Cyprian's *De Unitate Ecclesiae* in the *Apology*: "For all of the apostles were of like power among themselves, and the rest were the same as Peter was."[30] Here, Jewel emphasizes the total equality of episcopal authority given its essential oneness. In so doing, he discredits the papalist distinction between extraordinary power, that given by Christ to Peter, and ordinary power, which was delegated by Peter to the rest of the apostles. This distinction is the foundation for papal primacy, and Jewel argues it was totally unknown by Cyprian and other ancient bishops.[31] Not only is this distinction an innovation, it contravenes the Scriptures, the first four general councils, the church fathers, and the example of the primitive church, making it heretical. Throughout the *Apology*, Jewel inveighs against the specific claims of absolute papal power as plainly contradicting the canons of catholicity:

> And therefore, sithence the Bishop of Rome will nowadays so be called, and challengeth unto himself an authority that is none of his, besides that he doth plainly contrary to the ancient councils and contrary to the old fathers, we believe that he does give unto himself, as it is written by his own companion Gregory [the Great], a presumptuous, a profane, a sacrilegious, and an Antichristian name; that he is also the king of pride; that he is Lucifer, which preferreth

---

[27] See footnote #20 above. Pope Victor I (d. 199) threatened excommunication of eastern bishops over their refusal to observe Easter according to the practice of the Church of Rome.

[28] Jewel, *Works*, 3:284.

[29] Jewel, *Works*, 3:284.

[30] Jewel, *Works*, 3:286.

[31] Jewel, *Works*, 3:286.

> himself before his brethren; that he has forsaken the faith, and is the forerunner of Antichrist.[32]

Thus for Jewel, papal primacy and supremacy represent the very antithesis of catholicity.

In addition to Cyprian, Augustine, and Jerome, Jewel cites the first general council, the Council of Nicaea (325), which proclaimed: "The Bishop of Rome has no more jurisdiction over the church of God than the rest of the patriarchs, either of Alexandria or Antioch have."[33] This is of considerable significance because Nicaea I, as one of the first four general councils, defined the parameters of orthodoxy, and thus catholicity. Affirmed by a general council, the plural episcopate in which all bishops possess and exercise equal authority is a necessary and orthodox mark of catholicity. By defining orthodoxy, the general councils provided the boundaries of catholicity. The role and functions of councils in determining doctrine factor prominently in Jewel's conception of catholicity.

JEWEL'S REVISION OF CONCILIARISM IN HIS DOCTRINE OF CATHOLICITY

As has been discussed above, one criterion of orthodoxy employed by Jewel was the teaching of first four general councils. He understood these deliberative bodies to have represented the mind of the church and its understanding of the Word of God. As such, they stood for the bishop as vehicles of Catholic consent. Jewel argues throughout the *Apology*, however, that the general council is no longer a viable means of expressing Catholic doctrine, since no general council can represent the entire church. In fact, Jewel points out that at the previous session of the Council of Trent, only forty bishops attended[34]—hardly an expression of Catholic consensus. Moreover, whereas the four general councils granted liberty to all attendees to speak freely, Trent and other supposedly general councils presided over by the pope did not afford this liberty, thereby stifling all discussion and dissent.[35] All judgments rendered by the so-called council must be ratified by the sin-

32 Jewel, *Apology*, 26.

33 Jewel, *Apology*, 25.

34 Jewel, *Apology*, 125.

35 Jewel, *Apology*, 113.

gular authority of the pope himself.[36] Hence, in Jewel's estimation, the pope's total dominance of the council rendered any contribution to a genuine Catholic consensus out of the question. Finally, another deficiency of Trent, which further disqualifies it from the status of general council of the church, was its exclusion of civil magistrates from active participation in its proceedings.[37] The return of the properly catholic general council, for Jewel, therefore requires the reformation of the whole conciliar apparatus.

In part 6 of the *Apology*, using the ecclesiastical arrangement in England as an example, Jewel proposes a solution for recovering the necessary constructive role of councils. Jewel's program entails transferring the power of general councils to regional and national synods. Not only do regional and national synods have the capacity to substitute for general councils, they can even correct the errors of such pretended bodies like Trent, which Jewel contemptuously dubs a "silly little convent." Furthermore, regional and national synods can and should readily reform their territorial churches without awaiting a general council, the convening of which could take extensive time and the completion of which could be postponed repeatedly, as was the case with sessions of Trent. Even more importantly than this, participants can deliberate freely within the bounds of orthodoxy, arriving at a true consensus that can be translated into substantial reforms. In proposing this alternative to general councils, Jewel insists that he does so within the bounds of received Catholic tradition, evidenced by ancient regional and national synods that decided doctrinal and practical matters. such as those of Carthage under Cyprian as well as those of Ancyra and Gangra, which predate the general Council of Nicaea.[38] Furthermore, Jewel argues that regular meetings of bishops by way of regional and national synods constitute an important element of long-standing Catholic tradition, attested by the four general councils themselves, especially the Council of Nicaea's requirement that bishops meet together twice a year.[39] Although Catholic tradition sanctions and even requires the convening of regional and national synods to promote the well-being of churches, it should be

[36] Jewel, *Apology*, 113.

[37] Jewel, *Apology*, 113.

[38] Jewel, *Apology*, 124. According to Jewel, this is further evidenced by the regional North African synods in Carthage that condemned the Donatists and Pelagius in the fifth century, and the Synod of Frankfurt presided over by Charlemagne in 794.

[39] Jewel, *Apology*, 124.

noted that the suggestion that such assemblies act on the same par as general councils is one that is without precedent in ecclesiology up to this point.

The element within synods that elevates them to the level of general councils, and that empowers them to reject the pronouncements of pretended councils, is the participation and close supervision of civil magistrates. For Jewel, the defining quality of the first four general councils, that which gave them their unique and hence truly Catholic status, was that Christian emperors summoned them.[40] Interestingly, Jewel expounds his biblical doctrine of royal supremacy in connection with his understanding of regional and national synods. Jewel believes that the Scriptures mandate a Christian prince exercise authority over the church in his (or in the case of England in Jewel's day, her) realm.[41] Full participation by lay princes as well as their synods constitute obedience to the Old Testament command that they safeguard true religion according to the Word of God. This biblical doctrine of royal supremacy enabled Jewel to characterize Parliament's enacting of the Elizabethan Settlement as the work of a national ecclesiastical synod under the governance of the Queen as the godly prince. Whether the venerable bishop of Sarum would acknowledge it or not, the ascription of the power of general councils to regional and national synods originates with him, and thus stands as his unique contribution to Protestant ecclesiology.

CONCLUSION

John Jewel, as an apologist for the Protestant Church of England, directed his defense against a formidable institution in the midst of rapidly changing and perilous times. Jewel sought to vindicate his church's catholicity as Christian Europe transformed from a supposedly unified Christendom to a conglomeration of autonomous Christian states, each of which sought to define its identity by way of this fragmenting Christianity. Yet all of them claimed catholicity, leading to bitter conflict over what it meant to be "catholic." The Council of Trent sought to reinforce a catholicity defined by submission to the Roman Church, whose earthly head was the pope as

---

[40] Jewel, *Apology*, 116–19.

[41] See Gazal, *Scripture and Royal Supremacy*, ch. 5.

the Vicar of Christ. Protestant nations, and in this case, Elizabethan England sought another source of Catholic identity. Jewel provided this by appropriating the canons of early Christian tradition, defined by Vincent of Lerins. He claimed that catholicity consists in what has been believed always, everywhere, and by all, and he clarified this to include the Scriptures, the first four general councils, the writings of the church fathers, and example of the primitive church. As has been shown, for Jewel, this meant biblical truth as interpreted and applied by the early church; anything subsequent and containing no basis in or being contrary to catholicity so defined was heretical and thus rejected. This included most of Rome's "catholic" doctrines and practices. Jewel, following Cyprian, saw the catholic body of truth as preserved and protected by a plural episcopate, which Jewel understood to include all Protestant church leaders in Europe. Finally, Jewel endeavored to preserve what he deemed ancient catholicity by rejecting the general council, which had become unilaterally dominated by the pope and so was no longer a legitimate channel of genuine consent informed by antecedent tradition. The bishop's solution was to transfer the authority of general councils to regional and national synods that possess the necessary elements of true catholic councils, especially the supervision of the godly prince. With these conditions in place, even an apparently legislative body like England's Parliament could be legitimately regarded as a truly catholic national ecclesiastical synod because it legislates on the basis of received catholic truth. With all Protestant commonwealths of Europe working in tandem to reform themselves, they would together form the true, restored Catholic Church in Europe. Thus, in defending the orthodoxy of the Church of England, Jewel presented to Europe a church that had reformed itself back into catholicity.

BIBLIOGRAPHY

Gazal, Andre A. "'A Crime So Heinous': The Concept of Heresy in John Jewel's *Apology of the Church of England*." Paper presented at the Defending the Faith Conference, Salisbury, UK, September 17, 2014.

——. *Scripture and Royal Supremacy in Tudor England: The Use of Old Testament Narrative*. Lewiston, NY: Edwin Mellen, 2013.

Guarino, Thomas G. *Vincent of Lerins and the Development of Christian Doctrine*. Grand Rapids, MI: Baker, 2013.

Jenkins, Gary W. *John Jewel and the English National Church: The Dilemmas of an Erastian Reformer*. Burlington, VT: Ashgate, 2006.

Jewel, John. *Apology of the Church of England*. Translated by Ann Bacon, and edited by John Booty. New York: Church Publishing, 2002.

——. *The Works of John Jewel*. Edited by John Ayre. 4 vols. Cambridge: Cambridge University Press, 1845–1850.

Oberman, Heiko. "'*Quo Vadis, Petre*': Tradition from Irenaeus to *Humani Generis*." In *Dawn of the Reformation Essays in Late Medieval and Early Reformation Thought*, 269–96. Grand Rapids, MI: Eerdmans, 1992.

Tierney, Brian. *Foundations of the Conciliar Theory: The Contribution of the Medieval Canonists from Gratian to the Great Schism*. Cambridge: Cambridge University Press, 1968.

III: REFORMED CATHOLICITY AND THE ANALOGY OF BEING

Steven J. Duby, Grand Canyon University

INTRODUCTION

IN RECENT discussions among Roman Catholic, Eastern Orthodox, and Protestant theologians, the topic of the so-called analogy of being has played a significant role. Often Protestant theology, in the wake of Karl Barth, is portrayed as having little room for an analogical relationship between (sinful) creatures and God the Creator. In some circles this has yielded an assumption that a consistently Protestant approach to human knowledge of God will reject the project of natural theology and hold that human beings can know God only on the basis of God's grace given in Christ and the act of faith.

In light of this, this essay will argue that a Reformed Protestant approach to human knowledge of God does in fact have room for an "analogy of being" and can, in constructive dialogue with medieval and contemporary Roman Catholic theologians, pursue a truly catholic vision of the knowledge of God available by nature. Such a pursuit is catholic not only in the sense that it enables Protestants to find common ground with Roman Catholic and Eastern Orthodox believers in a secular society but also in the sense that it leads to an affirmation of what John Owen calls a "catholic" revelation of God to all humanity, a revelation that is preparatory for human beings to come to a saving knowledge of Christ.[1]

To make the case that Reformed Protestants can and should embrace a carefully defined—and catholic—analogy of being, I will attempt to do three things. First, I will summarize a traditional doctrine of analogy expounded by Thomas Aquinas and some Reformed orthodox theologians. Second, I will summarize Barth's critique of such a doctrine. Finally, in response to Barth, I will seek to explain how an essentially Thomistic (and broadly Reformed orthodox) view of analogy coheres with a Protestant rendering of nature, grace, and human knowledge of God.

THOMAS AND THE REFORMED ON ANALOGY

Thomas

Though we will focus our attention on analogy in Thomas and the Reformed, it is helpful to begin by briefly noting its place in Aristotle's thought. The Stagirite famously illustrates his understanding of analogy by using the example of health, observing different ways in which something might be called "healthy." One thing might be called "healthy" by preserving health, another by producing it, another by signaling it, another by in fact having it. Similarly, something may be called a "being" in different ways: for example, by being a substance, by being an "affection" or disposition of a substance, by being a quality of a substance, by being a generation or production of a substance or something that belongs to a substance. That subject that is healthy or has health is what is principally called "healthy," and those other things we call healthy are deemed such by reference to that principally healthy thing. Likewise, substance is principally called a being, and other things are called beings by way of an analogy or certain correspondence and similarity to substance. While substance exists per se and in its own right, a quality, for example, exists insofar as it inheres in a substance. "Being" is thus predicated in different modes according to a πρὸς ἕν analogy (an analogy "toward one" or by reference and likeness to a principal thing, i.e., substance). This form of analogy is often called an "analogy of attribution." In Aristotle's metaphysics, the πρὸς ἕν analogy

[1] John Owen, *Theologoumena Pantodapa*, in vol. 17 of *The Works of John Owen*, ed. William H. Goold (Edinburgh: T & T Clark, 1862), I.5.9–10, p. 51.

serves as a way to affirm the diversity of being while also securing the unity of being as a subject of scientific study. Because of the relationship of the various categories of being to a primal category (substance), being in its different modes can be studied in a single science.[2] Another form of analogy also appears in Aristotle's thought, where there is a correspondence between features of two things, in the sense that a feature of one is to it as a similar feature of another is to the other: *a* is to *b* as *c* is to *d*. A quality proper to one thing is analogous to a similar quality that is proper to another in that it is (proportionally) in its own substance as the other quality is (proportionally) in its substance.[3] This is often called an "analogy of proper proportion (or proportionality)."

In the thirteenth century Thomas continues the Christian development of Aristotle's reflections, discussing analogy both with respect to the relationships that exist among creatures and with respect to the relationship between creatures and God.[4] Thomas conveys his understanding of analogy

---

[2] Aristotle, *Aristotelis Metaphysica*, ed. W. Jaeger (Oxford: Clarendon, 1957), IV.1, 1003a–1005a, pp. 59–64.

[3] E.g, Aristotle, *Metaphysica*, XII.1071a, pp. 248–29.

[4] A number of studies of Thomas on analogy have appeared in recent times, often seeking to correct some misunderstandings associated with Cajetan's reading of Thomas. See, e.g., Hampus Lyttkens, *The Analogy between God and the World: An Investigation of Its Background and Interpretation of Its Use by Thomas of Aquino* (Uppsala, Sweden: Lundequistska, 1953); Gerald B. Phelan, *St. Thomas and Analogy* (Milwaukee, WI: Marquette University Press, 1941); George P. Klubertanz, *St. Thomas Aquinas on Analogy: A Textual Analysis and Systematic Synthesis* (Chicago: Loyola University Press, 1960); Battista Mondin, *The Principle of Analogy in Protestant and Catholic Theology* (The Hague: Martinus Nijhoff, 1963), esp. parts II–IV; Bernard Montagnes, *The Doctrine of the Analogy of Being according to Thomas Aquinas*, trans. E. M. Macierowski (Milwaukee, WI: Marquette University Press, 2004); Ralph M. McInerny, *Aquinas and Analogy* (Washington, DC: Catholic University of America Press, 1996); John F. Wippel, *The Metaphysical Thought of Thomas Aquinas: From Finite Being to Uncreated Being* (Washington, DC: Catholic University of America Press, 2000), pp. 65–93, 543–75. Some emphasize that Thomas's writing on analogy is focused on the semantic or logical level of inquiry (e.g., McInerny, *Aquinas and Analogy*; see also Laurence Paul Hemming, "*Analogia non Entis sed Entitatis*: The Ontological Consequences of the Doctrine of Analogy," *International Journal of Systematic Theology* 6 [2004]: 118–29), while others argue that it is directly bound up with certain ontological commitments (e.g., Wippel, *Metaphysical Thought of Thomas Aquinas*; cf. Lawrence Dewan, "St. Thomas and Analogy: The Logician and the Metaphysician," in *Form and Being: Studies in Thomistic Metaphysics* [Washington, DC: Catholic University of America Press, 2006], pp. 81–95; Alan Philip Darley, "Predication or Participation? What Is the Nature of Aquinas' Doctrine of Analogy?," *Heythrop Journal* 57 [2016]: 312–24).

across a range of works in his corpus. In *De Principiis Naturae*, he discusses the ways in which various things may stand in unity with one another. Beyond the stricter kinds of unity (in number, in species, in genus) there is unity or "agreement" (*convenientia*) by analogy.[5] A predicate, he writes, may apply to something univocally, equivocally, or analogically. In univocal predication, not only a common name but also a common *ratio* or definition of a name applies to two different things. In such a case, the predicate indicates a genus under which two things are located. In equivocal predication, only a common name (not the *ratio* or definition of it) applies to two different things. In analogical predication, there is a commonality of both the name and, in a qualified way (*non ex toto*), the diverse *rationes* of the name too. The commonality of the *rationes* consists in that they are all "referred to one thing" (*attribuuntur uni alicui eidem*) from which the feature named (e.g., health) is in some sense derived. That one thing to which a plurality of analogates are referred for their unity may be a particular end, a particular agent, or a particular subject. Of special importance here is the case in which the basis for analogical unity is a subject. For Thomas, *ens* is analogically predicated of quantity, quality, and other accidental instances of being because they have substance (*ens* in its primary mode) as their subject. "Being," Thomas reasons, is not a genus encompassing both substance and accidents because it applies to substance in a primary way (*per prius*) and to accidents in a derivative way (*per posterius*). Among beings there is a relative ordering and hierarchy, while a genus applies to its sundry species (e.g., animal to man and donkey) equally and without this relative hierarchy. Due to the relationship between substance and accidents, being is therefore not predicated univocally across the categories of being.[6] Thomas also adds that

---

For a mediating approach, see Gregory P. Rocca, *Speaking the Incomprehensible God: Thomas Aquinas on the Interplay between Positive and Negative Theology* (Washington, DC: Catholic University of America Press, 2004), pp. 127–34. I follow the second approach here, with an appreciative nod toward Rocca's way of explaining the relationship between the logical and ontological dynamics of analogy.

[5] Here *convenientia*, *analogia*, *proportio*, and *comparatio* all appear as roughly synonymous.

[6] It may be worth pausing to note that this means Thomas does not accept the metaphysical framework of Parmenides, whose monism was built upon the principle that beyond being there is only nonbeing. As Thomas unfolds the reasoning of Parmenides, he observes that nonbeing is nothing (*nihil*) and thus cannot produce diversity in being. Therefore, for Parmenides, since there is nothing to diversify being and since being is one, all being must remain one. Thomas, however, takes it

the principles of different beings agree "according to proportion": the matter of a substance, for example, relates to its substance like the matter of a quantity relates to its quantity.[7]

In a number of works, Thomas presents his view of analogy in relation to the question of theological language and the Creator-creature relationship. In the commentary on the *Sentences*, he writes that the unity of Creator and creature is "by a community not of univocation but of analogy." Analogical "community," though, is twofold: either by posterior things participating in a prior thing or by one thing receiving its existence and *ratio* from another. God does not participate with creatures in something prior to both Himself and creatures, so in the unity of Creator and creature just the latter sort of analogy applies: "The creature does not have existence except as it descends from the first being, nor is it called a being except insofar as it imitates the first being."[8] Later in this commentary, Thomas remarks that univocity assumes a "community according to the *ratio* of nature" with diversity according to (individual) existence, which community cannot apply in the case of God and creatures because God's nature is identical with His own existence. Accordingly, "being" is not predicated univo-

---

to be a fact that there are diverse beings and diverse categories of beings (substance and the various categories of accidents) in which beings have various modes of existing. He therefore denies that being is a genus that would have to be diversified by factors external to it (see Thomas Aquinas, *In Duodecim Libros Metaphysicorum Aristotelis*, ed. M.-R. Cathala and R. M. Spiazzi [Turin-Rome: Marietti, 1950], I.9, nn. 138–39, pp. 41–42; cf. Wippel, *Metaphysical Thought of Thomas Aquinas*, pp. 66–73, 87–89). In Thomas's view, then, being applies to the many, and its unity consists not in that it is a genus equally applicable to all things but rather in that, on the level of created being (or the "predicamental" level), it always stands in some correspondence or πρὸς ἕν analogy to substance (*In Metaphys.*, IV.1, nn. 535–44, pp. 151–52). To elaborate, in medieval philosophy and theology, to identify being as a genus applicable under the same *ratio* to the many would inevitably raise questions about (1) how being could be diversified (for a genus is differentiated by factors extrinsic to it) and (2) how it could remain a transcendental concept predicable equally and under the same *ratio* across the categories of things that in fact have diverse modes of existing. As noted below, when Duns Scotus defends the univocity of being, he will thus argue that his view does not require being to be a genus and does not stipulate that all beings have the same mode of existing in reality.

[7] Thomas Aquinas, *De Principiis Naturae*, in vol. 43 of *Opera Omnia*, Leonine ed. (Rome: Editori di San Tommaso, 1976), 6, pp. 46–47.

[8] Thomas Aquinas, *Scriptum super Libros Sententiarum*, vol. 1, ed. R. P. Mandonnet (Paris, 1929), prol., q. 1, a. 2 ad 2, p. 10.

cally of God and creatures. A predicate like being or knowledge is predicated analogically of God and creatures insofar as creatures imperfectly imitate God and are thus "like God" (even as God is, strictly speaking, not "like creatures").[9] In the same work, Thomas provides another ramification of analogy under three types: (1) analogy according to mental "intention" only (*secundum intentionem tantum, et non secundum esse*), where something is thought to belong to multiple things (with reference to a first) even though in reality it is properly in the first only; (2) analogy according to being only (*secundum esse et non secundum intentionem*), where something belongs to multiple things in reality in an analogical manner but is thought by the mind to apply to them univocally; and (3) analogy according to both intention and being (*secundum intentionem et secundum esse*), where something applies in an analogical manner to multiple things both in the intention of the mind and in reality. For Thomas, the third type of analogy is in view when being is predicated of substance and accidents and when various things (truth and goodness, for example) are predicated of God and creatures. Truth and goodness are in God and then in creatures by reason of greater and lesser degrees of perfection.[10] Clearly, Thomas is deploying the notion of analogy here in a way that underscores that a given perfection is not merely caused by God but also truly present in God Himself.[11]

In *De Veritate*, Thomas presents an alternative account of analogy. Once again he denies that something (in this case, knowledge) can be attributed to God and creatures univocally. However much creatures might imitate God, nothing can belong to creatures according to the same *ratio* with which it belongs to God, for all that is in God is identical with His own *esse*. Yet, pure equivocity is ruled out because some similarity between God and creatures is presupposed in God knowing creatures by knowing Himself and in our ability to learn about God by studying created beings. To explain how this analogical "community" does not undermine the Creator-creature distinction or the "infinite distance" between God and creatures, Thomas explains how analogy or *proportio* can have different meanings. On the one hand, "agreement according to proportion" can apply when two things have a proportion toward one another in that they have a "determined distance" or some mutual "habitude" between them.

---

[9] Thomas, *Sent.*, I.35.1.4 sol. and ad 6, pp. 819–21.

[10] Thomas, *Sent.*, I.19.5.2 ad 1, p. 492.

[11] Compare Wippel, *Metaphysical Thought of Thomas Aquinas*, pp. 549–50.

Thomas calls this an "agreement of proportion" (*convenientia proportionis*). For example, the number two has such a distance or habitude to the number one, in that two is its double. On the other hand, there may be an agreement not of two things proportionate to one another but of two proportions to one another. Thomas calls this an "agreement of proportionality" (*convenientia proportionalitatis*), and it echoes Aristotle's identification of an analogy in which *a* is to *b* as *c* is to *d*. Here Thomas gives an example: sight is to the eye as understanding is to the mind. Because creatures have no habitude or relation to God in which His perfection is determined by them, only this second form of analogy—an analogy of "proportionality"—can apply in the case of God and creatures: God's knowledge is to God as the creature's knowledge is to the creature. This "similitude of proportionality" does not compromise the "infinite distance" between God and the creature or entail a mutual habitude between them; creatures are like God, but, in accord with Isaiah 40:18 ("To whom then will you liken God?"), God is not like creatures.[12]

In later works, Thomas does not persist in limiting the Creator-creature analogy to that of "proportionality." He returns to the "analogy of attribution" in which the perfections of creatures are referred back to God.[13] To conserve space, this can be presented in a composite sketch of relevant portions of the *Summa contra Gentiles*, *De Potentia*, and the *Summa*

---

[12] Thomas Aquinas, *Quaestiones Disputatae De Veritate*, in vol. 22.1/2 of *Opera Omnia*, Leonine ed. (Rome: ad Sanctae Sabinae 1970), 2.11 corp. and ad, 1, 2, 4, pp. 78–80.

[13] It is worth noting that in light of Thomas's *De Veritate* Cajetan famously linked the analogy of proportionality to the analogy *secundum esse* described in Thomas's *Sentences* commentary and argued that the analogy of proportionality uniquely upholds that a given perfection is truly found in God Himself (see his *De Nominum Analogia. De Conceptu Entis*, ed. P. N. Zammit [Rome, 1952], III.23–30, pp. 23–30). On this point, his reading of Thomas is criticized by various authors (e.g., Montagnes, *Doctrine of the Analogy of Being*, pp. 120–40; McInerny, *Aquinas and Analogy*, pp. 3–29; Wippel, *Metaphysical Thought of Thomas Aquinas*, pp. 90n87, 553). However, for a more recent effort to explain Cajetan's own constructive aims in *De Nominum Analogia*, see Joshua P. Hochschild, *The Semantics of Analogy: Rereading Cajetan's* De Nominum Analogia (Notre Dame, IN: University of Notre Dame Press, 2010). In my view, it is important to recognize that Thomas's treatment of analogy in *De Veritate* is not his last word on the matter and that the analogy of attribution too can uphold the intrinsic character of God's perfections. At the same time, I believe that one helpful point made in the *De Veritate* treatment is that God and creatures have no *proportio* or determinate distance between them. While they do have an ontological relationship, it is not a mutually constitutive one.

Theologiae. Thomas stresses that nothing belongs to God and creatures univocally, for created effects are not formally "adequate" to the divine power by which they are wrought. God is an analogical agent who produces His likeness in His effects, but in only a limited fashion. For God's perfections are really identical with His own essence, while the creature's perfections (wisdom, goodness, power, and so on) are qualities added to essence. God has His perfections in an unlimited or "universal" way, while creatures have their various perfections by participation in God's perfection and thus in a limited or "partial" way. God's perfections "pre-exist" in Him in a simple and preeminent manner, while creatures' perfections exist in them in a divided manner. Moreover, the attributes used to signify God's perfections do not circumscribe or capture the fullness of those perfections. In addition, what is predicated univocally of two things is simpler than and prior to both of them, but, according to Thomas, nothing is—ontologically or conceptually—simpler than or prior to God. Univocity also assumes a parity in the modes of existing of two things, but God is His own *esse* and creatures exist only by participation in *esse.*[14] *Ens* (a term derived from the verb *esse*) therefore cannot be predicated univocally of God and creatures, for it is predicated of God in an absolute manner (essentially and *secundum prius*) and of creatures in a derivative manner (by participation and *secundum posterius*).[15]

---

[14] On the senses in which creatures participate in *esse*, see Wippel, *Metaphysical Thought of Thomas Aquinas*, pp. 120–21.

[15] Furthermore, for Thomas, since *esse* within the order of created being is the concrete actualization of essence, it is not included in genus or species but rather lies on the side of that which individuates things (see, e.g., *Quaestiones de Quolibet*, in vol. 25 of *Opera Omnia*, Leonine ed. [Rome: Commissio Leonina; Paris: Les Éditions du Cerf, 1996], II.2.2 [4], pp. 216–18; *Summa theologiae*, vols. 4–12 of *ibid.*, Ia.3.5 corp., p. 44). Thus, the meaning of the commonality of *ens* and *esse* within the horizon of created being might be summarized as follows. First, *ens* or *esse* commonly applies to various categories of things (delineated in the ten Aristotelian *praedicamenta*) by an analogical correspondence in which things in the nine accidental *praedicamenta* depend on substances. Given the evidently diverse modes of existing of substances, quantities, qualities, and so on, *ens* is not restricted to one genus and is not itself a genus equally and univocally applicable to all the categories of being. Second, *ens* or *esse* commonly applies to distinct individuals in that all individual things exist, but it is not a genus or species that accounts for the common determinations of a group of individuals. Rather, it can be said to apply similarly to individuals across categories or within a category, genus, or species by an analogy of proportionality (e.g., the *esse* of Peter is to Peter as the *esse* of John is to John) (compare Montagnes, *Doctrine of the Analogy of Being*, pp. 87–88; Wippel, *Metaphysical Thought of Thomas Aquinas*, p. 93, 545–56; Thomas Joseph White, "'Through Him All Things Were Made'

To put it differently, *ens* cannot be abstracted from God and the creature to function as a conceptual genus under which the two fall, for in its application to creatures it always "carries with it an awareness of it as ordered to…and as dependent upon the primary analogate" (i.e., God).[16] Pure equivocity, however, also is ruled out. For, among other things, it would conflict with the fact that knowledge of creatures leads to knowledge of God (so Rom. 1:20). Thomas therefore reiterates his commitment to analogy and distinguishes between two kinds of analogy of attribution. The first is an analogy of many to one (*multa ad unum*), in which the analogates both participate in something prior, which cannot occur when God is one of the analogates. The second is an analogy of one to another (*unum ad alterum*), which applies to God and creatures as creatures are entirely dependent upon God for all that they possess.[17] In these texts, it is evident that Thomas's deployment of the analogy of attribution (in its *unum ad alterum* form) (1) precludes any common factor in which God and creatures alike might participate, (2) assumes that the referring of created perfections back to God entails the presence of each perfection in a "preeminent" or "superexcellent" manner in God's own being, and (3) is built, at the predicative level, upon the ontological relationship of creatures to God, a relationship explicated in terms of causality and participation.

Early Reformed Authors

In the sixteenth and seventeenth centuries Reformed Protestants assessed the arguments of various medieval and Roman Catholic writers on the matters of analogy and univocity, including Thomas, Duns Scotus, Cajetan, Francisco Suárez, and others. The early Reformed certainly drew upon the

[John 1:3]: The Analogy of the Word Incarnate according to St. Thomas Aquinas and Its Ontological Presuppositions," in *Analogy of Being: Invention of the Anti-Christ or Wisdom of God?*, ed. Thomas Joseph White [Grand Rapids, MI: Eerdmans, 2011], pp. 265–6nn47–48). Outside the framework of created being altogether is God, who does not merely "have" *esse* in a generic or specific determination but rather in utter uniqueness and supremacy is his own unlimited act of being.

[16] Wippel, *Metaphysical Thought of Thomas Aquinas*, p. 571.

[17] Thomas Aquinas, *Summa contra Gentiles*, vol. 13 of *Opera Omnia*, Leonine ed. (Rome: ex Typis Riccardi Garroni, 1918), I.32–34, pp. 97–98, 102, 103–4; *De Potentia*, in *Quaestiones Disputatae*, vol. 2, 10th ed., ed. P. Bazzi et al. (Rome-Turin: Marietti, 1965), 7.7, pp. 202–5; *Summa Theologiae, Prima Pars*, in vol. 4 of *Opera Omnia*, Leonine ed. (Rome: ex Typographia Polyglotta, 1888), Ia.13.5, pp. 146–47.

resources of medieval philosophy and theology in an eclectic manner, but on this particular topic they essentially stood in continuity with Thomas's approach and criticized Scotus's doctrine of univocity.[18] Girolamo Zanchi, for example, writes that a univocal term is one that is the same in both name and *ratio* or definition when applied to multiple things. An analogical term is one that is the same in name and yet somewhat (but not entirely) diverse in *ratio* or definition when applied to multiple things. That to which an analogous term applies in a secondary or derivative sense has some "proportion" or "agreement" with some primary analogate so that it too receives the "name" ascribed to the primary analogate. According to Zanchi, predicates like "goodness" that are applied to God and to creatures are analogous, for in God goodness is "most perfect" and identical to the divine essence itself, while in creatures it is imperfect and an accident.[19] If such a predicate were purely equivocal (the same in name only when applied to God and creatures), this would presuppose a lack of order between God and the creature. However, "between God and things created by God there is a most beautiful order," in which God is both the efficient and the final cause of the creature: "from him and through him and to him are all things" (Rom. 11:36). It is by this order that created things make known something of God's eternal power and deity (Rom. 1:20). Like Thomas and Suárez, Zanchi is quick to clarify that this analogy between God and the creature is not an analogy of "many to one"—for "nothing is prior to God"—but rather an analogy of "one to another."[20]

In treating the features of a system of logic, Bartholomäus Keckermann discusses the notion of "similitude," observing that it can be "simple" (when one term is compared to another) or "complex" (when two propor-

---

[18] There has been discussion recently about whether some of the Reformed orthodox favored a Scotistic doctrine of univocity, but I am in agreement with the position of Richard Muller that the Reformed embraced an essentially Thomistic doctrine of analogy (see his "Not Scotist: Understandings of Being, Univocity, and Analogy in Early-Modern Reformed Thought," *Reformation & Renaissance Review* 14 [2012]: 127–50).

[19] Though Zanchi (unlike Suárez) does not explicitly distinguish here between an external and an internal sort of proportion or agreement that a secondary analogate might have with a primary analogate, he certainly assumes the attributes in view to be intrinsic to creatures, calling them accidents and perfections that are *in creaturis*.

[20] Girolamo Zanchi, *De Natura Dei, seu De Divinis Attributis* (Neostadii Palatinorum, 1598), I.10, pp. 28–30.

tionate terms are compared to another set of two proportionate terms). He identifies the former as the analogy of proportion but seems to assume that it must take the *multa ad unum* form, and then he identifies the latter as the analogy of proportionality. After this Keckermann comments that "God and creatures are said to differ in more than genus" but "agree" in analogous names insofar as the natures of creatures are "images" of God.[21] In his systematic theology, Keckermann roots this analogous "agreement" between God and creatures in God's causal activity: creatures as such have a "likeness" and "similitude" of God because "every effect is similar in something to its own cause."[22] Focusing on the particular question of "being" in his metaphysics, Keckermann denies that *ens* ("that which is" or "that which has essence") might be applied to God in an ordinary manner. God does merely "have" or instantiate some essence under which He is delimited but rather is His own essence; He is *super ens* and "supersubstantial." Elaborating on YHWH's question in Isaiah 40:18, 25—"To whom then will you compare me?"—Keckermann writes, "You must not think about me as a substance or accident or some species of being but as the one who is above every being or above every substance and accident."[23]

In Johann Alsted's metaphysics, he explicitly identifies equivocal, univocal, and analogical uses of the name "being." *Ens* is not strictly speaking a genus that is conferred upon its species "equally." It is only an "analogical" genus or can have only an analogical unity in its various applications to substance and accidents, to God and creatures. Alsted characterizes this as a πρὸς ἕν ("toward one") or ἀφ' ἑνὸς ("from one") analogy in that accidents depend upon substance to exist and creatures depend upon God to exist. Within this analogy or "order," "being" is predicated principally of God since He exists by His own essence and secondarily of creatures since they exist by participation in God's existence.[24] In his work

---

[21] Bartholomäus Keckermann, *Systema Logicae*, in vol. 1 of *Operum Omnium quae Extant* (Geneva, 1614), I.2.4, pp. 673–64; 2.5, p. 679.

[22] Bartholomäus Keckermann, *Systema S. S. Theologiae*, in vol. 2 of *Operum Omnium quae Extant* (Geneva, 1614), I.5, p. 80 (separate pagination).

[23] Keckermann, *Scientiae Metaphysicae Brevissima Synopsis et Compendium*, in vol. 1 of *Operum Omnium*, I.2, p. 2015.

[24] Johann Alsted, *Metaphysica* (Herbornae Nassoviorum, 1613), I.1, pp. 32–33. On *ens* as an "analogical genus," cf. Johannes Maccovius, *Metaphysica*, 3rd ed., ed. Adrianus Heereboord (Lugduni Batavorum, 1658), I.1, pp. 2–3. It may be worth emphasizing that Alsted, Maccovius, and others who call *ens* an "analogical" genus

on natural theology, Alsted sketches a method for speaking of God that initially might appear to diverge from an analogical approach: begin with the term *ens* (conceived as a genus) and then modify *ens* with a "term of difference," either *summum* ("highest") or some more particular qualifier that highlights God's absolute perfection. However, right after this Alsted clarifies that in God *ens* and essence are one and the same; God's existence is not a distinct "contraction" of a broader divine essence but just is His "most singular essence." According to Alsted, then, Scotus errs in claiming that *ens* is a univocal predicate. It is predicated of God first (*secundum prius*)—and must be predicated of Him since He does exist in an eminent manner—and of creatures in a derivative manner (*secundum posterius*).[25] Later in the same work Alsted states that a univocal view of the perfections predicated of God and creatures would require a "proportion" between them, by which he means a "parity" or "mutual" similarity. However, "between the finite and the infinite there is no proportion." These perfections are in creatures in a limited manner because creatures participate in God in a limited way, while the perfections are in God "supereminently."[26]

Toward the end of the period of Reformed orthodoxy, Peter van Mastricht illustrates well key features of a broadly Reformed approach to the question of analogy. He mentions the distinction between God's incommunicable and communicable attributes and comments that there is no "trace" (*vestigium*) of the former in creatures. In light of texts like Genesis 1:26–27, 2 Corinthians 3:18, and 2 Peter 1:4, the attributes described as "communicable" do have a *vestigium* in creatures. The communicable attributes, he adds, are not univocally or "equally" (*ex aequo*) predicated of God and creatures, for "between the infinite and the finite there is no proportion in any way." Nor are they equivocal, for knowledge of the creature does help to facilitate knowledge of the Creator. The communicable attributes, then, are analogically predicated of God and creatures. The thing signified by a given attribute is "principally" and "originally" in God and "participatively" and "with a degree of diminution" in creatures. Mastricht clarifies that such an attribute is not applied to God merely "causally" as if He only

---

mean that there is an analogical agreement between *ens* in its application to substance and accidents and to God and creatures, not that *ens* is a univocal concept or that God and creatures equally participate in some ontological principle.

[25] Johann Alsted, *Theologica Naturalis* (Antonius Hummius, 1615), I.3, pp. 31–32.

[26] Alsted, *Theologia Naturalis*, I.17, pp. 174–75.

caused the thing signified to be in creatures but did not have it in Himself. Instead, it is "truly," "essentially," "eminently" in God Himself.[27] Indeed, Mastricht points out in expounding the traditional "threefold way" (*via triplex*) of obtaining knowledge of God that if God is the cause of the various perfections in creatures, the perfections must belong eminently to God, for "no one can bestow upon another what he neither formally nor eminently has."[28] We could no doubt consider other writers in a historical examination of analogy and univocity, but with this sampling of medieval and early modern authors in hand, it is time now to offer some constructive remarks on the material en route to dealing with more recent treatments of analogy and univocity.

Karl Barth's Critique

Some of the modern concerns about analogy center on whether it upholds the otherness and sovereignty of God. Barth raises serious objections to the notion of an *analogia entis* in theology proper, particularly the Roman Catholic theologian Erich Przywara's account of it, calling it an "invention of the anti-Christ" and a decisive reason not to become a Roman Catholic.[29] Barth rejects Przywara's conception of the *analogia entis* because of his insistence upon a fundamental discontinuity between God and the world and his attendant commitment to theology as a discipline informed and governed not by general human experience of the (fallen) created order but by God's free revelatory activity in the person of Jesus Christ.[30] For Barth, there is no place for a general ontology that presumes to set the conditions for a Chris-

---

[27] Peter van Mastricht, *Theoretico-Practica Theologia*, 2nd ed. (Utrecht, 1724), II.5.7–8, pp. 94–95; cf. 12, pp. 96–97. Mastricht also denies that being in particular is a "univocal genus" (II.3.10, p. 79).

[28] Mastricht, *Theoretico-Practica Theologia*, II.2.19, p. 70.

[29] Barth, *Church Dogmatics,* ed. G.W. Bromiley and T.F. Torrance, trans. G.W. Bromiley et al. (London: T & T Clark, 2009), I/1, p. xiii. See Erich Przywara, *Analogia Entis: Metaphysics, Original Structure and Universal Rhythm*, trans. John R. Betz and David Bentley Hart (Grand Rapids, MI: Eerdmans, 2014). For more on Przywara and his relationship to Barth, see Johnson, *Karl Barth and the* Analogia Entis; John R. Betz, "After Barth: A New Introduction to Erich Przywara's *Analogia Entis*," in White, *Analogy of Being*, pp. 35–87.

[30] My sense of the overarching structure of Barth's view of analogy is indebted especially to Johnson, *Karl Barth and the* Analogia Entis (London: Bloomsbury, 2011).

tian description of God. All true talk about God can arise only on the basis of and in response to the Lord's free and gracious decision to address us in His Word. At this point Roman Catholicism, according to Barth, goes wrong in assimilating Christ the divine Word to the being of the church so that "grace becomes nature" and "the personal act of divine address becomes a constantly available relationship" within which an *analogia entis*, a "presence of a divine likeness of the creature even within the fallen world," can form the basis of our speech about God's being.[31] Roman Catholicism errs here because, in Barth's view, given the extent of human sin as apprehended by the Reformers, there can no longer be a "direct discernment of the original relation of God to man" that may then be subsequently "confirmed by the Gospel." All such knowledge of our relation to God is restored to us only in the special revelation of the gospel.[32] The "cosmos…stands in contradiction to God," and even when God does address us through creaturely means He communicates only indirectly to us because of our creaturely nature and our sinfulness and remains veiled in a manner that precludes the epistemic directness of an *analogia entis* between God and creatures.[33]

A little later in the *Church Dogmatics*, Barth discusses his reservations about an analogy of being in connection with the concept of the *imago Dei.* He contends that after the Fall there is "no conformity of man to God," "no point of contact between God and man" that might preserve in us an aptness to receive God's Word. In other words, human beings as creatures—creatures that are now fallen—have in their "humanity and personality" completely lost the *imago Dei.* The *imago Dei* is "not just, as it is said, destroyed apart from a few relics; it is totally annihilated." There is thus no *analogia entis*, no being that is common to God and humanity in its natural

---

31 Barth, *Church Dogmatics*, I.1, pp. 36–38, 40–44.

32 Barth, *Church Dogmatics*, I.1, p. 130; cf. IV.1, p. 177.

33 Barth, *Church Dogmatics*, I.1, pp. 166–69. Barth does later take into account the Roman Catholic theologian Gottlieb Söhngen's approach to the analogy of being, in which the *analogia entis* is drawn into the sphere of and grafted onto an *analogia fidei* where the *analogia entis* is based on the believer participating in Christ and becoming a child of God by faith (*Church Dogmatics*, II.1, pp. 79–84). Barth does not believe this to be an accurate representation of official Roman Catholic teaching, but the fact that he is very amenable to Söhngen's *analogia fidei* and Christ-centered *analogia entis* shows that he is willing to acknowledge a carefully defined ontological agreement of the creature with God.

and fallen state. The only similarity possible is one actualized by God in the event of revelation, in which God enables human persons to receive his revelation by faith. In that event there is a correspondence between the human decision to receive God's revelation and God's decision to bring human persons into fellowship with Himself. There emerges on the human side a correspondence to God parsed not in terms of deification but in terms of a "union with what is believed," which takes place, as justification by grace does, in the human person's apprehension of Christ by faith.[34]

In Barth's assessment of fellow Protestant theologian Johann Quenstedt on the topic of analogy, he seizes the opportunity to speak more about the relationship between the *analogia entis* and justification by grace. He takes Quenstedt to be representative of the Protestant orthodox and of Thomas and other medieval lights who affirm a doctrine of analogy. In Barth's judgment, Quenstedt rightly affirms an analogy of attribution between God and the creature by virtue of which our words (essence, spirit, goodness, justice, and so on) can be truthfully applied to God as well as creatures. However, Barth believes Quenstedt has failed to take up the analogy of attribution into a properly theological and, indeed, Protestant view of God's relationship to creatures. For Quenstedt asserts that the created analogate possesses its likeness to God not only by an extrinsic relation or habitude to God but by properly possessing that likeness in its own right in an intrinsic analogy of attribution. Barth regards this as inconsistent with Quenstedt's own Lutheran affirmation of justification by grace through faith and would like to have seen Quenstedt apply the logic of justification to "the problem of the knowledge of God." According to a Protestant doctrine of justification by grace, "what converts the creature into an analogue of God does not lie in itself and its nature." Instead, "what converts the creature into an analogue of God," what brings about humanity's fellowship with God, is the creature's reception of the grace of God that comes to us from without in the person of Christ. At the epistemological level, what enables us to know and speak of God is not mere observation of the created order but rather faith's apprehension of God in Christ. For Barth, Quenstedt is focused on determining how there might be some agreement or fellowship between God and creatures with respect to "being in general," while Barth seeks to understand such a fellowship with respect to "the particular being of grace" given only in God's revelation. In Quenstedt's

[34] Barth, *Church Dogmatics*, I.1, pp. 236–41.

framework, creatures as beings already are "relatively" what God Himself is "absolutely"; we have a "given and constant" similarity to God and have no need of revelation or faith to enjoy or discover a correspondence between ourselves and God. Barth therefore asks, "In this [intrinsic analogy of attribution] where is the freedom of the gracious God which Quenstedt knows so well when he speaks of [justification]?" The implication of Quenstedt's understanding of analogy, then, is that there is a "being in which God and man—the former absolutely, the latter relatively—participate," a being that is "superior to God" and determines what God and creatures are, what the relationship between them is, and what establishes the veracity of our speech about them. It is only by a "lucky inconsistency" that Quenstedt and the Protestant orthodox retain the Reformers' awareness of human sin and God's grace, and it would be far more consistent with Protestant sensibilities to see Christology as the "life-centre" of theology proper. Ultimately, Barth says, the doctrine of analogy in Quenstedt and the Protestant orthodox fails to align with the teaching of Scripture, for in Scripture "it is not a being common to God and man which finally and properly establishes and upholds the fellowship between them, but God's grace."[35]

It appears that Barth's underlying reason for viewing the agreement between God and creatures in conjunction with the doctrine of justification is that, in his understanding of it, the being of creatures is itself rooted in the grace of God, which is to be understood through the lens of the incarnation and justification. John 1:3 is significant here: all things were made through Christ.[36] On the one hand, creation is the "external basis" for the covenant of grace in which God establishes fellowship between humanity and Himself through Christ, in the sense that the existence of created being is presupposed in the actualization of human fellowship with God. On the other hand, however, the covenant of grace is the "internal basis" and presupposition of the existence of created being, for in God's purposes the covenant of grace takes priority and creation is "the theatre of the history of

---

[35] Barth, *Church Dogmatics*, II.1, pp. 237–43. Cf. Bruce L. McCormack, *Orthodox and Modern: Studies in the Theology of Karl Barth* (Grand Rapids, MI: Baker, 2008), pp. 177–79.

[36] See Barth, *Church Dogmatics*, II.2, pp. 91–3; III.1, pp. 29–31. In the latter section, Barth appeals to various writers of the tradition who in some way see creation as a work of God's goodness and grace (e.g., Augustine, Anselm, Thomas, Amandus Polanus).

the covenant of grace" and "the way to the covenant." Accordingly, Christ is the goal of creation and also "the beginning just because he is the goal" (cf. Eph. 1:10; Col. 1:15–16). It is particularly noteworthy in connection with the question of analogy that, for Barth, "that covenant is the goal of creation is not something which is added later to the reality of the creature...It already characterises creation itself and as such."[37] To be sure, Barth affirms with Genesis 1:31 that created being is good, but he hastens to add that it is such only because in actualizing it God has "justified" it in taking it up into his purpose of "instituting and fulfilling the covenant between the divine Creator and man." Creation thus shares in the perfection of God "as the arena, instrument and object of His living action" in Christ, and this can be known by us only as we apprehend in faith what God does in Christ.[38] In addition, given the Fall, "any tenable distinction between man as created by God and the sinful determination of his being is possible only if his sinful nature...is minimised." The only possible way now to see the true nature of humanity—and human persons are still God's handiwork—lies in seeing humanity as God's covenant partner through His revelation in Christ, the true and "proper" man.[39]

The positive content of the ontological agreement between humanity and God thus lies in human persons being in and like Christ and bearing witness to God's revelation in Christ: "To be a man is to be with Jesus, to be like Him. To be a man is to be in the sphere where the first and merciful will of God toward His creatures, His will to save and keep them from the power of nothingness, is revealed in action." Barth comments that "man *in abstracto*" (i.e., apart from "the divine will to pity, help and save") is defenseless against "the threat of surrounding non-being" but is secured by God in and only in the elect man Jesus Christ. Again, "Man *is* the being which is addressed in this way by God....He does not first have a kind of nature in which he is then addressed by God...He is from the very outset, as we may now say, 'in the Word of God.'"[40] In this schema, salvation is the "fulfilment of being," for created being "in itself" does not have "a part in the being of God." Put quite strikingly, "Created being as such needs salvation,

[37] Barth, *Church Dogmatics*, III.1, pp. 43–46, 94–97, 229–32. Cf. IV.1, p. 9–10.

[38] Barth, *Church Dogmatics*, III.1, pp. 366–88. Cf. IV.3.1, pp. 96, 114–23, 137–39, 163–64.

[39] Barth, *Church Dogmatics*, III.2, pp. 28–32, 40–46. Cf. III.2, pp. 124–25, 134–37.

[40] Barth, *Church Dogmatics*, III.2, pp. 145–51; cf. IV.1, pp. 92–93; IV.2, p. 19.

but does not have it: it can only look forward to it."[41] True human being, then, has a correspondence to God as human beings "give themselves to God" just as He has "given Himself for man." It is in gratitude and active obedience to the divine Word that human beings are aligned with God.[42] In other words, human beings, in living in loving fellowship and mutuality with one another, image Christ being for us as man, and Christ as man for us images the intradivine love between the Father and Christ the Son. Barth calls the similarity in these relationships an *analogia relationis*.[43] Indeed, in some of the latest material in the *Church Dogmatics*, Barth is prepared to say that Christians exist "in analogy and correspondence" to what Christ is as they are children of God made such by the original divine Son.[44]

A Reformed Protestant Response to Barth

How might we continue to utilize the helpful points in the Thomistic and early Reformed understanding of analogy and confirm that we can do this as genuinely Protestant thinkers who are true to our distinct tradition and also have a rightful place at the table of catholic Christianity? Here I will offer the following points in response to Barth's concerns.

First, while Barth's criticism of the *analogia entis* contains salutary reminders about the place of God's grace in conforming us to the image of His Son and about our dependence on special revelation in spiritual renewal and dogmatic theology, his understanding of the relationship between nature and grace is problematic and yields a lopsided Creator-creature analogy that is rooted in redemptive grace alone. In particular, I do not think that Barth's system of thought allows us sufficiently to understand creation or nature as a biblical category in its own right and as the stage on which the Fall and redemption (contingently) take place. To be sure, he does distin-

---

[41] Barth, *Church Dogmatics*, IV.1, p. 8.

[42] Barth, *Church Dogmatics*, III.2, pp. 182, 207; IV.1, pp. 41–42.

[43] Barth, *Church Dogmatics*, III.2, pp. 219–22, 267–69; cf. IV.1, pp. 191–92; IV.2, pp. 528–33; IV.3.2, pp. 597–607. On this aspect of Barth's account, see Bruce L. McCormack, "Karl Barth's Version of an 'Analogy of Being,'" in *Thomas Aquinas and Karl Barth: An Unofficial Catholic-Protestant Dialogue*, ed. Thomas Joseph White (Grand Rapids, MI: Eerdmans, 2013), pp. 122–23, 135–44. This theme is also central in the recent constructive proposal of Archie J. Spencer, *The Analogy of Faith: The Quest for God's Speakability* (Downers Grove, IL: InterVarsity Press, 2015), ch. 5.

[44] Barth, *Church Dogmatics*, IV.3.2, pp. 532–53.

guish between creation as such and the covenant of grace and does affirm the goodness of created being. But then he also comments that for humanity as such, humanity without reference to God's will *to save* (not merely God's will to give humanity an original righteousness or God's will to sustain and instruct humanity in the garden), "the fall and original sin are an ontological necessity" due to the "threat of surrounding non-being."[45] Or, even more poignantly, "Created being as such needs salvation."[46] It seems that in the logic of Barth's framework creation is not established and good in its own right, and created humanity as such does not image God and then only contingently fall into sin. Creation as such is brought into being and upheld at all only by *saving* grace.[47] However, the scriptural narrative of creation, sin, and redemption, together with the emphasis that the gracious work of God has a restorative character (e.g., Acts 3:21; Rom. 12:2; Eph. 4:24; Col. 3:10), requires us to confess an original goodness of created being as such, a fall into sin that is not ingredient in human nature as such and a redemptive recovery of something (i.e., human nature rightly ordered to God) that once existed and was good in its own right. In short, if Barth worried that in Roman Catholicism "grace becomes nature," I worry that in his account nature becomes grace—redemptive grace—over against the inner logic of the biblical economy.[48]

---

[45] Barth, *Church Dogmatics*, III.2, p. 146.

[46] Barth, *Church Dogmatics*, IV.1, p. 8.

[47] Barth does state that given God's will to save humanity and secure our fellowship with him, it is inexplicable that human beings would reject their Creator. Indeed, according to Barth, sin is in this sense an "ontological impossibility" (*Church Dogmatics*, III.2, pp. 146–47). However, insofar as the divine will to save presupposes sin from which humanity must be saved, the claim that this salvific will is fundamental to the being of creation would still imply that sin and the Fall are intrinsic to the very being of creation. It is similar with Barth's statement that in the Fall humanity "forfeits" God's "predetermined salvation" (IV.1, p. 10). If it is a forfeiting of not simply fellowship with God but rather *salvation*, this implies that creation by its very nature is fallen, for otherwise there would be no need of salvation.

[48] Keith Johnson has insightfully stressed that in the development of his theology Barth did eventually recognize the need to affirm some positive relationship between created (and fallen) humanity and God even before the incarnation took place. Barth aimed to secure this relationship without foregoing his Christ-centered notion of analogy and true knowledge of God by claiming that "the created order itself, and thus created human being as such, is a function of God's decision to reconcile sinful humans in and through Jesus Christ." This move is consummated in Barth's configuration of the doctrine of election where "Jesus Christ is both the

There is a broad sense in which all that God does is gracious, a broad sense in which creation or created being itself can be considered a work of grace since God owes nothing to creatures prior to their origin but nevertheless richly blesses them in the constitution and provisions of their natural life.[49] While Barth recognizes a distinction between grace taken in such a broad sense and grace taken in a redemptive sense,[50] he clearly emphasizes that nature is characterized from the outset by *redemptive* grace. But if this does disrupt the logic of the economy and call into question the restorative dimension of grace, then Barth's view of the nature-grace relation, whatever the merits of some of its constituent features, need not govern our approach to the doctrine of analogy.[51] If Barth's view of nature and grace is problematic, then so too is his construction of a parallel between the Creator-creature analogy and the doctrine of justification by grace and his concomitant assertion that there can be only an extrinsic analogy of attribution

---

subject and object of election and thus the beginning and end of creation" ("Natural Revelation in Creation and Covenant," in White, *Thomas Aquinas and Karl Barth*, p. 145). In this way, then, Barth does have a framework for affirming a Creator-creature analogy and a "natural revelation." I do not think this alleviates the problems with Barth's approach, though. There still appears to be in Barth's theology an assumption that the Fall is a necessary unfolding or feature of creation itself. If creation is established by reconciling grace, what about creation as such entails its enmity with God, an enmity that must be presupposed in the very notion of reconciliation? Also, I doubt that a "natural revelation" whose content is the saving work of Christ and whose content can be apprehended only within the sphere of the covenant of grace is meaningfully called "natural" in keeping with the way Paul describes the knowledge of God possessed (and distorted) by the human race at large in Romans 1:18–23. In addition, if one disagrees with Barth's unusual understanding of the role of Christ's humanity in election and believes that the immutability of God in the incarnation and the divine power of Christ's saving work are best established in a different manner, then his account loses much of its force.

[49] See Thomas, *ST*, Ia.21.4 corp. and ad 4, pp. 261–22. Among the early Reformed, see, e.g., Franciscus Junius, *De Theologia Vera* (Lugduni Batavorum, 1594), X, p. 65; Amandus Polanus, *Syntagma Theologiae Christianae* (Hanoviae, 1614), V.2, p. 256; Francis Turretin, *Institutio Theologiae Elencticae*, 2nd ed., vol. 1 (Geneva, 1688), V.11.16, p. 521. Yet see also the comments of Mastricht, *Theoretico-Practica Theologia*, II.17.14, p. 180 regarding the care with which God's works of nature and God's works of grace are to be distinguished.

[50] Barth, *Church Dogmatics*, IV.1, pp. 8–9.

[51] Of course, God's redemptive grace is more than restorative: it brings us not just back to the state of integrity but onward to the state of glory. Nevertheless, while this grace is more than restorative, it is not less.

between God and creatures. For created being participates in and displays the goodness and perfection of God even by virtue of its being created by God, not just by virtue of God's redemptive grace. Moreover, it seems to me that Barth's use of the concept of justification in his account of creation and analogy threatens to detach it from its customary (and indelibly forensic) usage in Scripture and Protestant dogmatics.

To say this is not to slip into a "Pelagian" approach to the matter of human fellowship with God. Created being that participates in and exhibits God's perfection is not something won by human merit; it is a gift. Nor does a likeness of created being to God entail that, after the Fall, natural knowledge of God by itself empowers us to attain to redeemed fellowship with God. Creatures know something of God but persistently suppress it (so Rom. 1:18–23) and need the renewing effects of the Word and Spirit of God to experience right fellowship with him (e.g., Rom. 12:2; 1 Cor. 2:6–16). Moreover, affirming that the creature enjoys a certain likeness to God simply by virtue of being created by God does not entail that after the Fall human beings can be justified in the Pauline sense by something residing within us. Human beings are still made in the image of God and yet the image is so marred by sin that we lack an inhering quality of righteousness or total fulfillment of God's law by which we might be acquitted and accepted by God our judge.[52] Our only hope lies in receiving by faith the righteousness of Christ that undoes the work of the first Adam (Rom. 5:12–21). One can affirm a similitude of human beings to God by virtue of creation, even one that endures after the Fall, and still embrace a robustly Protestant view of the *imago Dei* and Adam's fall. In such a view something belonging to the integrity of human nature itself (i.e., our original righteousness before God) is lost in the Fall so that there is a corruption of human nature itself, not just a loss of a supernatural gift apart from which human nature and natural human knowing would perhaps retain their wholeness.[53] In this connection, I think it reasonable to say that Barth's exposition of nature, grace, and analogy is not a necessary extension of

---

[52] A Roman Catholic author like White too can affirm this, even if disagreements between Rome and Protestantism on the doctrine of justification remain: "Our wounded natural capacity for God…can *in no way* procure for us the gift of justification or salvation," *Wisdom in the Face of Modernity: A Study of Thomistic Natural Theology*, 2nd ed. (Ave Maria: Sapientia Press, 2009), p. 283n103.

[53] On this element in Reformed theological anthropology, see, e.g., Turretin, *Inst.*, V.9–11, pp. 509–21.

Protestant soteriological commitments; on this point he is not so much being Protestant as he is being, well, Barthian.[54]

The end and therefore the original impetus of human existence certainly is union and communion with the triune God, but affirming this does not require us to say that the constitution of human nature is such that communion can be wrought only by *redemptive* grace. Furthermore, if one affirms that created human nature was good in its own right and did not necessarily include in its constitution an ordering toward saving grace, this does not entail that the work of the Son in establishing our fellowship with God is left as an afterthought on God's part. Even creation and our creaturely relation to God are brought about and upheld through the Son (so John 1:3–5; Col. 1:15–17; Heb. 1:2). Indeed, even if one believes that our fellowship with God would have been perfected by an incarnation of the Son even apart from the Fall, such an approach does not entail that human beings require salvation in order to have an analogical likeness and fellowship with God.[55] Furthermore, if we say that created human nature as such is good in its own right and images God even without reference to saving grace, and that the Fall and redemption are not ingredient in human nature as such or requisite for a Creator-creature analogy, we are not thereby positing two separate moments in the divine decree. To remain aligned with the logic of the economy, we can maintain that there is within the decree a logical priority of created human existence to the Fall and to God's saving work without suggesting that there is a disunity or chronological development within the decree. In other words, God's original and eternal plan for the human race does include the Fall (a fall permitted rather than authored by God) and redemption, but this simply does not mean that created human nature as such needed redemption in order to enjoy participation in God and fellowship with God. In sum, then, I think Barth's view of analogy understates the goodness of created being as such and the similarity to God that creatures have even by virtue of their simply being created by God.

---

[54] My sense of how being Protestant should shape one's view of the Creator-creature analogy is thus different from that of Johnson in *Karl Barth and the* Analogia Entis or Spencer in *Analogy of Faith.*

[55] For examples of this sort of approach, see Edwin Chr. van Driel, *Incarnation Anyway: Arguments for a Supralapsarian Christology* (Oxford: Oxford University Press, 2008); Joel R. Beeke and Mark Jones, *A Puritan Theology: Doctrine for Life* (Grand Rapids, MI: Reformation Heritage, 2012), ch. 9.

Second, while Barth is understandably concerned about human beings having license to take up whatever features of created being they like and attribute these to God (perhaps for self-serving ends), careful retrieval of an *analogia entis* does not justify such a practice. At this point it is important to distinguish between different ways in which an *analogia entis* and an analogous attribution of creaturely names to God might function in Christian theology. In this essay, I have no interest in suggesting that there is an *analogia entis* in the sense of a unity of divine and created being by common participation in a being superior to both. That would be an analogy of attribution of the *multa ad unum* sort rightly denied by Thomas, Zanchi, and others. That Barth assumes in his critique of Quenstedt that an intrinsic analogy of attribution must entail the *multa ad unum* schema reveals a serious misunderstanding of the historical usage of analogy. The *unum ad alterum* analogy of attribution that is invoked by Thomas and various early Protestant authors, and that I would commend in Christian *theologia* today, presses home the fact that creatures derive their being and perfections from the God who is entirely *a se*. It underscores the fact that God participates in nothing beyond Himself, nothing that we might purport to know first and then claim as a basis upon which we can (idolatrously) attribute to God's being whatever we like.

The analogy of attribution is also not meant to function here as a principle of dogmatic theology. It is not what generates dogmatic reasoning, what supplies its content, or what norms its claims about God. To deploy an older Protestant prolegomenon, the "external principle of knowing" (*principium cognoscendi externum*) in dogmatic theology is God's revelation in Holy Scripture. The "proximate" and "immediate" efficient cause of Christian knowledge of God developed in dogmatics is the Word of God. For "the first principle into which all theological dogmas are resolved is *Dominus dixit*."[56] Thus, the theologian does not begin his or her work by taking initiative to survey whatever potential creaturely analogues might seem helpful for description of God. Instead, bound from the beginning to the Word of God, the theologian reads Scripture and learns from Scripture the names and attributes that God would have us apply to Himself. But precisely in Scripture we also learn that God's works reflect His perfection, which helps us to understand why he authorizes us to use ordinary words in our speech about Him, and we are invited to recall our experience of creaturely wisdom

[56] Polanus, *Syntagma*, I.14, p. 16.

or justice, for example, in understanding the meaning of God's wisdom or justice, even as Scripture leads us to recognize the significant dissimilarity between (fallen) creatures and God and the distinct, analogical sense in which our words apply to God. There is thus a positive role for an (intrinsic) analogy of attribution not as a principle of dogmatics but as a resource to explicate how creaturely names are not arbitrarily applied to God and how they convey true knowledge of God. In addition, when the Christian believer is donning the "spectacles" of Scripture,[57] he or she can look out upon the natural world and, with the guidance of Scripture, perceive aright the many ways in which it discloses the majesty of its Creator. Indeed, it is by virtue of this (qualified) ontological analogy and the consequent analogical predication found in Scripture and Christian proclamation that someone outside the body of Christ and its patterns of speaking can first apprehend the gospel's verbal disclosure of God's triune identity and respond in faith.[58]

CONCLUSION

With these reflections on the concerns of Barth, I hope to have signaled at least that, whatever helpful cautions we might glean from his work, we need not let his concerns prevent us from appropriating the analogy of attribution (of the *unum ad alterum* sort) in the work of Christian theology and thus joining with other catholic believers in acknowledging a "catholic" revelation of God that is taken into account in the practice of dogmatics. Affirming and using that form of analogy does not automatically lead to neglecting the transcendence and otherness of God or our dependence on revelation for our knowledge of God, and it does not require that we compromise our

[57] For the metaphor, see John Calvin, *Institutes of the Christian Religion*, ed. John T. McNeill, trans. Ford Lewis Battles (Louisville, KY: Westminster John Knox Press, 1960), I.6.1, p. 70.

[58] On the apprehension of the gospel presupposing some (analogical) apprehension of God by nature and some prior grasp of the meaning of terms used in special revelation, compare the argument of Thomas Joseph White, "'Through Him All Things Were Made' (John 1:3)," in White, *Analogy of Being*, pp. 246–79, esp. p. 272n57. In general acquisition of knowledge of God, then, the analogy of being may feature earlier than Scripture in the order of discovery (with sundry infralapsarian distortions of the knowledge of God), though Scripture precedes it in the work of dogmatics.

Protestant convictions on sin and grace. David Bentley Hart has quipped, against Barth, that the *rejection* of the *analogia entis* is "the invention of antichrist" and perhaps "the most compelling reason for not becoming Protestant."[59] However, based on what we have seen here, I would suggest that affirming a Creator-creature analogy established by God's act of creation can and should be a point of common ground for Protestants, Roman Catholics, and Eastern Orthodox believers.

[59] David Bentley Hart, *The Beauty of the Infinite: The Aesthetics of Christian Truth* (Grand Rapids, MI: Eerdmans, 2003), p. 242.

BIBLIOGRAPHY

Alsted, Johann. *Metaphysica*. Herbornae Nassoviorum, 1613.

———. *Theologica Naturalis*. Antonius Hummius, 1615.

Aristotle. *Aristotelis Metaphysica*. Edited by W. Jaeger. Oxford: Clarendon, 1957.

Aquinas, Thomas. *De Potentia*. In *Quaestiones Disputatae*, vol. 2. 10th edition. Edited by P. Bazzi et al. Rome-Turin: Marietti, 1965.

———. *De Principiis Naturae*. In vol. 43 of *Opera Omnia*. Leonine edition. Rome: Editori di San Tommaso, 1976.

———. *In Duodecim Libros Metaphysicorum Aristotelis*. Edited by M.-R. Cathala and R. M. Spiazzi. Turin-Rome: Marietti, 1950.

———. *Quaestiones Disputatae De Veritate*. In vol. 22.1/2 of *Opera Omnia*. Leonine edition. Rome: Commissio Leonina, ad Sanctae Sabinae 1970.

———. *Quaestiones de Quolibet*. In vol. 25 of *Opera Omnia*. Leonine edition. Rome: Commissio Leonina; Paris: Les Éditions du Cerf, 1996.

———. *Scriptum super Libros Sententiarum*. Vol. 1. Edited by R. P. Mandonnet. Paris: Sumptibus P. Lethielleux, 1929.

———. *Summa contra Gentiles*. Vol. 13 of *Opera Omnia*. Leonine edition. Rome: ex Typis Riccardi Garroni, 1918.

———. *Summa Theologiae*. Vols. 4-12 of *Opera Omnia*. Leonine edition. Rome: ex Typographia Polyglotta, 1888.

Barth, Karl. *Church Dogmatics*. Edited by G.W. Bromiley and T.F. Torrance. Translated by G.W. Bromiley et al. London: T & T Clark, 2009.

Beeke, Joel R., and Mark Jones. *A Puritan Theology: Doctrine for Life*. Grand Rapids, MI: Reformation Heritage, 2012.

Betz, John R. "After Barth: A New Introduction to Erich Przywara's *Analogia Entis*." In *Analogy of Being: Invention of the Anti-Christ or Wisdom of God?*, edited by Thomas Joseph White, 35–87. Grand Rapids, MI: Eerdmans, 2011.

Cajetan, Thomas. *De Nominum Analogia. De Conceptu Entis.* Edited by P. N. Zammit. Rome: Angelicum, 1952.

Calvin, John. *Institutes of the Christian Religion.* Edited by John T. McNeill. Translated by Ford Lewis Battles. Louisville, KY: Westminster John Knox Press, 1960.

Darley, Alan Philip. "Predication or Participation? What Is the Nature of Aquinas' Doctrine of Analogy?" *Heythrop Journal* 57 (2016): 312–24.

Dewan, Lawrence. "St. Thomas and Analogy: The Logician and the Metaphysician." In *Form and Being: Studies in Thomistic Metaphysics.* Washington, DC: Catholic University of America Press, 2006.

Hart, David Bentley. *The Beauty of the Infinite: The Aesthetics of Christian Truth.* Grand Rapids, MI: Eerdmans, 2003.

Hemming, Laurence Paul. "*Analogia non Entis sed Entitatis*: The Ontological Consequences of the Doctrine of Analogy." *International Journal of Systematic Theology* 6 (2004): 118–29.

Hochschild, Joshua P. *The Semantics of Analogy: Rereading Cajetan's* De Nominum Analogia. Notre Dame, IN: University of Notre Dame Press, 2010.

Johnson, Keith L. *Karl Barth and the* Analogia Entis. London: Bloomsbury, 2011.

———. "Natural Revelation in Creation and Covenant." In *Thomas Aquinas and Karl Barth*, edited by Thomas James White, 129–56.

Junius, Franciscus. *De Theologia Vera.* Lugduni Batavorum, 1594.

Keckermann, Bartholomäus. *Scientiae Metaphysicae Brevissima Synopsis et Compendium.* In vol. 1 of *Operum Omnium quae Extant.* Geneva, 1614.

———. *Systema Logicae.* In vol. 1 of *Operum Omnium quae Extant.* Geneva, 1614.

———. *Systema S. S. Theologiae.* In vol. 2 of *Operum Omnium quae Extant.* Geneva, 1614.

Klubertanz, George P. *St. Thomas Aquinas on Analogy: A Textual Analysis and Systematic Synthesis.* Chicago: Loyola University Press, 1960.

Lyttkens, Hampus. *The Analogy between God and the World: An Investigation of*

Its Background and Interpretation of Its Use by Thomas of Aquino. Uppsala, Sweden: Lundequistska, 1953.

Maccovius, Johannes. *Metaphysica*. 3rd edition. Edited by Adrianus Heereboord. Lugduni Batavorum, 1658.

McCormack, Bruce L. "Karl Barth's Version of an 'Analogy of Being.'" In *Thomas Aquinas and Karl Barth: An Unofficial Catholic-Protestant Dialogue*, edited by Thomas Joseph White, 88–144. Grand Rapids, MI: Eerdmans, 2013.

———. *Orthodox and Modern: Studies in the Theology of Karl Barth*. Grand Rapids, MI: Baker, 2008.

McInerny, Ralph M. *Aquinas and Analogy*. Washington, DC: Catholic University of America Press, 1996.

Mondin, Battista. *The Principle of Analogy in Protestant and Catholic Theology*. The Hague: Martinus Nijhoff, 1963.

Montagnes, Bernard. *The Doctrine of the Analogy of Being according to Thomas Aquinas*. Translated by E.M. Macierowski. Milwaukee, WI: Marquette University Press, 2004.

Muller, Richard. "Not Scotist: Understandings of Being, Univocity, and Analogy in Early-Modern Reformed Thought." *Reformation & Renaissance Review* 14 (2012): 127–50.

Owen, John. *Theologoumena Pantodapa*. In vol. 17 of *The Works of John Owen*. Edited by William H. Goold. Edinburgh: T & T Clark, 1862.

Polanus, Amandus. *Syntagma Theologiae Christianae*. Hanoviae, 1614.

Phelan, Gerald B. *St. Thomas and Analogy*. Milwaukee, WI: Marquette University Press, 1941.

Przywara, Erich. *Analogia Entis: Metaphysics, Original Structure and Universal Rhythm*. Translated by John R. Betz and David Bentley Hart. Grand Rapids, MI: Eerdmans, 2014.

Rocca, Gregory P. *Speaking the Incomprehensible God: Thomas Aquinas on the Interplay between Positive and Negative Theology*. Washington, DC: Catholic University of America Press, 2004.

Spencer, Archie J. *The Analogy of Faith: The Quest for God's Speakability*.

Downers Grove, IL: InterVarsity Press, 2015.

Turretin, Francis. *Institutio Theologiae Elencticae.* 2nd edition. Vol. 1. Geneva, 1688.

Van Driel, Edwin Christiaan. *Incarnation Anyway: Arguments for a Supralapsarian Christology.* Oxford: Oxford University Press, 2008.

Van Mastricht, Peter. *Theoretico-Practica Theologia.* 2nd edition. Utrecht, Netherlands: Sumptibus Societatis, 1724.

White, Thomas Joseph. "'Through Him All Things Were Made' [John 1:3]: The Analogy of the Word Incarnate according to St. Thomas Aquinas and Its Ontological Presuppositions." In *Analogy of Being*, 246–79.

——. *Wisdom in the Face of Modernity: A Study of Thomistic Natural Theology.* 2nd edition. Ave Maria: Sapientia Press, 2009.

Wippel, John F. *The Metaphysical Thought of Thomas Aquinas: From Finite Being to Uncreated Being.* Washington, DC: Catholic University of America Press, 2000.

Zanchi, Girolamo. *De Natura Dei, seu De Divinis Attributis.* Neostadii Palatinorum, 1598.

IV:
ON ESCHEWING THE LABYRINTHS: WHY PROTESTANTS SHOULD NOT RESURRECT THE "SPIRITUAL READING" OF SCRIPTURE

Iain Provan, Regent College

FOR MANY Protestants, 2017 was a year of celebration: the five hundredth anniversary of the beginning of the Protestant Reformation. Yet this was not true of all. For some, the Reformation was not, in fact, a positive development in the history of the church that we should continue to celebrate. It was, instead, a tragedy whose occurrence we should lament.[1] It contributed significantly to the process by which the church lost its robust connection to "the Great Tradition": the "broad consensus of the church fathers and medieval theologians" concerning orthodox faith and life.[2] In so contributing, the Reformation helped to pave the way for the rise of the modern secular world[3]—a world in which, in Hans Frei's words, there has occurred a profound "eclipse of biblical narrative."[4] An entire premodern

[1] Hans Boersma, *Heavenly Participation: The Weaving of a Sacramental Tapestry* (Grand Rapids, MI: Eerdmans, 2011), 85, 104.

[2] Boersma, *Heavenly Participation*, xi.

[3] Here this Protestant thinking clearly converges with the kind of Roman Catholic analysis presented in recent, significant books by authors like Charles Taylor and Brad Gregory. Charles Taylor, *A Secular Age* (Cambridge, MA: Belknap, 2007); Brad S. Gregory, *The Unintended Reformation: How a Religious Revolution Secularized Society* (Cambridge, MA: Belknap, 2012).

[4] Hans W. Frei, *The Eclipse of Biblical Narrative: A Study in Eighteenth and Nineteenth*

world defined by and organized in terms of the great Christian story began to disappear, and a new, modern world began to emerge, in which the Bible gradually lost its cultural authority, and fewer and fewer people looked to synthesize with it the knowledge they were rapidly acquiring from other sources. What contemporary Protestants need to do now, on this analysis, is to reconnect themselves to the Great Tradition—to retrieve what was lost in the midst of the tumult of the sixteenth-century European church. At least in my friend and colleague Hans Boersma's case, the task is specifically to recover what he calls the ancient "Platonist-Christian synthesis"—the synthesis that preceded the rediscovery of Aristotle in the West and then his rise to dominance in high medieval theology.[5] Central to this project is the retrieval of an integrated, spiritually focused Bible for the church. In pursuit of this, we must reject the Protestant dismissal—a *fateful* one, which led ultimately to the development of a secular hermeneutic—of much of the pre-Reformation approach to the Bible. We must instead attempt the recovery of a sacramental approach to Scripture in which its literal meaning points to its spiritual meaning.[6] For the literal sense of Scripture so beloved of the magisterial Reformers is in fact only "the starting point (*sacramentum*) of a search for the greater, more christological reality (*res*) of the gospel," and it is only a sacramental hermeneutic that will allow us "to retain the centrality of the Bible while…rediscover[ing] its hidden spiritual depths."[7]

On this kind of view, then, the answer to the problem of the eclipse of biblical narrative is to get back behind the Reformation, which was in fact one of the significant causes of the eclipse. We must learn to inhabit once again an older, better, and more orthodox worldview, involving an older, better, and more orthodox hermeneutical method. And in this better method the allegorical reading of Scripture plays a central role, since the reader in question does not believe that the Word of God is only or even predominantly expressed in ordinary human words in their ordinary communicative intent. The reader believes, rather, that what God wishes to say through Scripture might be considerably different from what any of its human authors originally meant. As one contemporary scholar has summarized the prevailing view on this question in the pre-Reformation period:

Century Hermeneutics (New Haven, CT: Yale University Press, 1974).

[5] Boersma, *Heavenly Participation*, 33–39.

[6] Boersma, *Heavenly Participation*, 21–24, 137–53.

[7] Boersma, *Heavenly Participation*, 152–53.

"Spiritual meanings...were the golden hoard contained in the casket of the literal."[8]

Now I am both skeptical about this entire proposal and doubtful about the analysis upon which it is based. However, it is neither the entire analysis nor the entire proposal that is the subject of my deliberations in this essay.[9] Here I wish to focus on only one element of the larger proposal, asking this question: Should contemporary Protestants recommit to a pursuit of spiritual meaning in Scripture of the kind that significantly marked the pre-Reformation period—should we, like so many of our pre-Reformation forebears in the church, regard Scripture's literal meaning only as our "starting point" in the quest for "its hidden spiritual depths"?[10]

THE LITERAL SENSE

So confused and confusing has this debate become in our present environment that we cannot even begin this discussion without defining our terms. So what does it mean to read Scripture "literally"? What does it mean to read *any* text "literally"? Consider the following statement: "I was literally glued to my seat throughout the entire performance." What the writer means, of course, is that he was *metaphorically* glued to his seat throughout the entire performance. The addition of the word "literally" to this sentence is therefore unhelpful, if the author's purpose is one of clear communication. It encourages certain kinds of readers, in fact, to do what they might have done anyway, precisely because they pride themselves in reading texts literally. "He *says* he was glued to his seat," they might say; "we must take him at his word." These are the kinds of readers that Peggy Parish has in mind in her popular I Can Read! series of stories concerning "Amelia Bedelia."[11] Amelia *is* a certain kind of "literal reader." If her employers ask her

---

[8] Lesley Smith, "Nicholas Lyra and Old Testament Interpretation," in *Hebrew Bible / Old Testament: The History of Its Interpretation, 2: From the Renaissance to the Enlightenment*, ed. Magne Sæbø (Göttingen, Germany: Vandenhoeck & Ruprecht, 2008), 49–63 (55–56).

[9] Readers interested in an extensive analysis of the entire proposal should consult my recent book: Iain Provan, *The Reformation and the Right Reading of Scripture* (Waco, TX: Baylor University Press, 2017), from which the substance of the present essay is also drawn.

[10] Boersma, *Heavenly Participation*, 152–53.

[11] E.g., Peggy Parish, *Amelia Bedelia*, 50th anniversary ed. (New York: Greenwillow

to change the towels, for example, she will go out and buy new ones. When she makes a sponge cake, she puts in real sponges, and when she pitches a tent, she throws it into the forest. In this case, however, the word "literal" refers to a kind of reading that misses the point of a communication through failing to understand how language is being used. This being so—as Kevin Vanhoozer suggests—this kind of reading does not deserve to be called "literal" at all, precisely because it does *not* attend carefully to the communicative intent of the person who put the "letter" of the text on the page in the first place.

Vanhoozer proposes instead (and I concur) that we call this "literalistic" reading. For a truly literal reading pays attention to the "speech acts" of the author, and not just to words in themselves, whereas a literalistic reading focuses only on the latter. The literal sense of Jesus' statement, "I am the door," for example, is discovered not only by consulting a dictionary about what a word like "door" typically means in the language spoken by the author (which is indeed important), but also by paying attention to how that word is actually being used in a particular speech act. An author might well use a word like "door" metaphorically, but nevertheless intend to communicate "literal truth" (e.g., about Jesus) in the process. Literal reading makes room for this possibility. Literalistic reading does not. If this is so, then we should avoid using the word "literal," not only emphatically, but also as the opposite of words like "metaphorical." And so we should not say: "She failed to understand the metaphorical language in the poem and interpreted it literally." We should rather say: "In failing to understand the metaphorical language in the poem, she failed to interpret it literally." She missed the point of the literary communication.

"Literalistic" is of course a modern and not an ancient term, but the distinction I am drawing here is one that the Reformers certainly considered important. Luther is very interested in the ways that the biblical authors are "artists and poets," and he is attentive to phenomena in the text like Hebrew parallelism and metaphors. This is also true of Calvin. William Bouwsma tells us that "like earlier commentators in the tradition of Augustine's *De doctrina christiana*...Calvin regularly identified metaphor, allegory, personification, metonymy, synecdoche, and other tropes."[12] Calvin is in-

Books, 2013).

[12] William J. Bouwsma, *John Calvin: A Sixteenth-Century Portrait* (Oxford: Oxford University Press, 1988), 123. In "metonymy," the name of an attribute or adjunct is

deed impatient with those who fail to grasp that a faithful reading of Scripture must attend to such phenomena. This is well illustrated in the comments in his *Institutes of the Christian Religion* about "fanatical men" whose commitment to reading Scripture literally (as they see it) threatens to open the door to "a boundless barbarism [that] will overwhelm the whole light of faith."[13] It was necessary, rather, for the biblical exegete to possess a sound knowledge of rhetoric, without which, as he (Calvin) observed, "many supervacuous contentions will arise."[14] Reformation exegetes could sometimes disagree about *which* texts were meant to be read metaphorically, or in accord with some other figure of speech, but they do not disagree *that* the literal sense *included* such phenomena.

It becomes clear as we begin to develop this argument in this way that literal reading is never simply a matter of words or even sentences alone, read apart from their contexts. There is, first of all, the historical context—for words mean what they mean in particular languages at particular times. And this is why the Reformers urged their readers to attend closely to matters like the nature of the grammar and syntax of the original Hebrew and Greek texts that lay before them, and not simply depend on Latin translation. "Become a text critic," Luther advises his readers, "and learn about the grammatical sense, whatever grammar intends, which is about faith, patience, death, and life."[15] What God says in Scripture, He says in the ordinary language of those who lived in the past, and were indeed conditioned by that past—so we need to engage with that same past. Just a few years later, Luther tells Erasmus that "we must everywhere stick to the simple, pure, and natural sense of the words that accords with the rules of grammar and the normal use of language as God has created it in man."[16] The same idea is often expressed in Calvin's writings. In his search

---

substituted for that of the thing meant (as in "lend me your ears"). In "synecdoche," a part represents the whole, or vice versa (as in "Denver won by six runs," meaning "Denver's baseball team"). A "trope" is a figure of speech.

[13] R. M. Frye, "Calvin's Theological Use of Figurative Language," in *John Calvin and the Church: A Prism of Reform*, ed. Timothy George (Louisville, KY: Westminster John Knox, 1990), 172–94 (181), citing Calvin, *Institutes*, 4.17.23.

[14] Cited in Frye, "Figurative Language," 189.

[15] Martin Luther, *A Brief, Yet Clear Exposition of the Song of Songs* (1530–1531), as cited in Heinrich Bornkamm, *Luther and the Old Testament*, trans. E. W. and R. C. Gritsch, ed. V. I. Gruhn (Mifflintown, PA: Sigler, 1997), 92.

[16] Martin Luther, *The Bondage of the Will* (1525), *LW* 33:162.

for the mind of God in the writings of Paul, for example, Calvin keeps firmly in mind, writes Ward Holder, that "Paul was a first-century thinker who was conditioned by the cultures in which he moved and taught."[17]

There is the historical context, and then, secondly, there are the literary and the canonical contexts. Words mean what they mean in particular textual places—in paragraphs, and in books, and in the whole of Scripture. And to read them apart from these contexts is to fail to read them literally. The communicative intent of the authors of the books and of the shapers of the canon was that they should be read *in* such contexts—and, thereby, that we should hear the Word of God to us through them. This is certainly also what both Luther and Calvin believed; they would have regarded as incomplete any efforts of theirs to read "literally" any discrete section of a biblical book, had they not then proceeded to read it in its larger context. For example, "Calvin always believed that each book of the scripture represented a coherent effort at expression by its author."[18] We routinely find in his commentaries, therefore, attention to the nature of the whole as well as to the parts of a particular biblical book. Both Reformers would have regarded anything less than such efforts to read contextually as a failure to make the attempt to read fully "literally"—and they would surely have been right to believe so.

And this brings me finally in this section of the essay to the question of typology—sometimes called "figuration." Resemblance within the context of the whole biblical story is the key idea here. Within that context, into which Christians believers are now also to "read" themselves, certain persons or entities are, or ought to be, like each other in certain ways. Some of these resemblances involve a "lesser" and a "greater," leading some to suggest that "escalation" through time is the main defining feature of biblical typology. Yet it would be a mistake to assume that "escalation" is always or even normally in view when typological connections are present in Scripture. For this reason, Dan Treier's more neutral definition of typological reading is preferable. He proposes that we think of it simply as "iconic" mimesis, which preserves "a 'narrative coherence' between referents."[19]

---

[17] R. Ward Holder, *John Calvin and the Grounding of Interpretation: Calvin's First Commentaries* (SHCT; Leiden: Brill, 2006), 106.

[18] Holder, *Grounding*, 75.

[19] Daniel J. Treier, "Typology," in *Dictionary for Theological Interpretation of the Bible*, ed. Kevin J. Vanhoozer (Grand Rapids, MI: Baker Academic, 2005), 823–27 (825).

The main point here is to resist the idea that there is in the NT any generalized notion that God's dealings with Israel in the OT are any less real, or any less important in themselves, than his dealings with the church in the NT. It was precisely because of the tendencies of some typological reading in this direction that Luther can be found criticizing the approach, even though he himself was far from shy about making typological connections between biblical texts. God did not reveal Himself in the OT through figurative hints, Luther believed, nor did that body of literature merely provide images for a later Christ event. The Israelites lived their own substantive life of faith in response to God's revelation in OT events, *and then they also* prefigured NT realities. Likewise, however much the OT is considered in the NT to "point beyond itself," this is not at the cost of the reality or importance of God's dealings with his OT people. As Hans Frei puts it, in typology, "*without loss to its own literal meaning or specific temporal reference* [my emphasis], an earlier story (or occurrence) [becomes] a figure of a later one."[20]

This being so, it is clear that we should not drive a wedge between the literal and the typological, as some do. The literal and the typological or figurative are best understood, not as two *different* ways of reading, but as two aspects of the *same way* of reading. The latter comes into its own not so much at the level of sentence or paragraph, but at the level of larger entities like whole books and even collections of books. In Frei's words, typological reading involves "literalism at the level of the whole biblical story." Figuration should not be conceived of, he writes, as "being in conflict with the literal sense of biblical stories, [but as being]...at once a literary and a historical procedure, an interpretation of stories and their meanings by weaving them together into a common narrative referring to a single history and its patterns of meaning."[21] "Literal" and "typological" should not be considered as opposites, then. Nor were they generally considered to be so by the magisterial Reformers. Calvin's general commitment to this kind of large-scale contextual reading is well illustrated, for example, by his approach to Paul's letters in his commentaries; he is not only interested in reading well all of Romans as an entire book in itself, but also in reading it within the context of the whole corpus of the Pauline literature, and then of the whole of Scripture. In general, his belief is that "the story of Israel

---

[20] Frei, *Eclipse*, 2.

[21] Frei, *Eclipse*, 2.

repeats itself in the life of the (Christian) reader, and thus the words of the text are addressed not only to the characters in the story but also to Calvin and all readers."[22]

THE SPIRITUAL SENSE

This, then, is the literal reading of Scripture that the magisterial Reformers commended. In so doing, they set their face against the marked tendency among many of their ancestors in the faith, already described, to practice a spiritual, that is, an allegorical reading of the text that leaves the literal somewhat or entirely behind. And here, again, we must be particularly clear as to what we best mean by our words, because there have always been those (whether in ancient or modern times) who have wished to blur the distinction between allegorical and typological reading, representing *all of it together* simply as "spiritual reading." John O'Keefe and Rusty Reno, for example, frequently refer to "typology" in their book on early Christian interpretation of the Bible "without assuming a sharp distinction from allegory."[23] Allegory, they claim,

> is not conceptually or essentially distinct from typology. It is an extension of the typological strategy that does not limit itself to discerning patterns of and between events. Allegory is more fluid and ambitious. It seeks patterns and establishes diverse links between scripture and a range of intellectual, spiritual, and moral concerns.[24]

The attentive reader will note, however, that O'Keefe and Reno here deny a sharp distinction at one moment, only to reinforce its reality in the next. Typological reading is *indeed* best thought of as discerning "patterns within and between events [and I would add "persons" and "entities"] depicted within scripture." On the other hand, allegorical reading is *indeed* "more fluid and ambitious," moving beyond (and often well beyond) "pat-

---

[22] Kathryn E. Greene-McCreight, *Ad Litteram: How Augustine, Calvin, and Barth Read the "Plain Sense" of Genesis 1–3* (IST 5; New York: Peter Lang, 1999), 111–12.

[23] John J. O'Keefe and Russell R. Reno, *Sanctified Vision: An Introduction to Early Christian Interpretation of the Bible* (Baltimore: Johns Hopkins University Press, 2005), 20.

[24] O'Keefe and Reno, *Sanctified Vision*, 21.

terns…depicted within scripture."[25] It is for this reason that Dan Treier, having defined typological reading (as we have seen) as "iconic mimesis, which preserves a narrative coherence between referents," defines allegorical reading as "*symbolic*" mimesis (my emphasis), "which arbitrarily imposes a thoroughly ahistorical connection."[26] No doubt some will wish to quibble with the word "arbitrary," since allegorical reading can possess method. What is clear, however, is that the two kinds of reading described by O'Keefe and Reno are very different from each other. And whatever we may think of either, it does not help us in speaking and writing clearly about the rights and wrongs of various approaches to biblical hermeneutics if we already fudge distinctions by the language we use in describing them. *Typological reading is literal reading in a sense that we cannot plausibly ascribe to allegorical reading.* This is precisely because the former makes connections that internally illuminate the Bible as a coherent story, presenting its own distinctive view of the world, whereas the latter obscures those connections in making "sense of texts that have been *resituated* [my emphasis] within alien cultures and conceptual frameworks."[27] To put this in a different, but overlapping way:

> Typology emerges from the relationship between the two Testaments and centers in Christ as the fulfillment of the Old Testament. Allegory emerges from a flattening of the Scriptures into an atemporal whole, in which the same truth is to be found throughout. In this it reveals the vertical dualism of Platonism rather than the eschatological vision of Scripture.[28]

The Reformers certainly distinguished typology from allegory along such lines, and they had little time for the kind of "spiritual reading" that

---

[25] "Unlike typologies, allegories require significantly more interpretive investment capital.… Allegory involves so much interpretive ambition that it can create the impression that the real source of meaning is in the reader's imagination and not in the text itself." Indeed! O'Keefe and Reno, *Sanctified Vision*, 90.

[26] Treier, "Typology," 825.

[27] Kevin J. Vanhoozer, *Is There a Meaning in This Text? The Bible, the Reader, and the Morality of Literary Knowledge* (Grand Rapids, MI: Zondervan, 1998), 114.

[28] Craig G. Bartholomew, *Introducing Biblical Hermeneutics: A Comprehensive Framework for Hearing God in Scripture* (Grand Rapids: Baker Academic, 2015), 145.

was grounded in allegorical reading. Luther could be fierce, for example, when it came to this practice, to which in his earlier life as a monk he had been very much attached. He had come to believe, however, that such reading had led its proponents to miss the sense of Christ in Scripture even as they believed they had penetrated right to it. Recognizing that this approach had significant roots in the postapostolic church, Luther nevertheless believed that

> the allegorical methods with which Origen or Jerome sought to bring the Old Testament to the level of Christian taste and spirit in reality gave it the *coup de grace*: the allegorical interpretation killed the spiritual sense of the Old Testament.[29]

For Luther, the true spiritual sense was indeed none other *than* the literal sense. The Word of God has "a sure, simple, and unequivocal meaning upon which our faith may build without wavering";[30] it is "the one simplest meaning which we call the written one, or the literal meaning of the tongue."[31] John Calvin shared Luther's distaste for the allegedly nonliteral senses of the Bible, criticizing Origen and others who

> have seized the occasion of torturing Scripture, in every possible manner, away from the true sense. They concluded that the literal sense is too mean and poor, and that, under the outer bark of the letter, there lurk deeper mysteries, which cannot be extracted but by beating out allegories. And this they had no difficulty in accomplishing; for speculations which appear to be ingenious have always been preferred, and always will be preferred, by the world to solid doctrine.[32]

Calvin believed that Bible readers ought to have more reverence for

---

[29] Bornkamm, *Luther and the Old Testament*, 89–90.

[30] Martin Luther, *On the Papacy in Rome against the Most Celebrated Romanist in Leipzig* (1520), *LW* 39:83.

[31] Martin Luther, *Answer to Goat Emser* (1521), *LW* 39:178.

[32] John Calvin, *Commentaries on the Epistles of Paul to the Galatians and Ephesians*, trans. William Pringle (Grand Rapids: Eerdmans, 1948), 135—in a comment on Gal. 4:22.

the text than was displayed in such readings by "empty-headed creatures…[who in reading allegorically] change dogs into men, trees into angels, and convert the whole of Scripture into an amusing game."[33] They ought to pay more careful attention to the language, grammar, syntax, and historical context of its various passages, as well as to the various rhetorical devices employed therein as part of various authors' efforts to communicate with their intended audiences. They ought to attend, indeed, to what modern writers would call plot development in the biblical narrative.[34] This attention to the rhetoric of a text in the course of literary analysis in pursuit of "the writer's central arguments and concerns"[35] also characterizes the more systematically worked-out Protestant approaches of Philipp Melanchthon and Martin Bucer. It was Bucer who once famously referred to allegorical reading as turning Scripture into "a wax nose that can be twisted in any direction."[36] It is Melanchthon who once lampooned it as involving "labyrinths in which others show off their talents," and thereby unknowingly contributed to the title of this present essay.[37]

The Reformers, then, sought to sweep away all the other "senses" of the biblical text in favor of the literal or literal-historical sense, which could also be referred to as the "simple," or "genuine," or "natural" sense. It did not matter if notable Church Fathers had lent their authority to "spiritual" reading; the search for "deeper mysteries" beneath the surface of the biblical text had resulted only in the distortion of its message. It was a dangerous and indeed *unwarranted* way of approaching Scripture that should be rejected.

---

[33] John Calvin, *The First Epistle of Paul the Apostle to the Corinthians*, trans. John W. Fraser (Edinburgh: Saint Andrew Press, 1960), 187—in a comment on 1 Cor. 9:8–9.

[34] Note, for example, his attentiveness to such detail in his Genesis commentary, as described in Greene-McCreight, *Ad Litteram*, 107–18.

[35] John L. Thompson, "Calvin as a Biblical Interpreter," in *The Cambridge Companion to John Calvin*, ed. Donald McKim (Cambridge: Cambridge University Press, 2004), 58–73 (61).

[36] R. Gerald Hobbs, "Pluriformity of Early Reformation Scriptural Interpretation," in *HBOT*, 2:452–511 (461).

[37] Cited in Hobbs, "Pluriformity," 496, referring to a letter of October 29, 1556 (#6110) now found in Karl G. Bretschneider, ed., *Corpus Reformatorum,* 101 vols. (Halle, Germany: Schwetschke, 1841), 8:893–94.

THE REFORMERS AS RELIABLE GUIDES

Were the Reformers right? I believe that they were absolutely right. They were right, first of all, in their claim about the lack of any fundamental warrant for this kind of "spiritual reading" in apostolic teaching. In the NT, we find Jesus and his apostles reading OT Scripture predominantly, if not entirely, literally.[38] That is, they pay attention to the apparent communicative intention of Scripture as a collection of texts from the past, taking full account of the nature of the language in which these intentions are embedded and revealed as components of Scripture's unfolding covenantal story. They are not to be found reading it "spiritually," if by this we mean allegorically. This is true even in Galatians 4:21–31, where Paul uses the verb *allēgoreō* to refer to his reading of Genesis in that context. Already in ancient times Origen appealed to this passage in the course of defending his own allegorical approach to the biblical text, which owes a significant amount to his Jewish Alexandrian predecessor Philo. But in response, other ancient writers like John Chrysostom argued that in Galatians 4 Paul pursues a customary typological approach to the OT while *referring* to it (unhelpfully) using the verb *allegoreo*.[39] That is to say: *allegoreo* does not signify in Paul what it signifies in other ancient authors like Philo and his later fellow Alexandrians (such as Origen). And indeed, study of Philo's genuinely allegorical treatment of Genesis confirms this judgment. For whereas Paul reads Scripture literally in line with our earlier discussion of this term—reminding the Galatian Christians thereby of which distinctive story they find themselves in, and of which historical family they are members—Philo radically reshapes Scripture by way of allegorical reading in order to bring it into conformity with what was considered rational and virtuous by the Alexandrian Greeks of his day. Consider the following:

> When, therefore, you hear that Hagar was afflicted by Sarah, you must not suppose that any of those things befell her, which arise from rivalry and quarrels among women; for the question is not here about woman, but about minds; the one being practised in the branches of elementary instruction, and the other being devoted to the labours of virtue.[40]

---

[38] For a full defense of this proposition, see further Provan, *Reformation*, 107–50.

[39] John Chrysostom, *Commentary on Galatians*, 4.24 (*NPNF* 1, 13:34).

[40] Philo, *De congressu eruditionis gratia (On the Preliminary Studies)*, 180, in *WP*, 320.

Philo clearly does not read Scripture literally; Paul clearly does. Insofar as the Church Fathers and later medieval Christians then proceed also to read Scripture literally, they reflect basic apostolic hermeneutical practice. And it is this long Christian tradition of attending to the literal sense of Scripture as its foundational sense in which the Reformers rightly situate themselves, looking back in particular to Augustine's *On Christian Doctrine.* They were right to hold that this literal reading, including typological reading, is warranted, but that nonliteral reading of the kind to which the influential Origen so extensively resorted in the third century is not.

They were correct, too, about the danger of the latter. For the fact of the matter is—and the Reformers themselves well understood this—that exegesis in which the reader consciously sets his face against the literal sense of a Scriptural passage while claiming the leading of the Holy Spirit in his reading threatens in the end to undermine the very apostolic authority to which it appeals—as well as the authority of the OT Scriptures that the apostles presuppose. For if we are to conceive of a significant gap opening up between the communicative intention of a human author and the communicative intention of God, how then are we to gain reliable access through those texts to what God is saying? Moreover, if the Holy Spirit can operate in this way in *those* texts, why not also in others? Why not in all the Scriptures, including the apostolic writings? Perhaps what God really wishes to say is hidden beneath the surface of all of them and cannot be grasped by attention to ordinary human language *at all.* Perhaps what God really wishes to say looks quite different from what appears on the surface of the human text *everywhere.*

The further we press the agenda of this "spiritual" Bible reading, the more we recognize the seriousness of the threat to what we came to believe on the basis of literal reading in the first place—and who is to say how far the agenda is to be pressed? Once the allegorical train leaves the station and starts running along its tracks, where will it be forced to stop, and by whom? The author of the text cannot fulfill this role, since he was never informed about the departure of the train in the first place. And certainly if the train runs far enough without interference, any text, however authoritative it might once have been, will inevitably end up "saying" what another, newly authoritative text is saying. About this new text, incidentally, one thing can be said with complete certainty, even before it is written: that it, at least, will be subject only to literal reading. Not a breath of allegory will disturb its literal tranquility. For throughout history and down to the present time, one never finds readers allegorizing genuinely authoritative texts to which they ascribe primary authority, even if they claim otherwise. The texts that possess primary authority are always read literally, even if texts immediately surrounding them are read in other ways. Allegorizing only befalls texts that require domesticating in relation to primary authorities—texts that need to be made to say something, against their grain, in an important narrative that is alien to them. Allegorizing only occurs, as O'Keefe and Reno disarmingly put it, "when the literal meaning of a text is seen to run in a wrong or unhelpful direction…[when] the reader is unhappy with the literal meaning"[41]—and "wrong or unhelpful" are of course measured in terms of an authority that lies elsewhere. So it was in the beginning, when allegorical reading was first invented in Greece in order to subjugate an old text (Homer) to a new one (largely Plato). So it is now:

> To construct an allegory or to read allegorically is certainly also to express one's own ideology and worldview in conscious or unconscious dialogue with—or, perhaps, in opposition to—the text from which one's allegory is ostensibly drawn.[42]

Allegory, writes David Dawson, "is not so much about the meaning or lack of meaning in texts as it is a way of using texts and their meanings to situate oneself and one's community with respect to society and culture."[43] As O'Keefe and Reno themselves admit, this is what makes any "interpretive move that directs attention away from the literal sense…a dangerous game. Allegorical readings, especially of obscure or offensive texts, are prone to spin out of control."[44]

A certain degree of awareness of the threat thus posed to the authority of Scripture by "spiritual reading" is already apparent in patristic times.

---

[41] O'Keefe and Reno, *Sanctified Vision*, 103.

[42] John L. Thompson, *Writing the Wrongs: Women of the Old Testament among Biblical Commentators from Philo through the Reformation* (Oxford: Oxford University Press, 2001), 243—in the course of describing Gale Yee's opinion, but apparently agreeing with her.

[43] David Dawson, *Allegorical Readers and Cultural Revision in Ancient Alexandria* (Berkeley: University of California Press, 1992), 236.

[44] O'Keefe and Reno, *Sanctified Vision*, 93.

It is apparent *even though* so many of the Christian leaders in those early centuries had been educated in classically Hellenistic ways, and *even though* the appropriateness of at least some degree of allegorical reading of ancient literature seemed to them self-evident.[45] Even someone like Didymus the Blind, a devoted follower of Origen who allegorizes constantly in his teaching, recognizes the threat, insisting that the cross of Christ (at least) cannot be subject to this treatment: "If the cross is allegorized, the resurrection has to be allegorized, too. But if the resurrection is allegorized, everything that took place is like a dream."[46] It is precisely against this background, toward the end of a patristic period in which not a few writers give the impression of deciding on such matters arbitrarily, that Augustine's *Christian Doctrine* seeks to formulate guidelines for Scripture reading; and in this work he is a strong advocate of reading Scripture according to its literal sense. Readers should resist the temptation to evade the imperatives of the text read literally by appealing to a nonliteral sense. Only when it proves impossible to read individual texts literally in line with the thrust of the whole biblical story (and its major injunctions to love both God and neighbor), Augustine proposes, should the text be read in a different manner. Here a strong intuition about the potentially injurious effects of "spiritual reading" on the authority of Scripture results in a serious attempt to rein it in.

So the Church Fathers were *somewhat* aware of the problem. However, it is only with the benefit of hindsight—as readers who do not share directly in the pagan Graeco-Roman inheritance into which the Fathers were all inducted by way of upbringing and education[47]—that we can fully recognize its seriousness. It is only now that time has passed that we can look back and see the numerous ways in which Scripture's ability to function authoritatively, both in patristic times and in the Middle Ages, was not merely *threatened* but actually *compromised* by "spiritual" reading. Handled in such a manner, Scripture could not effectively challenge its readers. The literal sense could all too easily be ignored where it conflicted with favored

---

[45] Henning G. Reventlow, *History of Biblical Interpretation, Volume 1: From the Old Testament to Origen*, trans. Leo Perdue, RBS 50 (Atlanta: Society of Biblical Literature, 2009), 33–40; 2:5–6, 26.

[46] Cited in Henning G. Reventlow, *History of Biblical Interpretation, Volume 2: From Late Antiquity to the End of the Middle Ages*, trans. James O. Duke, RBS 61 (Atlanta: Society of Biblical Literature, 2009), 31.

[47] "[A] pagan rhetorical education was still a matter of course even for Christians in the fourth century" (Reventlow, *Biblical Interpretation*, 2:33).

prevailing ideas and ethical norms, and a "spiritual reading" could all too easily be found that conformed to them. Under such circumstances, Scripture could not function as an entity that is "breathed out by God and profitable for teaching, for reproof, for correction, and for training in righteousness, that the man of God may be complete, equipped for every good work" (2 Tim. 3:16–17)—even though this is what its Christian readers sincerely believed it to be accomplishing. Thomas Aquinas may well wish to claim in the thirteenth century, then, that "nothing necessary to faith is contained under the spiritual sense which is not elsewhere put forward by the Scripture in its literal sense."[48] But the fact is that a significant amount of what is represented as authentic Christian belief in the patristic literature and afterward is not obviously grounded in Scripture read in its literal sense at all: for example, the idea that the body is less important than the soul, or marriage less worthy than celibacy; that erotic desire and passion are problematic, and are to be suppressed; that the goal of existence is the ascent of the soul to God. It is not the literal reading of Scripture that drives these ideas. For these ideas to flourish, Scripture must be read in ways that its human authors (not being Greeks themselves) cannot be shown to have intended. The Bible must be allegorized so as to conform it to Plato and his ancient friends. Even today, apparently—for many theologians—to do the opposite is unthinkable. It is the philosophers who are running the show—not Scripture.

Into the significant "gap," then, between the voice of the human author and the voice of God in Scripture that was opened up by Bible readers in the postapostolic church came a considerable number of ideas that cannot be grounded in the literal sense of the biblical text—even though the literal sense was widely agreed to be the foundational sense. Scripture resists these ideas, but they entered into mainstream Christian discourse nevertheless, because whereas texts read literally can, like dogs, "bite back" at the reader—challenging his or her current ideas—texts read "spiritually" cannot. The faulty ideas in question are not, moreover, marginal or trivial. In the examples cited, they go right to the heart of what it means to be a human being, and how best to live our lives in pursuit of God-ordained goals. This is a fairly central matter of concern in Scripture. Particularly on such crucial matters pertaining to Christian faith, then—and others like them—one would indeed have hoped (to quote Aquinas) that more of the

[48] Aquinas, *Summa Theologiae*, 1.1.10.

Church Fathers might have found in Scripture "contained under the spiritual sense" only that which is "elsewhere put forward…in its literal sense." One would have hoped that, even had they believed that the apostles indulged to some small degree in the nonliteral reading of Scripture, they would have been alert to the dangers of attempting more of it. Evidently, however, this was often not the case; and to that extent, wittingly or not, the Church Fathers undermined the authority of Scripture, including the authority of the apostles, even as they appealed to it. So did many of those who followed them in the Middle Ages. So do many now.

CONCLUSION

And so we come to my conclusion. The Reformers well understood that the long Christian tradition of reading Scripture nonliterally lacked convincing apostolic warrant. They also comprehended how it undermined the authority of Scripture. Scripture could all too easily come to be understood, not as the very word of God (as the apostles believed)—"the loftiest and noblest of holy things," in Luther's words[49]—but as an embarrassing problem to be solved by subtle, labyrinthine hermeneutical maneuvers. By the beginning of the sixteenth century the Reformers had indeed accumulated many more examples of the ways in which this was the case than were even conceivable by the end of the fifth, and they perceived clearly that the very nature of Christian faith, as well as general access to it, were at stake in this question of "how should we read." They were surely correct to reject such "spiritual reading," and in doing so they rightly drew on much of what earlier writers like Augustine had already said about it. It was not the Reformers, in taking up such a position, but others before them in taking up theirs, who in some measure or another stepped away from the apostolic tradition. And in due course the Roman Catholic Church has itself moved officially and significantly in the same "reformed" direction, as documents like the papal encyclical *Divino afflante Spiritu* make clear in urging renewed theological interpretation of Scripture based on the literal sense.[50] Its purpose, we

[49] Richard B. Hays, *Reading Backwards: Figural Christology and the Fourfold Gospel Witness* (Waco, TX: Baylor University Press, 2014), 1, quoting the preface to the German translation of the Pentateuch (1523).

[50] Pope Pius XII, "Encyclical Letter Promoting Biblical Studies, *Divino afflante Spiritu*," in *The Scripture Documents: An Anthology of Official Catholic Teachings*, ed. Dean P.

read, is to "reduce to silence those who, affirming that they scarcely ever find anything in biblical commentaries to raise their hearts to God, to nourish their souls or promote their interior life, repeatedly urge that we should have recourse to a certain spiritual and, as they say, mystical interpretation."[51] This is hardly a ringing endorsement of the "spiritual reading" of Scripture.

Likewise, contemporary Protestants ought not to seek to resurrect a "spiritual reading" that pursues Scripture's nonliteral in addition to its literal sense. We ought to eschew these "labyrinths in which others show off their talents." Our true calling, I believe, is instead to continue to seek a deeper understanding of the literal sense of Scripture in precisely the manner of the Reformers' teaching—and, indeed, where necessary to read it even more literally, and more consistently literally, than they were able to do.[52]

Béchard (Collegeville, MN: Liturgical Press, 2002), 115–39.

[51] *Divino afflante Spiritu*, 125.

[52] On this important point see further Provan, *Reformation*, 216–25.

BIBLIOGRAPHY

Bartholomew, Craig G. *Introducing Biblical Hermeneutics: A Comprehensive Framework for Hearing God in Scripture.* Grand Rapids: Baker Academic, 2015.

Boersma, Hans. *Heavenly Participation: The Weaving of a Sacramental Tapestry.* Grand Rapids, MI: Eerdmans, 2011.

Bouwsma, William J. *John Calvin: A Sixteenth-Century Portrait.* Oxford: Oxford University Press, 1988.

Bretschneider, Karl G., ed. *Corpus Reformatorum,* 101 vols. Halle, Germany: Schwetschke, 1841.

Calvin, John. *Commentaries on the Epistles of Paul to the Galatians and Ephesians.* Translated by William Pringle. Grand Rapids: Eerdmans, 1948.

———. *The First Epistle of Paul the Apostle to the Corinthians.* Translated by John W. Fraser. Edinburgh: Saint Andrew Press, 1960.

Chrysostom, John. *Commentary on Galatians.* In "Saint Chrysostom," vol. 13 of *Nicene and Post-Nicene Fathers*, Series 1. New York: Charles Scribner's Sons, 1914.

Dawson, David. *Allegorical Readers and Cultural Revision in Ancient Alexandria.* Berkeley: University of California Press, 1992.

Frei, Hans W. *The Eclipse of Biblical Narrative: A Study in Eighteenth and Nineteenth Century Hermeneutics.* New Haven, CT: Yale University Press, 1974.

Frye, R. M. "Calvin's Theological Use of Figurative Language." In *John Calvin and the Church: A Prism of Reform*, edited by Timothy George, 172–94. Louisville, KY: Westminster John Knox, 1990.

Greene-McCreight, Kathryn E. *Ad Litteram: How Augustine, Calvin, and Barth Read the "Plain Sense" of Genesis 1–3.* IST 5; New York: Peter Lang, 1999.

Gregory, Brad S. *The Unintended Reformation: How a Religious Revolution Secularized Society.* Cambridge, MA: Belknap, 2012.

Hays, Richard B. *Reading Backwards: Figural Christology and the Fourfold Gospel Witness.* Waco, TX: Baylor University Press, 2014.

Hobbs, R. Gerald. "Pluriformity of Early Reformation Scriptural Interpretation." In *Hebrew Bible / Old Testament: The History of Its Interpretation, 2: From the Renaissance to the Enlightenment*, edited by Magne Sæbø, 2:452–511. Göttingen, Germany: Vandenhoeck & Ruprecht, 2008.

Holder, R. Ward. *John Calvin and the Grounding of Interpretation: Calvin's First Commentaries.* SHCT; Leiden: Brill, 2006.

Luther, Martin. *A Brief, Yet Clear Exposition of the Song of Songs*, 1530–1531. In Heinrich Bornkamm, *Luther and the Old Testament*, translated by E. W. and R. C. Gritsch, and edited by V. I. Gruhn . Mifflintown, PA: Sigler, 1997.

——. *Answer to Goat Emser* (1521). In Vol. 39 of *Luthers Works.* Edited by Eric W. Gritsch. Philadelphia: Fortress Press, 1970.

——. *The Bondage of the Will* (1525). In *Career of the Reformer III.* Edited by Philip S. Watson. Vol. 33 of *Luther's Works.* Philadelphia, PA: Fortress Press, 1957

——. *On the Papacy in Rome against the Most Celebrated Romanist in Leipzig* (1520). In Vol. 39 of *Luthers Works.* Edited by Eric W. Gritsch. Philadelphia: Fortress Press, 1970.

O'Keefe, John J. and Russell R. Reno. *Sanctified Vision: An Introduction to Early Christian Interpretation of the Bible.* Baltimore: Johns Hopkins University Press, 2005.

Parish, Peggy. *Amelia Bedelia.* 50th anniversary edition. New York: Greenwillow Books, 2013.

Philo. *De congressu eruditionis gratia (On the Preliminary Studies).* Translated by Monique Alexandre. In *Oeuvres de Philon d'Alexandrie.* Paris: Ed. du Cerf, 1967.

Pius XII, Pope. "Encyclical Letter Promoting Biblical Studies, *Divino afflante Spiritu.*" In *The Scripture Documents: An Anthology of Official Catholic Teachings*, edited by Dean P. Béchard, 115–39. Collegeville, MN: Liturgical Press, 2002.

Provan, Iain. *The Reformation and the Right Reading of Scripture*. Waco, TX: Baylor University Press, 2017.

Reventlow, Henning G. *History of Biblical Interpretation, Volume 1: From the Old Testament to Origen.* Translated by Leo Perdue. RBS 50. Atlanta: Society of Biblical Literature, 2009.

———. *History of Biblical Interpretation, Volume 2: From Late Antiquity to the End of the Middle Ages.* Translated by James O. Duke. RBS 61. Atlanta: Society of Biblical Literature, 2009.

Smith, Lesley. "Nicholas Lyra and Old Testament Interpretation." In *Hebrew Bible / Old Testament*, 49–63.

Taylor, Charles. *A Secular Age*. Cambridge, MA: Belknap, 2007.

Thompson, John L. "Calvin as a Biblical Interpreter." In *The Cambridge Companion to John Calvin*, edited by Donald McKim, 58–73. Cambridge: Cambridge University Press, 2004.

———. *Writing the Wrongs: Women of the Old Testament among Biblical Commentators from Philo through the Reformation.* Oxford: Oxford University Press, 2001.

Treier, Daniel J. "Typology." In *Dictionary for Theological Interpretation of the Bible*, edited by Kevin J. Vanhoozer, 823–27. Grand Rapids, MI: Baker Academic, 2005.

Vanhoozer, Kevin J. *Is There a Meaning in This Text? The Bible, the Reader, and the Morality of Literary Knowledge*. Grand Rapids, MI: Zondervan, 1998.

V:
BIBLICAL INTERPRETATION AND NATURAL KNOWLEDGE: A KEY TO SOLVING THE PROTESTANT PROBLEM

David Haines, Veritas International University

INTRODUCTION

IN HIS first theological treatise *On the Son*, Gregory Nazianzus, an important patristic theologian, provides a powerful defense of the divinity of Jesus Christ, answering a number of different attacks. At one point in the treatise, he notes how many of those who deny the divinity of Christ have latched onto New Testament passages that describe Jesus in terms which are only appropriately said of a human being—experiencing hunger, sleep deprivation, sorrow, and so on. They used these biblical descriptions to deny the divinity of Jesus Christ. Nazianzus refutes these arguments by laying down an important interpretative principle: "To give you the explanation in one sentence:—What is lofty, you are to attribute to the divinity, to that nature in Him which transcends sufferings and the body; but all that is humble, you are to attribute to the composite condition of Him who for your sakes emptied Himself and became flesh—yes, it is no worse to say, was made human and afterwards was also exalted."[1] Another example of the same is found in his fifth theological oration, *On the Holy Spirit*, where he confronts figurative or anthropomorphic language about God. Here he says:

---

[1] Gregory Nazianzus, *On the Son 1*, in *Five Theological Orations*, trans. Stephen Reynolds (n.p.: Estate of Stephen Reynolds, 2011), 64.

> Some things have no existence but are spoken of [in the Scriptures]; other things which do exist are not spoken of; some neither exist nor are spoken of, and some both exist and are spoken of. Do you ask me for proof of this? I am ready to give it. According to Scripture, God sleeps and awakens, is angry, walks, has the cherubim for His throne. And yet when has He ever been subject to such things [as sleeping and waking and anger]? Have you ever heard that God has a body [that walks and sits on a throne]? These are figures of speech, not realities. For we have designated as well as possible the things of God by reference to things of our own...In short, the various powers or activities of God have been pictured for us by various bodily images.[2]

If Nazianzus is right, then there seems to be something that we know about the divine nature and about humans, prior to reading the Scriptures, which allows us to properly interpret those passages that describe God and the Christ, and which allows us to distinguish literal predication from metaphorical or anthropomorphic/anthropopathic predication.

Contemporary Trends in Theology

Jumping ahead some sixteen hundred years, we turn to Mark Sheridan's 2015 book *Language for God in Patristic Tradition: Wrestling with Biblical Anthropomorphism*. In this book, Sheridan seeks to show how the patristic theologians dealt with anthropological descriptions of God in the Bible.[3] For Sheridan, these theologians interpreted these descriptions of the divine "theologically," that is, the Bible was interpreted in light of what was known about the nature of God—and the Scriptures were explained based upon an interpretative principle that could be named the appropriate predication

---

[2] Gregory Nazianzus, *On the Holy Spirit*, in *Five Theological Orations*, trans. Stephen Reynolds (n.p.: Estate of Stephen Reynolds, 2011), 112–13. John Calvin, for example, in his commentary on Paul's Epistle to the Romans, says that "*wrath* is attributed to God, by a figure which we call anthropopathy." Jean Calvin, *Commentaires sur l'épître aux Romains*, in *Commentaires de Jean Calvin sur le Nouveau Testament* (Paris: Librairie de Ch. Meyrueis, 1855), 3:25. My translation. In French we read, "*Ire* est attribué à Dieu par un figure qu'on appelle Anthropopathie."

[3] Mark Sheridan, *Language for God in Patristic Tradition: Wrestling with Biblical Anthropomorphism* (Downers Grove, IL: InterVarsity, 2015), 17.

principle—"that which can be appropriately said of God."[4] Sheridan explains that the early church and patristic fathers interpreted the Bible "theologically," by noting, first of all, that God is not at all like men, and secondly, that He condescends to man's weakness by describing Himself and his actions in ways that are easily understood by man (analogy, symbolism, etc.). The author goes on to develop what we have called the appropriate predication principle and argues that theological interpretation is necessary even today.

Though Sheridan rightly sees the combination of "theological interpretation" and the appropriate predication principle as the only way to recognize that a description is a symbolic or anthropomorphic accommodation, and not a literal description of God, he does not seem to realize that, to interpret the Bible in this way, is to *already possess* some prior knowledge of the natures of both that which is predicated, and that of which the predication is made.[5] In other words, in order to properly interpret biblical descriptions of God, one must already possess prior knowledge of the divine nature. The one question that Sheridan does not answer, and it is a very important question, is: How do we arrive at that proper understanding of the nature of God that becomes the norm for proper biblical interpretation and doctrinal formulation, for distinguishing between literal descriptions of God and anthropomorphic or symbolic descriptions of God? This question is not answered. Sheridan does not even hint at the fact that this is a question that must be asked. The idea that we get, from Sheridan, is that the patristic theologians inherited, from nowhere, an idea of the nature of God, which was then used as the norm for biblical interpretation. Is it possible that natural knowledge of God may have had a role to play in interpreting the Bible and formulating the doctrine of God?

In his 2017 book *All That is in God: Evangelical Theology and the Challenge of Classical Christian Theism*, James Dolezal sounds the alarm concerning the contemporary abandonment of classical theism among prominent evangelical theologians in the Reformed tradition. He notes that "the contemplative approach to theology proper treats God as an ahistorical being and seeks to

---

[4] Sheridan, *LGPT*, 213–15, 224–26. The name of the principle is my invention.

[5] For example, to recognize that "God walked in the garden" is an anthropomorphism (or, at very least, does not imply that God, by nature, is endowed with legs), one must already know (1) what "walking" is and implies, and (2) that God is not such that, by nature, "walking" can be appropriately predicated of him.

discover the timeless truths about Him by thinking through the implications and entailments of those things He has revealed to us in creation and Scripture."[6] He states, rightly, that "part of the reason many evangelical theistic mutualists do not recognize that they have already adopted a form of ontological becoming in God is because they have lost sight of what 'being' means."[7] Having mentioned the use of creation in coming to know something of God, Dolezal does not go on to show how "creation" might help in formulating an orthodox doctrine of God. Rather, the rest of his book is an attempt to apply a "theological interpretation" to Scripture in such a way that all of the classical divine attributes can be shown to be taught in the Bible.[8] He notes, for example, that "our theology should enable us to discern the various accommodated and nonliteral ways in which God speaks to us about Himself in biblical revelation."[9] He begins by explaining what is meant by divine simplicity—that all that is in God is God—and then moves on to draw some consequences from this definition.[10] As with Sheridan, we want to ask Dolezal, How do you know that God is *actus purus*, simple, immutable, and impassible? Where do your "theological concepts," which you use to interpret the Bible theologically, come from? After all, even some important Reformed theologians of the past, such as Charles Hodge,[11] have

---

[6] James Dolezal, *All That Is in God: Evangelical Theology and the Challenge of Classical Christian Theism* (Grand Rapids, MI: Reformation Heritage Books, 2017), xv. He later notes that the job of the theologian is both to gather "the various truths about God that are spread throughout nature and Scripture," and then to arrange "the doctrines so as to form a single coherent doctrine of God." Dolezal, *ATIG*, 37.

[7] Dolezal, *ATIG*, 7.

[8] Dolezal does nuance his work with the claim, in a footnote, that "in claiming that divine simplicity is a biblical doctrine, it does not follow that one can only arrive at this doctrine by considering the biblical witness…Even so, many things witnessed and entailed in God's disclosure of Himself in nature are also witnessed and entailed in the disclosure of Himself in Scripture." Dolezal, *ATIG*, 44–45fn17.

[9] Dolezal, *ATIG*, 21.

[10] Dolezal, *ATIG*, 40–41.

[11] Charles Hodge says, for example, "Here again we have to choose between a mere philosophical speculation and the clear testimony of the Bible, and of our own moral and religious nature. Love of necessity involves feeling, and if there be no feeling in God, there can be no love." Charles Hodge, *Systematic Theology* (1940; repr., Peabody, MA: Hendrickson, 2003), 1:428–29. He goes on to state that God "may be cold, insensible, indifferent, or even unconscious; He ceases to be God in the sense of the Bible, and in the sense in which we need a God, unless He can love as well as know and act." Hodge, *ST*, 1:429. A. H. Strong, the reformed Bap-

rejected doctrines such as impassibility, because this doctrine is (1) not clearly articulated in the Scriptures, and (2) the opposite of this doctrine seems to be clearly articulate in the Scriptures. How, then, do we know that God is impassible? Is it possible that natural knowledge of God has a role to play in interpreting the Bible and in doctrinal formulation?

This tendency, to pay lip service to natural knowledge, and then to continue as if every doctrine could be supported by a couple of proof texts from Scripture,[12] and "inferences" based upon these proof texts, is common among modern and contemporary theologians who wish to maintain classical theism. Others, however, such as the proponents of open theism, revel in pointing out that the proof texts actually say less than what they need to say, if they are to support classical theism. They go on to proclaim that classical theism imposes Greek philosophy on the Bible. This, of course, is an instance of the pot calling the kettle black, as they simply impose a different philosophy on Scripture. It seems that it has become all too easy to read one's "theological" or "philosophical" preferences into the Scriptures, and then be overjoyed at the discovery that the Bible teaches your theological or philosophical preferences. Catholics, open theists, classical theists, Arminians, and Calvinists of all sorts, all find warrant for their theological schools in the Bible and arrive with proof texts to back up their claims. But, how do we know who is properly interpreting Scriptures, and, therefore, is propounding true, orthodox, doctrine? This brings us to what some have called, the Protestant problem.

---

tist theologian, follows Hodge in denying immutability because of love: "The love of God involves also the possibility of divine suffering." A. H. Strong, *Systematic Theology: A Compendium*, 3 vols. in 1 (1907; repr., Old Tappan, NJ: Fleming H. Revell, 1979), 266. He goes on to argue that God is passible, and able to suffer, because the Bible clearly describes God as having emotions such as mourning and anger. Strong, *Systematic Theology: A Compendium*, 266.

[12] I am not suggesting that "proof-texting" is inherently wrong, but, rather, that we must be careful about how we do it. We need to cite our sources properly. If a doctrine is based upon natural knowledge, but can be shown to (1) not contradict the teaching of Scripture, and (2) help us to better understand Scripture, then, rather than saying that this is a doctrine that is "supported" by (or found in) the Scriptures, we need to say be honest, and say that it is based upon natural knowledge. See Michael Allen and Scott R. Swain, *Reformed Catholicity: The Promise of Retrieval for Theology and Biblical Interpretation* (Grand Rapids, MI: Baker Books, 2015), 117–41, for an interesting look at the practice of proof-texting.

The Protestant Problem

Orthodoxy might be defined as right belief. A person would be considered *fully orthodox* if he adheres to all those doctrines that are necessary for true Christian belief and denies none (implicitly or explicitly) of the doctrines that are necessary for true Christian belief. Though the desire is to be, ultimately, fully orthodox, most people are not. Our definition of orthodoxy, however, seems to cause significant problems for Protestantism as a whole. The problem could be broken down as follows: (1) The definition of "orthodoxy" seems to imply that there must be an official *extrabiblical* list of doctrines containing a minimum of true Christian teachings to which a person must adhere to be considered orthodox. (2) As has often been noted, Protestantism (due to the doctrine of *sola scriptura* coupled with the priority of individual interpretation as led by the Holy Spirit) seems to make it impossible for there to be any official extrabiblical list containing a minimum of true Christian teachings to which a person must adhere to be considered orthodox. Alister E. McGrath and Darren C. Marks, in the *Blackwell Companion to Protestantism*, note that "the 'Protestant problematic' (Karl Rahner) is that it places priority on individual conscience in response to revelation—in the Bible and the experience of salvation—as its defining characteristics. As such it must create the possibility, but not the necessity, of interpretative difference in doctrine, practice and polity."[13]

The Protestant problem, to be very clear, is:

> 1. If the Scriptures is the only infallible and ultimate authority for Christian doctrine and practice;
>
> 2. And, if much of the Bible must be interpreted by individual human beings;
>
> 3. And if there is no authoritative and infallible interpretation of the Bible, but every individual is free to interpret the Bible as he wills;
>
> 4. Then, it would appear that there can be no certainty about which doctrines should be accepted as true (funda-

[13] Alister E. McGrath and Darren C. Marks, "Introduction: Protestantism—the Problem of Identity," in *The Blackwell Companion to Protestantism*, ed. Alister E. McGrath and Darren C. Marks (Oxford: Blackwell, 2004), 14.

mental or secondary), and which doctrines can be left as a matter of opinion.

5. There can, therefore, be no such thing as Protestant orthodoxy.

6. We cannot, therefore, distinguish between false teachers and true teachers of the church; between those who are truly Christian, and those who are not; and so forth.

In other words, to be able to say that a person is, or is not, in line with the teaching of the Bible, there must be some agreement on the clear teachings of the Bible. If we are not able to come to an agreement on the teachings of the Bible, because the individual is the authority over the interpretation, then we could never say that some one person is, or is not, in line with the teaching of the Bible.

Now, it must be recognized that any approach to solving the Protestant problem must be multifaceted. Some of the subjects that must be discussed include the doctrine of *sola scriptura* and the notion of individual interpretation; the interaction between the individual and interpretative communities; the role of Christian doctors and of the Holy Spirit both in the interpretation of Scripture and in teaching the church; the art of skillful textual reading; and how we should understand theological authority, truth, infallibility, certainty, and so forth. Part of the solution to the Protestant problem is, I propose, found in the role that natural knowledge plays in biblical interpretation and doctrinal formulation. In this essay, I will argue that natural knowledge of man, God, and the universe is necessary for biblical interpretation and doctrinal formulation, and is a key element in solving the Protestant problem.

WHAT IS NATURAL KNOWLEDGE?

What Do We Mean by Natural Knowledge?

It is not the purpose of this essay to delve into a technical discussion of the nature of knowledge. Some, claiming to follow Plato, propose that knowledge is, put quite simply, justified true belief.[14] Socrates, of course,

---

[14] Jonathan Barnes, for example, notes that "the standard account of knowledge, around which all recent work has been done, defines knowledge as justified true

rejected this definition of knowledge.[15] Others, such as Alvin Plantinga, sought to revise this definition, claiming that knowledge is warranted true belief.[16] It is common, in the Thomistic-Aristotelian tradition, to describe knowledge as the union between the knower and the known.[17] Aquinas, for example, states that truth is found in "the conformity of thing and intellect."[18] For the purposes of this essay we will limit our understanding of knowledge to the judgment, and state that, for our purposes, knowledge is a true judgment; or, to borrow Aristotle's formulation, "To say of what is that it is not, or of what is not that it is, is false, while to say of what is that it is, and of what is not that it is not, is true."[19] That is, a person has knowledge when they predicate X of Y, and it is the case that Y is X.

But what is natural knowledge? This question is as sticky as the question about the definition of knowledge, because what one means by "natural" knowledge all depends upon what one means by "nature" or "natural." Now, many people use the word "nature" to refer to the wildlands, the forests, the mountains—anything that is still left untouched by mankind; and, more broadly, to the entire sensible universe. C. S. Lewis cautions us, however, that the word "nature" has so many different meanings that we cannot just assume, when we come across it in some writing, that the author is using it in this sense.[20] Lewis notes, after having explained the various meanings of *natura*, *kind*, and *phusis*, that "the best clue [when seeking to discover what an author means by "nature"] is to ask oneself in

---

belief." Jonathan Barnes, *Introduction to Contemporary Epistemology* (1985; repr., Oxford: Blackwell, 1997), 23. Cf. Robert Audi, *Epistemology: A Contemporary Introduction to the Theory of Knowledge*, 2nd ed. (2003; repr., New York: Routledge, 2004).

[15] Plato, *Theaetetus*, trans. M. J. Levett, ed. Myles Burnyeat (Indianapolis, IN: Hackett, 1990), 348.

[16] See Alvin Plantinga, *Warrant and Proper Function* (Oxford: Oxford University Press, 1993).

[17] Frederick D. Wilhelmsen, for example, says that "knowledge is an immaterial act uniting the knower with the thing known." Frederick D. Wilhelmsen, *Man's Knowledge of Reality: An Introduction to Thomistic Epistemology* (Englewood Cliffs, NJ: Prentice Hall, 1956), 79.

[18] Thomas Aquinas, *Truth*, trans. Robert W. Mulligan (1954; repr., Cambridge: Hackett, 1994), 1:6.

[19] Aristotle, *Metaphysics*, Bk. IV, ch. 6 (1011b26–28).

[20] C. S. Lewis, *Studies in Words*, 2nd ed. (1967; repr., Cambridge: Cambridge University Press, 2008), 42 (hereafter cited as *SW*).

each instance, what is the implied opposite to nature."[21] Some possible ways of understanding "nature" or "natural," using this tactic, include:

> 1. The "that which is." Not *that* it is, but *what* it is. The "essence" element of the "existing essence."[22] That which is *a part of a thing* from the conception or beginning of its existence. That which is necessary to this X in order for this X to be an X.[23] For example, nature as opposed to, or contrasted with, existence.[24]

---

[21] Lewis, *SW*, 43.

[22] Which is, of course, what Aristotle means by *ousia* (which is sometimes translated as "substance").

[23] "X is, by nature, Y." Aristotle says, for example, "All men by nature desire to know." Aristotle, *Metaphysics*, Bk. I, ch.1. Craig A. Boyd, in an article on the relationship between faith and reason, seems to recognize this understanding of the term "nature," when he says that "nature" could refer to "a metaphysical understanding of the term that captures the important elements of the empirical but also considers an important teleological dimension that certain animals, especially humans, may have." Craig A. Boyd, "The Synthesis of Reason and Faith," in *Faith and Reason: Three Views*, ed. Steve Wilkens (Downers Grove, IL: Intervarsity, 2014), 134. Not only does Augustine use the word "nature" in this manner, but he ascribes the creation of all natures to God: "God, therefore, made all natures, not only those which were to abide in virtue and justice, but also those that were to sin." Augustine, *On Free Will*, in *Augustine: Earlier Writings*, ed. and trans. J. H. S. Burleigh (Louisville, KY: SCM, 1953), 190–91. Later in the same work he notes that all natures are, per se, good, and then goes on to explain what he means by the word "nature": "Therefore, it is true to say that any nature, so far as it is such, is good. If it is incorruptible it is better than what is corruptible. But if it is corruptible it is doubtless good since it becomes less good as the process of corruption goes on. Every nature is corruptible or incorruptible. Therefore every nature is good. And by 'a nature' I mean what is also usually called a substance. Every substance is either God or comes from God because every good thing is either God or from God." Augustine, *On Free Will*, 193. C. S. Lewis, in his masterful exposition of the meaning of "nature" in *Studies in Words*, notes that "by far the commonest native meaning of *natura* is something like sort, kind, quality, or character." Lewis, *SW*, 24. On the following page, Lewis notes, "Horace can speak of *humana natura*, the character common to all men…A class or species has a *natura*, and so has a particular or an individual." Lewis, *SW*, 25. Finally, he notes that "those who wish to go further back will notice that *natura* shares a common base with *nasci* (to be born); with the noun *natus* (birth); with *natio* (not only a race or nation but the name of the birth-goddess); or even that *natura* itself can mean the sexual organs—a sense formerly born by English nature, but apparently restricted to the female. It is risky to try to build precise semantic bridges, but there is obviously some idea of a things *natura* as its original or 'innate' character." Lewis, *SW*, 25. Lewis continues by noting that the

2. The *manner* in which one comes to possess something.[25] We can distinguish between two uses of the term "nature" when used to speak of "how" one comes to possess or to know something. First of all, (2a) a person could come to possess or know Y in a manner that is neither fabricated, nor due to nurture or hard work.[26] Secondly, (2b) a person could come to possess Y, or to know something about Y, through his own hard work or reflections, rather than from some other sort of intervening source (human, angelic, or divine). We could distinguish, for example, between

---

English word "kind" is very similar in meaning to the word *natura* (Lewis, *SW*, 26ff.). Turning to the Greek word *phusis*, Lewis notes how it came to mean, quite early on, something similar to nature[1]. Lewis quotes Aristotle to the effect that "'whatever each thing is like (*hoion hekaston esti*) when its process of coming-to-be is complete, that we call the *phusis* of each thing.' On this view a thing's *phusis* would be what it *grows* into at maturity." Lewis, *SW*, 34. That which it grows into at maturity is the *telos* of the thing.

[24] This is the way that we use the word "nature" when properly describing the Trinity. See Francis Turretin, *Institutes of Elenctic Theology*, trans. George Musgrave Giger, ed. James T. Dennison Jr. (Phillipsburg, NJ: P&R, 1992), 1:253. Here he says, "The absolute consideration of God (as to his nature and attributes) begets the relative (as to the persons)...Here occurs the word *ousias* or 'essence' and 'nature' which denotes the whatness (*quidditatem*) of a thing."

[25] Lewis seems to be referring to this way of understanding the word "nature" when he notes that "behaviour is *unnatural* or 'affected,' not simply when it is held to be a departure from that which a man's *nature* would lead to of itself, but when it is a departure for the worse." Lewis, *SW*, 43. The implied opposite of "unnatural," in this case, is the way in which a thing normally acts, or does things, that which comes naturally to it. He brings this point out explicitly when he notes, referring to a comment made by Aristotle in his *Politics*, that "this, as it is one of the oldest, is one of the hardiest senses of *nature* or *natural*. The nature of anything, its original, innate character, its spontaneous behaviour, can be contrasted with what it is made to be or do by some external agency." Lewis, *SW*, 45. Note that there is a bit of overlap between nature[1] and nature[2] in Lewis's comment here.

[26] "X came about Y naturally." Or "X is a natural Y." Or, "This X came from nature." Lewis provides us with a great example of this notion when he describes "nature" as that which the teacher works on in the student, contrasted with what comes about without effort: "Quintilian says that in oratory *natura* can do much without training but training can do little without *natura* (II, xix). The *nature* in question is of course the 'given' capacity in the pupil, what the teacher finds to work upon. Addison speaks of 'the rustic part of the species who on all occasions acted bluntly and *naturally*': no efforts of their own had modified their given behaviour (given by temperament, environment, and the passions) in the direction either of refinement or affection." Lewis, *SW*, 46–47.

knowing about Jesus from having lived within Him (such as was the case with his apostles) and knowing about Jesus through divine revelation (as is the case with everyone other than those who lived with Jesus in the first century). Thus, the manner in which one comes to knowledge of X is "natural" rather than "supernatural" or "divine."

3. The sum of all contingent, sensible, beings—the *universe*.[27] Nature, in this sense, can be cultivated, possessed, protected, and studied.[28] When nature[3] is studied, one can learn both about that which is immediately evident to the

---

[27] Lewis, in his discussion of the Greek *phusis*, suggests how this word (which is often translated in English as "nature") came to refer to the sum of all that exists. "The pre-Socratic Greek philosophers had had the idea of taking all the things they knew or believed in—gods, men, animals, plants, minerals, what you will—and impounding them under a single name; in fact, of regarding Everything as a thing, turning this amorphous and heterogeneous collection into an object or pseudo-object. And for some reason the name they chose for it was *phusis*." Lewis, *SW*, 35. He later notes that this use of the word *phusis* opened the door for talking about something beyond nature: "By (so to speak) inventing Nature the old thinkers had made it possible, or at least facilitated, the question whether there is anything else." Lewis, *SW*, 38. Lewis goes on to note how this was done in Platonism, Aristotelianism, and Christianity. In Aristotle, for example, we are told that there are two things outside of *phusis*: "First, things which are unchangeable, but cannot exist 'on their own.' These are the subject-matter of mathematics. Secondly, there is one thing which is unchangeable and does exist on its own. This is God, the unmoved mover; and he is studied by a third discipline." Lewis, *SW*, 39. Lewis later notes, in a distinction between nature as the uninterfered with and the unnatural as the interfered with, that the common distinction between man and nature is very much a fabrication of man's daily experience: "What keeps the contrast alive, however, is the daily experience of men as practical, not speculative beings. The antithesis between unreclaimed land and the cleared, drained, fenced, ploughed, sown, and weeded field...That is why *nature* as 'the given,' the thing we start from, the thing we have not yet 'done anything about,' is such a persistent sense. *We* here, of course, means man. If ants had a language they would, no doubt, call their anthill an artifact and describe the brick wall in its neighbourhood as a *natural* object. *Nature* in fact would be for them all that was not 'ant-made.' Just so, for us, *nature* is all that is not man-made; the *natural* state of anything is its state when not modified by man." Lewis, *SW*, 45–46.

[28] This use of the word "nature" often has the first letter capitalized. The natural sciences study "nature" in order to better understand it and those things that are a part of nature (which are natural). Boyd refers to this understanding of the term nature when he says that "nature" could refer to "the object of various scientific inquiries that focuses upon explanations of how natural objects and living beings act and are acted upon." Boyd, "Synthesis of Reason and Faith," 134.

senses, and about that which is not immediately evident to the senses. Using nature in this third sense, we could postulate that a person can come to know Y about some aspect of nature itself or about its cause, from their study of nature or some aspect of nature, rather than from their study of nonsensible beings.

4. Nature can also be understood, in the theological sense underlined by Craig Boyd, as "a principle of corruption resulting from a primeval fall of humanity wherein the active power of nature is contrasted with the restorative powers of grace."[29] Note that we are not, here, talking about human nature per se, but to that state and capacities of human nature[1] post-Fall, in contrast to the effect of grace upon fallen nature[1]. Turretin notes that sin affects humans as an accident that inheres in the human nature, but not as an essential part of the human nature.[30]

5. Other ways in which the word "nature" is, or has been, used, as noted by Lewis in comparison with the implied opposites, include: (a) "'Having due affection,' or *pius*."[31] (b) The absence of reason in man,[32] or, more precisely,

---

[29] Boyd, "The Synthesis of Reason and Faith," 134. Lewis also mentions the distinction between nature and grace, though he doesn't take a position that is necessarily cynical, as we see in Boyd's comment. Nature, as contrasted with grace, may refer to what is "simply human" as opposed to what is caused by divine grace; or it may refer to what is decadent and depraved. Lewis notes, first of all, that "human nature (man as he is of himself) can be contrasted not only, as above, with man as he can become by moral effort but with man as he can be refashioned by divine grace." Lewis, *SW*, 53. In discussing various authors, he says that "what is here depreciated or discounted as 'but natural' is nothing depraved or sub-human; on the contrary it is something, on its own level and in its own mode, lawful, commanded, entirely good." Lewis, *SW*, 53.

[30] Turretin, *Institutes of Elenctic Theology*, 1:636. Here he states that "the orthodox constantly maintain that sin is to be distinguished from the substance itself, as an accident and vicious quality from its subject." Turretin is faithful to Augustine, who said, "So we use the word 'nature' in a double sense. Properly speaking, human nature means the blameless nature with which man was originally created. But we also use it in speaking of the nature with which we are born mortal, ignorant and subject to the flesh, which is really the penalty of sin. In this sense the apostle says: 'We also were by nature children of wrath even as others' (Eph. 2:3)." Augustine, *On Free Will*, 203.

[31] Lewis, *SW*, 43.

[32] Lewis notes some uses of the word "nature": where "a contrast between *nature*

> that which "man shares with (the rest of) *nature*, what he has only because he is a creature and not because he is a special creature, is *natural* in contradistinction to his specific, specially created, differentia [reason]."[33] (c) Lewis also mentions, in relation to the arts, that nature is used to refer to the real original, as opposed to the artistic imitation;[34] in relation to law, that nature is used to refer to what something really is, as opposed to how it is viewed by the laws;[35] in relation to society, that nature is used to refer to uncivilized, as opposed to how man lives in governed society (so, *nature* would mean uncivilized or uncultivated, as opposed to civilized and cultured).[36] (d) "Nature" or "natural" is also contrasted with the "supernatural," which, in common language, is often taken to refer to anything that involves immaterial entities, be it God, angels, or even ghosts.[37] Lewis suggests that this use of supernatural is because experience of these beings is not ordinary or normal.[38]

Most of our comments will turn around the first three uses of the word "nature." Note, then, that nature^{3} is the sum of all contingent beings. Each of these contingent beings has a nature^{1}, the "that which it is," which is the source of their intelligibility, activity, and so forth, and which, when known through abstraction, allows human knowers to classify them. It is nature^{1} that determines what a being does, or is able to accomplish, naturally^{2}. Nature^{3} can be studied for itself or can lead, through inference (a function that is natural^{2b} to humans), the knower to understand truths that

---

and reason" is suggested, and "the idiot is a *natural* for lacking it [reason]." Lewis, *SW*, 49. Lewis comments that "since the *nature* of man was defined as 'rational animal,' it seems very odd that the absence, or opposite, of reason in him should be *natural*." Lewis, *SW*, 49. The oddness disappears when we understand that we are comparing, in a sense, two aspects of men: that which they share with all other animals (which we could call natural), and reason (the specific difference).

[33] Lewis, *SW*, 49.

[34] Lewis, *SW*, 54–58.

[35] Lewis, *SW*, 58–62. In this section he distinguishes between natural law, and the laws of nature.

[36] Lewis, *SW*, 62–64.

[37] Lewis, *SW*, 64–68.

[38] Lewis, *SW*, 66.

transcend that which is empirically observable in nature^{3} itself.[39]

When we talk about natural knowledge, we are combining primarily the second and the third descriptions. *Natural knowledge* refers to those true judgments that humans obtain *through* their reasoned observations (as opposed to mediated through some other source, such as Scripture—thus, natural^{2b} observations) *of* the universe of sensible beings (nature^{3}). Humans are able to obtain such knowledge naturally (nature^{2b}) because of what they are (nature^{1}). It is not important to discuss whether this knowledge is obtained through simple unscientific observation or through extended scientific or philosophical study (as both are natural$^{1\&2b}$ human functions). So defined, it might seem evident that we should rule out any knowledge that humans might have been born with (such as innate ideas), however, it might be argued that innate ideas are inherent to human nature.[40] Note that, most theologians would agree that though the Fall affects all humans, it does not destroy nature^{1},[41] nor nature^{3},[42] though it does negatively affect

---

[39] Each of these statements may be, and are, debated in philosophical discourse. However, these statements allow us to better understand how we can use the one term "nature" to refer to different beings, states of being, etc.

[40] Innate ideas have found a place in the works of some Reformed theologians, though others have denied the existence of innate ideas. One might postulate that it is their adherence to a predominantly platonic or Cartesian epistemology that brought some to accept the notion of innate ideas, or, inversely, their adherence to a predominantly Aristotelian-Thomistic epistemology that brought others to reject the notion of innate ideas. Be it noted, however, that even if we accept the notions of "innate ideas," this type of innate knowledge would still qualify as "natural knowledge"—that is, as truths which humans possess by nature^{1} (by virtue of what they are). John Calvin himself would agree with this point: "There is within the human mind, and indeed by natural instinct, an awareness of divinity." John Calvin, *Institutes of the Christian Religion*, trans. Ford Lewis Battles, ed. John T. McNeill (Louisville, KY: Westminster John Knox Press, 1960), 1:43.

[41] If nature^{1} were destroyed, then there would be no particular humans in existence. Theodore Beza makes exactly this point in his work known as *Questions et Reponses Chrestiennes*, arguing that human volition and intellection were not entirely effaced, for if they had been entirely destroyed and rendered useless, then the human being would also have been entirely destroyed: "Neither the intelligence nor the will are removed, as I have just stated, otherwise the soul would perish, and would no longer exist today." Theodore de Bèze, *Questions et Responses Chrestiennes* (Eustace Vignon, 1584), 42–43. My translation.

[42] Genesis 3 and Romans 8 state that somehow, nature^{3} is affected by the Fall, but not destroyed.

nature^{2}—what man, by nature^{1}, is able to accomplish.[43] As such, the Fall does not destroy, though it does limit, the human ability (nature^{2}) to seek, discover, and possess truth.

When we talk about *natural knowledge*, therefore, we are referring to those true judgments that humans possess, not through superhuman intervention or revelation, nor through human fabrication (as in imaginative literature), but through reasoned observations about the sensible universe. Note that humans are a part of the sensible universe, thus, true judgments about humans, which are obtained through reasoned observations of humans, would count as natural knowledge. In fact, introspection—an individual humans reasoned observations of its interior states—would also be considered natural knowledge. The content of this natural knowledge may be quite varied and includes not only those truths that are observed (Socrates is a man. This shape is a triangle. This animal is a cat. This animal is a sheep), but also those truths that are inferred (Socrates will die. This shape has three interior corners. This animal has narcissistic tendencies. This animal is stupid). Thus, the notion of natural knowledge cannot exclude, by definition, inferred knowledge of supernatural beings or realities (beings or realities that are not a part of nature^{3}), though the nature^{1} of supernatural beings might limit *how* humans acquire knowledge about them, and how much knowledge humans can acquire about them. Furthermore, the notion of natural knowledge excludes the possibility that humans come to possess "natural" knowledge through the intermediary of supernatural beings (as in divine revelation through dreams, visions, etc.). Natural knowledge is gained through natural human powers of cognition and is arrived at through human observations of the universe of sensible beings, and human reasoning about these observations.

That we are, thus far, in accord with traditional Christian teaching could be demonstrated by a survey of most of the great theologians of Christianity,[44] pre-Reformation, Reformation, and post-Reformation; how-

---

[43] See Pietro Martyr Vermigli, *Common Places*, trans. Anthonie Marten (1574), 15. De Bèze, *Questions et Responses Chrestiennes*, 42–43. John Flavel, *A Blow at the Root; or, The Cause and Cure of Mental Errors*, in *The Whole Works of Rev. Mr. John Flavel* (London: W. Baynes and Son, 1820), 3:427–28.

[44] For the views of some of the most important early Reformed thinkers, see David Haines, "Natural Theology in Reformed Orthodoxy," in *Philosophy and the Christian: The Quest for Wisdom in the Light of Christ*, ed. Joseph Minich (Lincoln, NE: Davenant Press, 2018), 250–91.

ever, for the sake of space, we will consider only one theologian of interest. The Puritan John Flavel (1627–1691), in *Sermon 7* of his work entitled *The Method of Grace*, rightly distinguishes between natural and supernatural knowledge.[45] Flavel notes that there is a natural knowledge even of spiritual things—that is, that even unregenerate men are able to attain to some knowledge of spiritual truths via the natural light of reason.[46] Spiritual knowledge is that experiential knowledge of God's grace that is possessed only by true believers.[47] Flavel does not deny that many great, yet unregenerate, thinkers possess knowledge of truths about spiritual things; but, says Flavel, reassuring the believers, "One dram of knowledge of the best and most excellent things, is better than much knowledge of common things."[48] Indeed, says Flavel, one may have much knowledge of the world, man, and God, all of which is true, and still be condemned to hell.[49] "So it is here, a little spiritual knowledge of Jesus Christ, that hath life and savour in it, is more than all the natural, sapless knowledge of the unregenerate, which leaves the heart dead, carnal, and barren: it is not the *quantity*, but the *kind*, not the *measure*, but the *savour*."[50] These comments are placed in the context of his explanation of why many unbelievers possess accurate knowledge of spiritual things. We turn, now, to our next question: What is the role of natural knowledge in biblical interpretation and the development of Christian doctrine?

---

[45] John Flavel, *Sermon 7*, in *The Method of Grace*, in *The Whole Works of Rev. Mr. John Flavel* (London: W. Baynes and Son, 1820), 2:124.

[46] Flavel, *Sermon 7*, 2:124.

[47] Flavel, *Sermon 7*, 2:124.

[48] Flavel, *Sermon 7*, 2:124. See also John Flavel, *Sermon 23*, in *The Method of Grace*, in *The Whole Works of Rev. Mr. John Flavel* (London: W. Baynes and Son, 1820), 2:324.

[49] Flavel, *Sermon 7*, 2:124.

[50] Flavel, *Sermon 7*, 2:124.

IS THERE A PLACE FOR NATURAL KNOWLEDGE IN CHRISTIAN DOCTRINE?

Natural Knowledge in Biblical Interpretation and the Formation of Doctrine

In our introduction, we mentioned some recent works of theology that emphasize a theological interpretation of Scripture. This theological interpretation of Scripture reads the Bible through the lens of established doctrines. Michael Allen and Scott R. Swain, for example, seek to provide an argument supporting "a 'ruled reading' of Holy Scripture on the basis of Reformed theological and ecclesiological principles."[51] Such an attempt is neither without precedent (most of the early church fathers, such as Tertullian and Irenaeus, attacked heretical interpretations of Scripture by pointing out, among other things, that they were not reading the Scriptures according to the symbol of the faith), nor entirely without justification (those doctrines that are clearly taught in Scripture, and have been expressed in the ecumenical creeds, should provide an interpretative paradigm for Scripture). We also noted how Sheridan drew attention to, and how Gregory Nazianzus used, the interpretative principle of the early church fathers: the appropriate predication principle. The questions that need to be asked are, How do we know that the Bible should be interpreted this way? How do we know that some particular predicative statement about God does or does not adequately describe the divine nature? To respond, "We use theological interpretation and the appropriate predication principle" does not quite answer the question, even though it is proposed as a serious response. Such a response is not necessary, I propose, for natural knowledge provides us with the answer to these questions. Consider the following.

The Role of Natural Knowledge in Biblical Interpretation

Many modern theologians, especially those associated with presuppositionalism, but also theologians such as Charles Hodge, Augustus H. Strong, and Wayne Grudem, have been known to reject, or reinterpret, the classical at-

---

[51] Allen and Swain, *Reformed Catholicity*, 96.

tributes of God (such as impassibility and immutability) for no other reason than that they are not clearly taught in Scripture. These theologians show great confidence in their abilities to properly interpret Scripture, rejecting, as unnecessary and unbiblical, all natural knowledge about God. For these theologians, all one needs, to be orthodox, is the Bible, properly interpreted. This, however, is an overly simplistic view of how one arrives at doctrinal orthodoxy. On the contrary, in order to properly interpret Scripture, as helpful as it is to have a solid foundation in theological and biblical studies, there are some more fundamental truths that the interpreter must already know. The interpreter must possess, in other words, natural knowledge. Commenting on just this point, James Barr points out that

> not only does the Bible have to be interpreted, but interpretation goes on within the Bible itself. Much of the Bible, perhaps all of the Bible is the product of interpretation. But the consequence of this has not always been noticed: the more we stress the importance of interpretation, the more we render probable the influence of something like natural theology. Influenced by the dialectical theology, people have been inclined to think of interpretation as something that followed and expounded the contours of revelation without going in any way outside this narrow channel of thought. Interpretation, seen in this way, not only interprets revelation but interprets it solely by the use of categories which themselves derive from revelation and are internal to it. Some of the peculiar contortions of modern interpretative theory are probably half-conscious attempts to demonstrate this. But it would really be very strange if there was interpretation which used no categories whatever that were external to the material being interpreted.[52]

Barr concludes, rightly, that

> even if there is no natural theology in the Bible at all, but only revelational theology, it cannot produce a total picture of God except through the activity of the theological interpreter. But that interpreter must use his own thoughts,

[52] James Barr, *Biblical Faith and Natural Theology* (Oxford: Oxford University Press, 1993), 150.

> reason, instincts, and experience in order to grade, to select, to bring together, to order, and to raise to higher levels the material with which he or she works. The interpreter will have to draw conclusions from the scripture which it itself does not make express; and this drawing of conclusions will depend on the categories, methods, and anterior preferences of the interpreter. Thus, the theologian who fully denies natural theology may nevertheless be constructing an "idol" out of scriptural materials just as much as the natural theologian is constructing an "idol" out of other materials.[53]

Indeed, even the most basic attempt to interpret Scripture requires, as a precondition,[54] that the interpreter be in possession of a number of

---

[53] Barr, *Biblical Faith*, 152.

[54] It is important to distinguish between a precondition and a presupposition, as these two terms are, all too often, confused. A *precondition* is a "state of being" of extra-mental reality that must be present before some other state can arrive or come to be. For example, before you can buy a used book at the used bookstore on the other side of the street, there must be a used bookstore across the street. The existence of a used bookstore on the other side of the street is a precondition for the possibility of buying a used book in that bookstore. Philosophers often note that this is a metaphysical term, as it is referring to mind-exterior reality, regardless of human knowledge of that reality. A *presupposition* speaks not of a state of extra-mental reality, but, on the contrary, of a mental state. That is to say, a presupposition is some affirmation that must be believed before another affirmation can be believed. "Pre-suppose-ition": We "suppose" something before we suppose something else. It is a belief that one accepts as true or false before accepting, or being able to accept, some other belief as true or false. (For example, to believe that God hears your prayers, we must at least presuppose (1) that there is a God, and (2) that He can understand your way of expressing yourself. (1) and (2) are implicit in the statement that "God can hear your prayers." So, if you do not believe that there is a God, then you will not believe, either, that "God can hear your prayers.") It is worth noting that because presuppositions are mind states, this term is, properly, an epistemological term referring to components of human knowledge. Note that your beliefs may or may not be grounded in reality. If God does not exist (in mind-exterior reality), then the belief (mental state) that there is a God is false. But, this belief is a necessary presupposition for the belief that God can answer your prayers. It is entirely possible to be fully convinced of the truth of some belief, based upon your adherence to a false presupposition. Beliefs are inherently intentional; they are "of" or "about" other things. You determine the falsity of a presupposition or belief not by comparing it with your other beliefs (which, if some incoherency were to be discovered, would only go to show that you are incoherent in holding certain beliefs), but by comparing your belief with that "about which" you hold the belief.

important types of natural knowledge. The interpreter must, first of all, have naturally[2b] acquired *linguistic knowledge*, that is, a basic knowledge of (a) at least one language in which the Bible was translated (though knowledge of the original languages is to be preferred), (b) the grammar of the language in question, (c) the syntax of the language in question, (d) linguistic tools (such as analogy, metaphor, hyperbole, etc.), and (e) knowledge of the basic principles of textual interpretation. Humans possess linguistic abilities naturally (nature[1]) but must learn how to properly use these linguistic abilities. We are naturally (nature[1]) linguistic, but we learn (naturally[2a&b]) the languages we speak. When a human being is reading the Bible in a learned language, they are gaining knowledge (both about the history of the natural[3] world, and about that which is beyond nature[3]) in a natural (nature[2b]) way.

Knowledge of some language (even the original languages of the biblical texts), however, is not sufficient for the interpreter to gain a proper understanding of Scripture. Another precondition for interpretation is that the interpreter has *sufficient naturally[2a&b] acquired experience and knowledge of the world (nature[3])* that they will be able to understand the meaning of the words that are used in the Bible. This knowledge is, first of all, clearly natural knowledge; and, secondly, is gained through life experience, in conjunction with learning a language. Augustine, in his treatise *The Teacher*, demonstrates that words, as signs, signify the thing they correspond to. Indeed, we come to know the meaning of words by relating them to natural things.[55] The implication of this for biblical interpretation is obvious. Without natural knowledge of sensible and knowable things, humans cannot understand the words of Scripture. Conclusion: natural knowledge is a necessary condition for the right interpretation of Scripture. Augustine says, for example:

> If we consider this a little more closely, perhaps you will find that nothing is learned even by its appropriate sign. If I am given a sign and I do not know the thing of which it is the sign, it can teach me nothing. If I know the thing, what do I learn from the sign? When I read (Dan. 3:27: LXX Dan. 3:94): "Their *saraballae* were not changed," the word, *saraballae* does not indicate what it means. If I am told that some covering of the head is so called, would I know what a head is, or a covering, unless I knew already?

[55] Augustine, *The Teacher*, in *Augustine: Earlier Writings*, ed. and trans. J. H. S. Burleigh (Louisville, KY: SCM, 1953), 92–93.

> Knowledge of such things comes to me not when they are named by others but when I actually see them. When these two syllables first struck my ear, *ca-put,* I was as ignorant of what they meant as I was of the meaning of *saraballae* when I first heard or read it. But when the word, *caput,* was frequently repeated, observing when it was said, I discovered it was the name of a thing well known to me from my having seen it. Before I made that discovery the word was merely a sound to me. It became a sign when I had learned the thing of which it was the sign. And this I had learned not from signs but from seeing the actual object. So the sign is learned from knowing the thing, rather than vice versa.[56]

A little later, he summarizes his point: "We learn the force of the word, that is the meaning which lies in the sound of the word, when we come to know the object signified by the word. Then only do we perceive that the word was a sign conveying that meaning."[57] One can only conclude, that for Augustine, natural reason, which is clearly given by God to all humans,[58] is not only a necessary aid in all theological discussion, but that it is a necessary precondition for biblical interpretation. Without the faculty of reason, it is impossible to know the particular sensible things of reality, to come to know other truths based upon our sensible knowledge, or even to read, let alone properly interpret, the Scriptures. Those areas of natural knowledge that are necessary to properly interpret Scripture include, among other things, (a) geography (The geography of the Middle East? What is a "tree," a "desert," a "city," a "mountain"?), (b) geology (such as the precious stones mentioned in Revelation 21:18–21), (c) zoology (What is a donkey, a horse, a lion, and a lamb?), (d) the different cultures of the time, (e) the food of the time (Why do we not put new wine in an old wine sack?), (f) nature^3 in general (Why do we compare the life of a man to the grass? Does grass live long, or only for a little while?), (g) world history (Who are the Romans, Greeks, Egyptians, Babylonians?), and so on. At this point it is worth noting that this knowledge of the natural world (nature^3) is necessary not only for interpreting metaphors, similes, and any other form of poetic

---

56 Augustine, *The Teacher*, 93.

57 Augustine, *The Teacher*, 94.

58 Augustine, *On Free Will*, 149.

comparison, but also for interpreting any text that refers the reader to the natural world. Without this natural knowledge, the comparisons are lost on us, and the biblical teaching loses its power, or, at worst, is twisted and deformed. Let's consider a couple of examples. In order to understand the lesson given by Solomon when he exhorts us to become like the ant, we need to have a general idea of what an ant is, what it does, and how these natural truths might portray some spiritual truths we need to learn.[59] In order to fully grasp the extent of what Jesus is teaching us when he tells us to look at the birds and the flowers in order to understand the providence of God, we need to know what birds and flowers are, how they live, how long they live, and how this should reassure us about divine providence.[60] Without this type of natural knowledge, a person will be unable to understand biblical statements such as David's claim that he hides himself under the wings of the Lord,[61] or the biblical descriptions of Jesus as the lion of David or the lamb of God.[62]

There is a third type of natural knowledge that is also necessary for biblical interpretation. That is what we might call *philosophical or theoretical knowledge*. The interpreter must have some knowledge of what is being referred to when the Bible uses words such as, (a) nature[63] (What does the Bible mean when it speaks of nature? Of sin nature, the nature of man, or the divine nature?), (b) spirit (What does the Bible mean when it speaks of the Holy Spirit, the spirit of man, or when it says that God is spirit?), (c) time (How can one possibly discuss eternity, if one does not understand what time is?) (d) various political concepts (monarchy, theocracy, etc.), and (e) various moral concepts (just, love, good, evil, etc.). The Bible does not define any of the terms mentioned above but, rather, assumes that the reader understands the words that the Bible is using, and that to which they refer. Some people might suggest that one can discover the meaning of the words by studying other writings of the same time (this work is done for us

---

[59] Prov. 6:6–11.

[60] Matt. 6:26–34, Luke 12:27–31.

[61] Ps. 17:8, 57:1.

[62] Rev. 5:5–6.

[63] Often the word that is used to translate is the Greek *phusis*, which typically is taken to refer to the "that which something is and is common to all Xs which are that something" (see Rom. 1:26, 2:14, 27, 11:24, 1 Cor. 11:14, Gal. 2:15, 4:8, Eph. 2:3, etc.).

by those who compile lexicons and dictionaries of ancient languages). That is all well and good; however, (1) the ability to recognize words in different languages with different meanings is accomplished via natural human abilities (nature[1&2]) to speak and analyze human languages that are a part of nature[3] and natural (nature[1]) to humans, and, (2) lexicons do not tell us what words mean, nor that to which they refer, but, rather, word equivalencies. The word "tree" in English is used in roughly the same way as the word *arbre* in French. This does not, however, tell you what a "tree" or *arbre is*, only how the word is *used*.[64] Lexicons are only useful if you already know—natural knowledge—what the words in one of the languages indexed in the lexicon refer to. Lexicons do not replace experience and reflection.

A fourth type of natural knowledge that seems to undergird biblical interpretation has to do with predicative statements about the divine nature. This type of natural knowledge is commonly called natural theology—*natural knowledge of the divine nature*. It is this natural knowledge of nature[3] that leads us to some knowledge of the divine nature[1], and that, I propose, undergirds and makes possible the appropriate predication principle, and, ultimately, theological interpretation. That is, we know that predicative statement Y cannot be appropriately said of God because we already know, from nature[2] or nurture (through human instruction), (a) what Y is, and (b) that God is not Y. For example, we know what changing emotions or passions are, and that they cannot be appropriately predicated of God, not because we learned from Scripture that God is impassible, but, rather, because we learned from nature[3] that the divine nature[1] is impassible. The same could be said of divine simplicity, divine immutability, and numerous other divine attributes that are not explicitly affirmed in the original language manuscripts of the biblical texts.[65]

---

64 This is a nominal definition.

65 This statement is important, as some theologians use proof texts which (in some translations) make it seem as if the Bible is explicitly predicating, for example, omniscience, immutability, or atemporality, of God, when, in fact, the actual terms in the original languages do not quite say what theologians would like them to say. An interesting example is divine immutability. Many modern and contemporary theologians who adhere to divine immutability, rather than refer to arguments based on natural knowledge, prefer to cite Bible verses that say that God does not change. This, of course, opens the door, for opponents of divine immutability, for the comment that these verses, interpreted in their context, are not talking about the immutability of the divine nature, but, rather, of the unchanging faithfulness of God to His promises. This is, indeed, what these verses are saying. One might re-

Without natural knowledge of God, the appropriate predication principle and theological interpretation are useless. If we do not already know that to be spirit implies to be immaterial and incorporeal, then we will take the Bible at face value when it talks about the body, hands, eyes, and mouth of God. God must, then, be a physical corporeal being. That Jesus says that God is spirit[66] will not cause a problem, because the Bible does not say that spirits are immaterial and incorporeal beings. We will simply assume that God is a spiritual being with a physical body, which, of course, sounds very much like a Greek god. If we do not already know that God is impassible, we will not learn this from the Bible, which portrays God as constantly changing emotions. Appealing to the confessions, church tradition, or theological interpretation (all good things) will not help, for they appeal to Scripture for their doctrinal affirmations, and the question becomes, Why should we accept the confessional, traditional, or theological interpretation of the Scriptures in their application to the doctrine of God? It turns out that the confessional, traditional, or theological interpretation of Scripture relies on the appropriate predication principle, which, as we have already shown, relies upon natural knowledge. In the end, either we appeal to natural knowledge of God or to personal preference.

There is one final aspect of biblical interpretation that we must consider before we move on: the very *hermeneutical principles* that we so meticulously apply to Scripture in order to arrive at "biblical" teaching. The purpose of interpretation is to understand some communication. Hermeneutics is the science that studies the principles that must be followed when interpreting a communication, and the art of properly applying them. It is important to understand that the principles of hermeneutics are not inspired. They are, in fact, natural principles that are determined not by divine inspiration, but by the nature of communication itself; nor are they revealed by divine inspiration, but, rather, they are discovered by human beings as they read and seek to understand different forms of communication. Divinely inspired biblical poetry must be interpreted in the very same way that we interpret the poems of Robert Burns or Samuel Taylor Coleridge. The

---

ply, "Well, God is absolutely faithful to His promises because He is immutable." This is also true but is not explicitly stated in the Bible; and, furthermore, it is a false inference to move from "faithfulness to one's promises" to "absolutely immutable." How then do we know that God is immutable if not from Scripture?

[66] John 4:24.

historical books of the Bible are interpreted in the very same way that we interpret the *Gallic Wars* of Caesar. The epistles of Paul are written in the same way as other letters in the first century, and we interpret them in the same way. The hermeneutical principles by which we properly interpret Scripture were not handed down to us on a divine platter but were dug out of the earth through natural human reflection as we set about interpreting and understanding human communication.

It seems, therefore, that many types of natural knowledge are necessary for proper biblical interpretation and for the proper articulation of Christian doctrines. In other words, a necessary precondition for doctrinal orthodoxy is natural knowledge. Those forms of natural knowledge that we mentioned were natural linguistic knowledge and ability, knowledge gained through one's lived experience of the created world, philosophical or theoretical knowledge gained either through private reflection or through instruction, knowledge of hermeneutical principles, and, interestingly enough, some natural knowledge of the divine nature (which we most often call natural theology).

Interestingly enough, we are not the first to notice the major role that natural knowledge plays in the founding and forming of Christian doctrine. We have already quoted John Flavel, Augustine, and many others, on this point, but another important theologian, B. B. Warfield, makes the very same point in two articles he wrote. In his article "The Idea of Systematic Theology," he says, for example, "Apologetical Theology prepares the way for all theology by establishing its necessary presuppositions without which no theology is possible—the existence and essential nature of God, the religious nature of man which enables him to receive a revelation from God, the possibility of a revelation and its actual realization in the Scriptures."[67] Warfield says essentially the same thing in his article "The Task and Method of Systematic Theology," where he states, "Whether such a being as God exists needs to be ascertained, and if such a being exists, whether He is knowable; whether such creatures as men are capable of knowing Him, and, if so, what sources of information concerning Him are accessible. This is the task of apologetical theology."[68] That which apologetical theology

[67] Benjamin Breckinridge Warfield, "The Idea of Systematic Theology," in *Studies in Theology*, vol. 9 of *The Works of Benjamin B. Warfield* (1932; repr., Grand Rapids, MI: Baker Book House, 2000), 64.

[68] Benjamin Breckinridge Warfield, "The Task and Method of Systematic Theolo-

demonstrates is nothing other than naturally known truths about nature[3], human nature[1], and the divine nature[1]; that is, it is the role of apologetical theology, according to Warfield, to lay down those truths of natural knowledge that are necessary for the truth of fundamental Christian doctrines. Warfield elaborates on this point by noting three major presuppositions that are held by those who engage in exegetical, biblical, historical, practical and systematic theology—presuppositions that are established and proved by natural or apologetical theology: "(1) The affirmation that theology is a science presupposes the affirmation that God is, and that He has relation to His creatures."[69] He shows the importance of this presupposition as follows: "Were there no God, there could be no theology; nor could there be a theology if, though He existed, He existed out of relation with His creatures. The whole body of philosophical apologetics is, therefore, presupposed in and underlies the structure of scientific theology."[70] The second presupposition is, "(2) The affirmation that theology is a science presupposes the affirmation that man has a religious nature, that is, a nature capable of understanding not only that God is, but also, to some extent, what He is."[71] The third is, "(3) The affirmation that theology is a science presupposes the affirmation that there are media of communication by which God and divine things are brought before the minds of men, that they may perceive them and, in perceiving, understand them."[72]

It seems evident, therefore, that proper biblical interpretation and orthodox doctrinal formulation are not possible without natural knowledge. As such, it seems that we are warranted to say (1) that a theological interpretation of Scripture is not possible without natural knowledge, (2) that the appropriate predication principle is not applicable to Scripture without some natural knowledge of the divine nature[1], human nature[1], and the created universe, and (3) that, therefore, it is impossible, without natural knowledge, to determine what one must believe in order to be orthodox. This is true regardless of whether one is Reformed, Catholic, or Eastern Orthodox. Natural knowledge, accessible to all of humanity, is what makes

---

gy," in *Studies in Theology*, vol. 9 of *The Works of Benjamin B. Warfield* (1932; repr., Grand Rapids, MI: Baker Book House, 2000), 91.

[69] Warfield, "The Idea of Systematic Theology," 55.

[70] Warfield, "The Idea of Systematic Theology," 55.

[71] Warfield, "The Idea of Systematic Theology," 55.

[72] Warfield, "The Idea of Systematic Theology," 55.

it possible to properly interpret Scripture so as to arrive at a clear articulation of those doctrines that are necessary for orthodoxy. This is an important point: every human being has access, by the very fact of being alive and being able to use their senses, to the created universe. Human nature[1] is such that we desire to know. Human experience of the created universe (including introspection, learning a language and learning to read, etc.) give the individual human being every tool they need to be able to properly interpret the Scriptures, and, this, without having to appeal to an infallible magisterium.

Interestingly enough, in his debates with Roman Catholic theologians about the nature of the Eucharist, Thomas Cranmer (1489–1556), an early English Reformer, consistently referred to naturally known truths to illuminate and prove his arguments.[73] Armed with natural knowledge, the Christian exegete and theologian is able to distinguish between metaphorical, allegorical, anthropological, anthropopathic, and literal predication. Arriving at the proper interpretation of the texts because of their natural knowledge (of human nature, the divine nature, and the universe), they are then able to skillfully articulate doctrine, and refute heresy. This is not a natural religion, but natural knowledge in the service of theology. We do not need an infallible magisterium, but a recognition of the role that natural knowledge plays in biblical interpretation. Natural knowledge, therefore, seems to be a key element in the solution to the so-called Protestant problem. It may, in fact, be that key that makes it possible to, at the same time, lay down the limits of orthodoxy, avoid the necessity of an infallible magisterium, and avoid religious pluralism. This brings us to our final point, the place of natural knowledge within orthodoxy.

Natural Knowledge in the Hierarchy of Christian Doctrine

A *doctrine* is, broadly, any truth that is commonly accepted in some area of study, or that is proposed by some person as true. All Christians recognize,

---

[73] See Thomas Cranmer, "A Defence of the True and Catholic Doctrine of the Sacrament of the Body and Blood of Our Saviour Christ," in vol. 2 of *The Remains of Thomas Cranmer*, ed. Henry Jenkyns (Oxford: University of Oxford Press, 1833), 317, 333, 354, and Thomas Cranmer, "An Answer of Thomas unto a Crafty and Sophistical Cavillation Devised by Stephen Gardiner," in vol. 3 of *The Remains of Thomas Cranmer*, ed. Henry Jenkyns (Oxford: University of Oxford Press, 1833), 31, 53.

explicitly or implicitly, that there is a hierarchy of Christian doctrines. That is, that there are some doctrines that are more important than others.[74] It seems that we can articulate three broad levels of doctrines: (1) fundamental doctrines, (2) secondary doctrines, and (3) tertiary doctrines. There are a couple of points that need to be mentioned prior to distinguishing between these three levels. First of all, a doctrine that does not distinguish Christianity from any other religion or system of thought could not be considered a fundamental doctrine. Second, a doctrine whose acceptance, ignorance, or negation has absolutely no effect on Christian doctrine, or on the life of the Christian, cannot be considered a fundamental or secondary doctrine. Finally, any doctrine based upon a very questionable or highly debated interpretation of the Bible, or of nature, could not be more than a tertiary doctrine.

With these distinctions in mind, *fundamental or primary doctrines* are those doctrines that distinguish Christianity from all the other religions of the world, that are necessary for the truth of other distinctive doctrines, and that are accepted by the great majority of theologians. *Secondary doctrines* are those doctrines that do not necessarily distinguish Christianity from all other religions in the world, but that are necessary for the truth of the fundamental doctrines, or that flow necessarily from the fundamental doctrines. The denial of a secondary doctrine directly affects the fundamental doctrines. *Tertiary doctrines* are those truth claims, about both the Bible and nature[3], that do not directly affect either fundamental or secondary doctrines. The question of which doctrines fit into which levels of the hierarchy is one that must be considered in order to answer the "Protestant problem," and it is directly related to the question of natural knowledge.

The question we need to ask is: Where do beliefs about the natural world, which are not revealed in the Holy Scriptures, fit in the hierarchy of Christian orthodoxy? The most common knee-jerk reaction, of those to whom this question is posed, would be, "They fit into the third level." Indeed, we could, right away, dismiss several types of beliefs about the natural world, as being unnecessary for Christian orthodoxy, such as the color of the leaves of a maple tree in autumn, photosynthesis, the law of gravity, or

[74] Richard A. Muller, for example, notes that "orthodoxy consists in the faithful acceptance both of the fundamental articles and of those other, secondary doctrines, that sustain and serve to secure the right understanding of the fundamental articles." Richard A. Muller, *Scholasticism and Orthodoxy in the Reformed Tradition: An Attempt at Definition* (Grand Rapids, MI: Calvin Theological Seminary, 1995), 21.

the weight of a stone in my driveway. These are all truths that can be known by man, and which are about the natural world; however, they could not qualify as fundamental doctrines or secondary doctrines for Christianity. These are facts that are true for everyone, all religions, all thought systems, at all times. However, whether true or false, they have no effect either on fundamental or secondary doctrines, nor on Christian practice.

What we need to ask, however, is if all truths that can be known through, or about, the natural world are of this nature[1]. I propose that the answer to this question, in light of what we have seen thus far, is no. B. B. Warfield, as I noted above, would certainly agree with me that there are two types of truths about the natural world that directly affect both Christian doctrines and Christian practices: (1) metaphysical and epistemological doctrines, and (2) doctrines about human nature[1] and morality. These two types of truth so affect both Christian doctrine and practice as to drastically modify even the most fundamental doctrines.

In the first category, we could include, at least, (a) metaphysical and epistemological realism—that there are real natures[1], individualized in particular things, that can be known, and that are foundational to knowledge, rational discourse, "human" morality, and even the possibility of scientific research,[75] and so forth; (b) that one God, the creator of the whole universe, exists; (c) that truths about nature[3] can be objectively known; (d) that language communicates truths about reality and that man, by nature[1], is capable of both communicating and receiving communication.

In the second category, we could include, at least, (a) that the human being is composed, by nature[1], in one way or another, of a body and a spirit; (b) that the human being has an intellect and will, and can be said, in one way or another, to be "free" in his choices; (c) that the human species is composed of two sexes, male and female, which are distinguished by their sexual organs; (d) that the human being is able to recognize the morality, good or evil, of his actions.

Consider, briefly, what might bring us to the conclusion that these philosophical positions, known through the rational observation of nature[3], are necessary for Christian theology. Beginning with the first category, it seems (a) that Christian theology, and in fact the Bible, presupposes metaphysical and epistemological realism, as it takes for granted that there are

---

[75] See David Oderberg, *Real Essentialism* (New York: Routledge, 2007), 19–20, 33–34.

true natures[1] that can be known by man. It would seem that metaphysical and epistemological realism is necessary for: any coherent discussion concerning the divine nature[1]; the creation of the world; a coherent and orthodox explanation of the doctrine of the Trinity and the hypostatic union of the divine and human natures in Jesus Christ; all discussion concerning sin; all discussions concerning morality; and, among others things, the efficacy of the sacrifice of Jesus Christ for the human race (where "race" refers to all those particular beings who are of the same nature[1]—the human nature[1]). If it is not the case that (b) one God, the creator of the whole universe, exists, then Christianity is false; but, according to some (such as the apostle Paul in Romans 1:19–20) we are able to know, through our rational observation of nature[3], that one omnipotent creator God exists.[76] Finally, (d) if language does not communicate truths about reality, then how could the Bible communicate truth about reality? Moreover, if language does not communicate truths about reality, but only our perceptions of reality, or, worse, if language participates in the creation of reality, then any attempt at preaching, evangelism, discourse about theology, and so on will ultimately fail. It would be impossible, if such is the case, to communicate or discuss truths concerning God, man, and the work of Jesus, among other things. It would seem, then, that, at very least, these three aspects of natural knowledge, if they are false, render other, if not all other, fundamental Christian doctrines false.

Turning to the second category, (a) the Bible affirms that man is, at least, composed of body and spirit. That is to say, man is not simply a material body, but, rather, he also has a soul (which is the seat of his will and his intellect). That man is essentially (nature[1]) composed of body and spirit seems to lend support to doctrines concerning the incarnation of Jesus; and seems to be necessary for the doctrine of a future bodily resurrection, and the eternal heavenly state. If (b) man does not have an intellect, and, therefore, rational abilities, then he would not be able to receive a rational communication from God (such as the Bible). If man does not have a will, with some implied freedom of choice (whatever is meant by that), then he cannot be condemned for having acted voluntarily against the divine will (ex-

[76] It is worth noting that though Romans 1:19–20 does assume natural knowledge of God, it is not explicit about how that knowledge is obtained (whether it be by discursive reasoning, or through some form of intuitive noninferred recognition of the divine).

cept in the sense that an inventor throws into the trash an invention that does not work as he wanted it to. In such a situation, there is no moral judgment, only the judgment that it does not work.). It appears, therefore, to be necessary, for the doctrine of divine judgment against man, as well as for the doctrine of divine revelation, that man has, naturally[1], an intellect and will, and, some form of freedom of choice. That (c) humanity is composed of two distinct sexes is necessary for the Christian doctrine of marriage, for the teachings concerning the respective roles of men and women in the church and in the family, and even for the incarnation of Jesus Christ (who was born as a male). That (d) human beings are able to recognize what is morally right and wrong, at least to a limited extent, seems to be necessary not only for the condemnation of men as sinners, but also for the truth of certain scriptural truth claims (see Romans 1:32, 2:15–16). It would seem, then, that the four natural observations about man are necessary for Christian doctrine, since, if they are false, other fundamental Christian doctrines are also false, and some Christian practices (such as marriage) are rendered impossible, or worthless.

Furthermore, it follows that though some truths of natural knowledge do not affect Christian doctrines or practices, others do. It could be said that, not only do some of these beliefs have a great effect on other Christian doctrines as well as on Christian practice, but that some of those doctrines that distinguish Christianity from any other religion (fundamental or primary doctrines) could not be true unless certain doctrines of natural knowledge are also true. A further consequence would be that natural knowledge is not only necessary for biblical interpretation, the proper formation of doctrine, and for properly laying down the limits of orthodoxy, but, more importantly, some naturally known truths about nature[3], and its cause, may actually be necessary for orthodoxy. Though they may not be fundamental or primary doctrines, it would appear that there are a number of naturally known truths that qualify as secondary doctrines, and, thus, are necessary for full orthodoxy.

CONCLUSION

We set out to prove that natural knowledge (of man, God, and the universe) is necessary for biblical interpretation and doctrinal formulation, and, therefore, that it is a key element in a well-rounded solution to the Protestant problem. We began by explaining just what is meant by "nature," and how this term is used in relation to natural knowledge. We then asked whether there was any room, in Christian theology, for natural knowledge. In answering this question, we discovered not only that the answer is affirmative, but, in fact, that it is impossible, without natural knowledge, to either interpret divinely revealed Scripture, or to formulate doctrine coherently. This implies that natural knowledge is necessary for any attempt at determining the limits of orthodoxy. We then pushed our reflections a little bit further and discovered that some truths that qualify as natural knowledge are necessary for orthodoxy (e.g., that one God exists, that man is naturally[1] religious and able to receive communication from God).

How does all this help solve the so-called Protestant problem?[77] The Protestant problem is that, if *sola scriptura* and the principle of individual interpretation are true, then it seems impossible to ever know for certain that some doctrines are necessary elements of Christian belief. The protestant problem turns out to be based, in part, on failing to recognize the role of natural knowledge in biblical interpretation and doctrinal formulation. This natural knowledge includes not only truths that are known about the divine nature[1], human nature[1], and the created universe (nature[3]), but, also, the principles of interpretation that we use to properly interpret Scripture. Natural knowledge is, indeed, necessary for the proper articulation and defense of the fundamental doctrines of the Christian faith. Natural knowledge undergirds both the theological interpretation of Scripture, and the appropriate predication principle. Due to its very nature, we are able to rationally defend and articulate natural knowledge by appealing to that of which it speaks—the divinely created universe. This means that the fundamental articles of the Christian religion, many of which are accepted by faith, are upheld and supported by rationally defensible articles of natural knowledge. When, for example, the doctrine of divine impassibility is questioned, due to lack of scriptural support, one need not attempt to twist the Scriptures in order to prove this doctrine; but, rather, we can lean on that which can be known of the divine nature[1] from nature[3], and demonstrate that the only God that exists is the immutable, impassible, creator of this universe who so readily reveals His existence and divine nature.

If this essay has been successful, then we have shown, not only that

[77] Many of the reflections mentioned in this essay will be further developed in a manuscript I am preparing for publication on this subject: *Protestant Orthodoxy: How Do We Know What We Must Believe?*

natural knowledge is a necessary element for solving the Protestant problem, but, also, that it is necessary for biblical interpretation and doctrinal formation. If we, as classical theists, are to be coherent in our theology, then we must bite the proverbial bullet and accept the fact that natural knowledge—truths that are known through the natural sciences, the social sciences, and philosophy—has an essential role to play in biblical interpretation and doctrinal formulation. When the contemporary nonclassical theist accuses classical theists of using philosophy to help them interpret Scripture, rather than scurry around like a scared rabbit, classical theists should proudly congratulate the naysayers for having realized what is going on, and invite them to join the classical theists in consistently affirming the orthodox doctrine of God.

BIBLIOGRAPHY

Allen, Michael, and Scott R. Swain. *Reformed Catholicity: The Promise of Retrieval for Theology and Biblical Interpretation.* Grand Rapids, MI: Baker Books, 2015.

Aquinas, Thomas. *Truth.* Vol. 1. Translated by Robert W. Mulligan. 1954. Reprint, Cambridge: Hackett, 1994.

Aristotle. *Metaphysica.* Edited by W. Jaeger. 1957. Reprint, Oxford: Oxford University Press, 2010.

Audi, Robert. *Epistemology: A Contemporary Introduction to the Theory of Knowledge.* 2nd ed. 2003. Reprint, New York: Routledge, 2004.

Augustine. *On Free Will.* In *Augustine: Earlier Writings*, edited and translated by J. H. S. Burleigh, 102–17. Louisville, KY: SCM, 1953.

——. *The Teacher.* In *Augustine: Earlier Writings*, edited and translated by J. H. S. Burleigh, 64–101. Louisville, KY: SCM, 1953.

Barnes, Jonathan. *Introduction to Contemporary Epistemology.* 1985. Reprint, Oxford: Blackwell, 1997.

Barr, James. *Biblical Faith and Natural Theology.* Oxford: Oxford University Press, 1993.

Boyd, Craig A. "The Synthesis of Reason and Faith." In *Faith and Reason: Three Views*, edited by Steve Wilkens, 131–59. Downers Grove, IL: Intervarsity, 2014.

Calvin, Jean. *Commentaire sur l'épître aux Romains.* In vol. 3 of *Commentaires de Jean Calvin sur le Nouveau Testament*, 5–268. Paris: Librairie de Ch. Meyrueis et co., 1855.

Calvin, John. *Institutes of the Christian Religion.* Vol. 1. Translated by Ford Lewis Battles. Edited by John T. McNeill. Louisville, KY: Westminster John Knox Press, 1960.

Cranmer, Thomas. "An Answer of Thomas unto a Crafty and Sophistical Cavillation Devised by Stephen Gardiner." In vol. 3 of *The Remains of Thomas Cranmer*, edited by Henry Jenkyns, 24–554. Oxford: University of Oxford Press, 1833.

———. "A Defence of the True and Catholic Doctrine of the Sacrament of the Body and Blood of Our Saviour Christ." In vol. 2 of *The Remains of Thomas Cranmer*, edited by Henry Jenkyns, 275–463. Oxford: University of Oxford Press, 1833.

De Bèze, Theodore. *Questions et Responses Chrestiennes*. Eustace Vignon, 1584.

Dolezal, James. *All That Is in God: Evangelical Theology and the Challenge of Classical Christian Theism*. Grand Rapids, MI: Reformation Heritage Books, 2017.

Flavel, John. *A Blow at the Root; or, The Cause and Cure of Mental Errors*. In vol. 3 of *The Whole Works of Rev. Mr. John Flavel*, 413–92. London: W. Baynes and Son, 1820.

———. *Sermon 7* in *The Method of Grace*. In vol. 2 of *The Whole Works of Rev. Mr. John Flavel*, 121–40. London: W. Baynes and Son, 1820.

———. *Sermon 23* in *The Method of Grace*. In vol. 2 of *The Whole Works of Rev. Mr. John Flavel*, 318–27. London: W. Baynes and Son, 1820.

Gregory Nazianzus. *On the Son 1*. In *Five Theological Orations*, translated by Stephen Reynolds, 45–70. Estate of Stephen Reynolds, 2011.

———. *On the Holy Spirit*. In *Five Theological Orations*, translated by Stephen Reynolds, 97–123. Estate of Stephen Reynolds, 2011.

Hodge, Charles. *Systematic Theology*. Vol. 1. 1940. Reprint, Peabody, MA: Hendrickson, 2003.

Lewis, C. S. *Studies in Words*. 2nd ed. 1967. Reprint, Cambridge: Cambridge University Press, 2008.

McGrath, Alister E. and Darren C. Marks. "Introduction: Protestantism—the Problem of Identity." In *The Blackwell Companion to Protestantism*, edited by Alister E. McGrath and Darren C. Marks, 1-19. Oxford: Blackwell, 2004.

Muller, Richard A. *Scholasticism and Orthodoxy in the Reformed Tradition: An Attempt at Definition*. Grand Rapids, MI: Calvin Theological Seminary, 1995.

Oderberg, David. *Real Essentialism*. New York: Routledge, 2007.

Plantinga, Alvin. *Warrant and Proper Function*. Oxford: Oxford University Press, 1993.

Plato. *Theaetetus*.Translated by M. J. Levett. Edited by Myles Burnyeat. Indianapolis, IN: Hackett, 1990.

Sheridan, Mark. *Language for God in Patristic Tradition: Wrestling with Biblical Anthropomorphism*. Downers Grove, IL: InterVarsity, 2015.

Strong, Augustus H. *Systematic Theology: A Compendium*. 3 vols. in 1. 1907. Reprint, Old Tappan, NJ: Fleming H. Revell, 1979.

Turretin, Francis. *Institutes of Elenctic Theology*. Vol. 1. Translated by George Musgrave Giger. Edited by James T. Dennison, Jr. Phillipsburg, NJ: P&R, 1992.

Vermigli, Pietro Martyr. *Common Places*. Translated by Anthonie Marten. 1574.

Warfield, Benjamin Breckinridge. "The Idea of Systematic Theology." In *Studies in Theology*. Vol. 9 of *The Works of Benjamin B. Warfield*, 49–87. 1932. Reprint, Grand Rapids, MI: Baker Book House, 2000.

———. "The Task and Method of Systematic Theology." In *Studies in Theology*, 91–105. Vol. 9 of *The Works of Benjamin B. Warfield*. 1932. Reprint, Grand Rapids, MI: Baker Book House, 2000.

Wilhelmsen, Frederick D. *Man's Knowledge of Reality: An Introduction to Thomistic Epistemology*. Englewood Cliffs, NJ: Prentice Hall, 1956.

VI: WHAT HAPPENED IN THE SEARCH FOR LITURGICAL CATHOLICITY?

Christopher Dorn, First Presbyterian Church (Holland, MI)

THE MODERN liturgical and ecumenical movements were intimately bound up together. The principal concern of the liturgical movement was recovering the meaning of the Eucharist as the rite by which Christians renew their unity with Christ and one another. The liturgical movement further maintained that the ultimate goal of all sound liturgy is to unite Christians with the church in all times and in all places; thus, it was ecumenical or "catholic" to its core.[1] One American participant in these movements recognized this relationship, observing that "some see in the liturgy not only a bridge over which men may join the ranks in the Body of Christ with Christians of every century, but also the means by which a divided Christendom may be healed of its many divisions."[2]

This essay will consider the two movements as constituting a single complex, without reducing the one to the other. This will allow us to pose

---

[1] The terms "catholic" and "ecumenical" are virtually synonymous, since both are used to refer to a "whole" extended in space and time. Under this aspect we may understand these terms in the sense of the Vincentian Canon: that which applies everywhere (*ubique*), always (*semper*), and for everyone (*omnibus*).

[2] Garrett C. Roorda, "Worship and Liturgy in the Reformed Church in America," in *A Companion to the Liturgy: A Guide to Worship in the Reformed Church*, ed. Garrett C. Roorda (New York: Half Moon, 1917), 1. For this and for also what follows, see also Christopher Dorn, *The Lord's Supper in the Reformed Church in America: Tradition in Transition* (New York: Peter Lang, 2007), 95–107.

the following question: What happened in the search for liturgical catholicity in the Presbyterian and Reformed churches in North America?

If the question concerns the "what," that is, the progress and outcome of the search, it is relatively easy to answer. It plausibly began in 1909 at the World Eucharistic Congress in Malines, Belgium, where the Belgian Benedictine Dom Lambert Beauduin argued that, by means of corporate prayer, the liturgy binds individual Christians to the one, visible church for which Jesus prayed in John 17:20–23. Historians consider this event to signal future Roman Catholic participation in the liturgical movement.[3] Alternatively, we may locate the beginning in 1910, when Charles Henry Brent, the Protestant Episcopal Church (USA) bishop in the Philippines, called the General Convention of his denomination to join churches across the globe in assembling at a world conference to examine their differences. This has been regarded as the catalyst for the ecumenical movement.[4] The climax may be the Faith and Order Conference in Lima, Peru, in 1982, from which came the publication *Baptism, Eucharist and Ministry* (*BEM*), by far the most widely disseminated document to have come out of these movements before or since.[5] Or, alternatively, we may find it in 1993, when the Presbyterian Church (USA) published the latest revision of its *Book of Common Worship* (*BCW*),[6] which Methodist liturgical scholar James White lauded as "the state of the art in North American liturgical revision."[7]

If the question is rephrased slightly so that the "what" reads as "what in the world" or "whatever" happened, then it can be interpreted with reference to the apparent or real frustration of the search's aim. That makes it

[3] See, e.g., Bernard Botte, *From Silence to Participation: An Insider's View of Liturgical Renewal*, trans. John Sullivan (Washington, DC: Pastoral Press, 1988), 10.

[4] Tissington Tatlow, "The World Conference on Faith and Order," in *A History of the Ecumenical Movement: 1517–1948*, vol 1., ed. Ruth Rouse and Stephen Charles Neill (Geneva: World Council of Churches, 1954), 407.

[5] Faith and Order Paper No. 111 (Geneva: World Council of Churches, 1982).

[6] Presbyterian Church (USA), *Book of Common Worship* (Louisville, KY: Westminster John Knox Press, 1993). For an overview of the welter of material contained in this voluminous service book, which totals over 1,100 pages (!), see Harold M. Daniels, "The Making of the *Book of Common Worship* (1993)," in *To Glorify God: Essays on Modern Reformed Liturgy*, ed. Bryan D. Spinks and Ian R. Torrance (Edinburgh: T&T Clark, 1999), 31–53.

[7] James White, *Christian Worship in North America: A Retrospective: 1955–1995* (Collegeville, MN: Liturgical Press, 1997), 89.

harder to answer. We have speculated in earlier research that the twentieth-century liturgical renewal in North American Presbyterian and Reformed churches, which culminated in the *Book of Common Worship* (1993), has reached its end.[8] Indeed, already within a decade of its publication, its principal architects found it necessary to draw up a "Proposal for Structuring Advocacy of Service Book Use in Reformed Churches." What in the world *happened*? The authors became aware of certain Presbyterian congregations whose worship distressed them. They concluded that without a network of pastors and congregations committed to implementing historic Christian worship as set forth in the *BCW*, worshipping congregations would not enjoy the fruit of their liturgical labors.[9] And yet, even if the reception of the "catholic" forms into the worship life of existing Presbyterian congregations was and remains uneven, it must be acknowledged that the *BCW* has exerted a profound influence on the liturgical sensibilities of many in the Presbyterian Church (USA), as well as in American Protestantism more broadly. But before we determine the significance of this fact, let us return to the question as it appears in its first iteration: *What* happened?

LITURGICAL CATHOLICITY: THE PROGRESS AND OUTCOME OF THE SEARCH

Brent's call for a global assembly of churches was heeded. The General Convention adopted a resolution to appoint a joint commission to invite "all Christian Communions throughout the world which confess our Lord Jesus Christ as God and Saviour" to a "world conference." In 1920, representatives from participating churches met in Geneva to make preparations. Finally, in 1927 the first World Conference on Faith and Order was held in Lausanne, Switzerland. Never before had an assembly of church leaders so comprehensive taken place: over four hundred delegates from Orthodox, Reformation, and free church traditions came together at this historic event to discuss articles of faith that united and divided them.

---

[8] See Christopher Dorn, "A Liturgical Legacy from the Presbyterians: Introducing the Association for Reformed & Liturgical Worship," *New Mercersburg Review* 47 (Fall 2012): 33.

[9] Harold Daniels, "In God's Own Time—The Birthing of the AR&LW," unpublished paper. See also Dorn, "Liturgical Legacy," 32–34.

The Lord's Supper received passing attention at Lausanne and at the subsequent world conference in the context of a general consideration of the sacraments. But it was only in 1938 when the "continuation committee" constituted at Edinburgh decided to take up the "liturgical question." In the following year, the committee appointed two international theological commissions, of which the first was to study the "ways of worship" of the major Christian traditions and the second "intercommunion." The chaos of the war years prevented their members from carrying out their tasks with dispatch; it was not until 1950 that final reports were approved and distributed to delegates to the third world conference (1952 in Lund, Sweden) as a basis for their discussions.[10]

Ways of Worship

Because the papers of the first commission are most germane to our subject, they will be our exclusive focus here. They were compiled and published in a volume titled *Ways of Worship*, and their content reflects an already emergent consensus among ecumenical leaders about the marks of liturgical catholicity.[11] This could hardly have been otherwise, since the studies that proved to have the greatest impact on the liturgical reforms, by this time widespread in member churches, had already been published. Among the most outstanding include Yngve Brilioth's *Eucharistic Faith and Practice, Evangelical and Catholic* (1926, 1930), Odo Casel's *The Mystery of Christian Worship* (1932), and Gregory Dix's *The Shape of the Liturgy* (1945). What are these marks?

The first is the sacramental character of worship. This does not refer in the first instance to the sacraments of baptism and Lord's Supper, but rather to the "mystery" of worship, in which grace is communicated through it. From this vantage point, the act of preaching, performed in the expectation that God will use human words to communicate His grace, is "sacramental" in character. But the recognition of the "sacramentality" of the event of worship generally led to a renewed appreciation of the Lord's Supper in the member churches, which began to promote more frequent celebration of this sacrament.

---

[10] Dorn, *Lord's Supper*, 95–98.

[11] Pehr Edwall, Eric Hayman, and William D. Maxwell, eds., *Ways of Worship: The Report of a Theological Commission on Faith and Order* (London: SCM, 1951).

The second is the patterning of worship after models drawn from the apostolic and patristic eras. The liturgical movement stimulated a return to the biblical and postbiblical sources. This involved intensive study, especially of the New Testament and liturgies from the fourth and fifth centuries. These liturgies became the gold standard of a truly ecumenical order of worship, not least because of the conviction that they display the purity and strength of the undivided church.

Retrieval of these patristic sources led to renewed attention to the structure and elements of the Eucharistic Prayer. The use of the Eucharistic Prayer in the celebration of the Lord's Supper therefore came to constitute the third mark. Consideration of the content of the classic Eucharistic Prayers prompted many to contend that, in the celebration of the Lord's Supper, the worshipping assembly makes a memorial not only of Christ's atoning death, but also of His life, resurrection, ascension, and session at the right hand of God. In addition to these elements of the prayer is the Parousia, in contemplation of which the churches sought to recover the eschatological significance of the Lord's Supper. For their part, the representatives of the Reformed churches pointed out that the Institution narrative that the sixteenth-century Reformers drew from 1 Corinthians 11:23–26 for their forms for the Lord's Supper contains the words: "For as often as you eat this bread and drink the cup, you proclaim the Lord's death *until he comes*" (v. 26; italics mine).

The fourth mark is worship's sacrificial character. Many expressed the desire to revisit the Reformation controversies over the sacrifice of the Mass. Luther and Calvin had vehemently rejected the notion of Eucharistic sacrifice because, for them, it derogated from Christ's once-for-all sacrifice on the cross (see Heb. 7:27; 10:10). But the works of Brilioth, Casel, and Dix, among others, suggested to the churches that the terms of the problem might be reconceived. The sacrifice of the cross is not repeated in the celebration of the Lord's Supper, but rather reactualized. Moreover, the liturgical actions of communion and self-offering are integral to each other: they express the reality that one does not participate in the saving death of Christ apart from the self-dispossession that His death entails (see 2 Cor. 5:14).[12]

---

[12] On this subject it is worth mentioning the important two-volume study on Eucharistic sacrifice by the outstanding ecumenist Max Thurian. Thurian played a leading role in the preparation of *BEM* and drafted the liturgy used at the Faith and Order Conference at Lima, Peru (1982). Later known as the "Lima Liturgy," it has

SELF-CRITICISM OF THE REFORMED CHURCHES

Measured against these marks, the liturgical principles and worship practices of the Reformed churches were defective. Or, at least, that was the consensus of the Reformed contributors to the volume *Ways of Worship*.

The German Swiss pastor Arthur Graf complained that the dimension of mystery was absent from Reformed worship. He believed this absence an unfortunate legacy from the Reformers, whom he alleged distrusted anything not transparent to reason. He saw this "rationalizing attitude" reflected in the phrase "explanation of the mystery," which entered into the vocabulary of the Christian faith for the first time in the sixteenth century. This didacticism is embodied in the traditional forms for the Lord's Supper, characterized by the insertion of "verbal and learned expositions" of the meaning of the atoning death of Christ. The people must understand the celebration. For this reason, the sacrament became transmuted into a "doctrine" that has to be "discerned and known" rather than a mystery to be contemplated and adored. This had the effect of reducing the celebration to a catechism.[13]

The French pastor and liturgical scholar Richard Paquier attributed this development to a flawed theological conception of the sacraments. The Reformers regarded the sacraments as a seal and a pledge of God's grace that the word alone suffices to convey. For this reason, they conceived of sacraments as no more than a *verbum visibile*; they were a necessary pedagog-

---

enjoyed widespread use in worshipping assemblies seeking to embody the marks of liturgical catholicity as defined in the twentieth-century liturgical and ecumenical movements. See Max Thurian, *The Eucharistic Memorial*, trans. J. G. Davies, Ecumenical Studies in Worship no. 7 (London: Lutterworth, 1960). See also Theresa Berger, "Lima Liturgy," in *Dictionary of the Ecumenical Movement*, ed. Nicholas Lossky et al. (Geneva: World Council of Churches, 2002), 694–95.

13 Edwall, Hayman, and Maxwell, *Ways of Worship*, 232–34. It is interesting to contrast Graf's view here with that of the Roman Catholic priest and theologian Romano Guardini, whose book *The Spirit of the Liturgy* (1918; English translation 1930) established him as one of the most influential leaders of the liturgical movement. For Guardini, Protestantism embodies a pragmatic spirit that has "abandoned objective religious truth and has increasingly tended to make conviction a matter of personal judgment, feeling and experience." Possessed by this spirit, it no longer recognizes a "body of dogma which can be handed on in tradition, but right action as proof of the right spirit." Romano Guardini, *The Spirit of the Liturgy*, trans. Ada Lane (New York: Crossroad, 1998), 89–90.

ical aid that God graciously provides for frail human beings, unable otherwise to understand the promises of Christ in the word preached. But this reduction of the sacraments to another form of the word could only precipitate the collapse of the former into the latter. That lay behind the infrequent celebration of the Lord's Supper in ordinary Lord's Day worship in the subsequent centuries. This tendency should not have been unexpected, since in the last analysis there was no qualitative difference for the Reformers between the word and the sacraments.[14]

Nevertheless, the tendency Paquier noted was contrary to the original intention of the Reformers, who sought to recover the unity of word and sacrament in worship. In this connection, the Dutch comparative religions scholar Gerardus van der Leeuw noted that John Calvin desired weekly celebration of the Lord's Supper. For Calvin, the infrequent participation of the people of God in the sacrament was a defect inherited from Rome and needed to be overcome by the reform. This desire resonated with van der Leeuw, who insisted the New Testament features the Supper as the nucleus of Christian worship. Thus, there is no basis for regarding the Supper as a "special occasion;" the biblical evidence suggests that "every gathering of the members of the Body of Christ is essentially a gathering at the Table."[15]

Reflection on the New Testament witness also convinced these contributors that the traditional form for the Lord's Supper, passed down from Calvin and the Reformers, posed problems. The exclusive connection drawn between Christ's death and the Supper imbued the celebration with a somber mood. The form did not convey the joy that accompanied breaking bread in the New Testament church (Luke 24:30–35; Acts 2:46). The form's composers failed to appreciate that the sacrament is celebrated between the "Resurrection Supper of the Lord with his disciples and the eschatological Supper of the Lamb."[16] Consequently, the Reformed churches should celebrate the Supper joyfully as a "meal with the Risen Lord and an anticipation of the messianic Supper of the returning Lord."[17] Thus, the Swiss church historian Julius Schweizer urged the churches to compose new forms, instructing the people in the joy and hope appropriate to the occasion.[18]

---

[14] Edwall, Hayman, and Maxwell, *Ways of Worship*, 242.

[15] Edwall, Hayman, and Maxwell, *Ways of Worship*, 226.

[16] Edwall, Hayman, and Maxwell, *Ways of Worship*, 132.

[17] Edwall, Hayman, and Maxwell, *Ways of Worship*, 132.

[18] Edwall, Hayman, and Maxwell, *Ways of Worship*, 132.

Dissatisfaction with the traditional Reformational Eucharistic form combined with the rediscovery of New Testament Eucharistic themes no doubt helps explain the attraction of the classic Eucharistic Prayers of the fourth and fifth centuries. The celebration should begin not with a solemn exhortation addressed to the people, but rather with joyful praise and thanksgiving addressed to God. We have already noted that these prayers contain themes consistent with what the contributors highlighted in their observations of the biblical material. It is therefore not surprising to see that, by the mid-twentieth century, Eucharistic Prayers began to appear in the service books of Presbyterian and Reformed churches in Europe and North America.

RECEPTION OF THE LITURGICAL CONSENSUS IN NORTH AMERICAN REFORMED AND PRESBYTERIAN CHURCHES

The extent to which this consensus penetrated into the minds of those appointed to worship commissions in Reformed and Presbyterian churches in North America is evident already by the 1960s. In 1968 the Reformed Church in America (RCA) published *Liturgy and Psalms*. In 1970, a joint publication of the United Presbyterian Church in the USA, the (southern) Presbyterian Church in the United States, and the Cumberland Presbyterian Church appeared under the title *The Worshipbook: Services*.[19] Both succeeded in integrating word and sacrament in Lord's Day worship and in providing orders modeled on the classic Eucharistic liturgies of the patristic era. *Worshipbook* contains texts of the Lord's Prayer, the Apostles' and Nicene Creeds, the introductory dialogue of the Eucharistic Prayer, and so forth drawn from the International Consultation on English Texts, an ecumenical body composed of members representing Roman Catholic and Protestant churches in twenty countries. It also includes a three-year lectionary, adapted from the Roman Catholic *Ordo Lectionum Missæ* (1969), which came out of the reforms of the Second Vatican Council (1962–1965).[20]

---

[19] The United Church of Christ and the Reformed Church in America participated in the preparation of this service book at the beginning but did not continue in the process. See Marsha M. Wilfong, "Reformed Worship in the United States of America," in *Christian Worship in Reformed Churches Past and Present*, ed. Lukas Vischer (Grand Rapids, MI: Eerdmans, 2003), 137.

[20] Dorn, "Liturgical Legacy," 30.

The following two decades witnessed the high-water mark of these developments. We have already mentioned the document *BEM*, which the World Council of Churches' Commission on Faith and Order approved at Lima, Peru, in 1982 for transmission to member churches.[21] The product of decades of patient dialogue, *BEM* sums up the ecumenical consensus on the meaning and practice of baptism, Eucharist, and ministry. It hardly needs to be said that the Eucharist is explained in terms that presuppose the classic Eucharistic liturgies of the fourth and fifth centuries: the Eucharist involves thanksgiving to the Father, memorial of Christ, invocation of the Spirit, communion of the faithful, and anticipation of the kingdom. The responses to this text came from more than 190 churches, filling six volumes. No doubt this astonishing engagement indicates the high level of interest in liturgical matters among churches at this time.

Unsurprisingly, this decade featured a profusion of new service books in North America. The United Church of Christ published the *Book of Worship* in 1986. The RCA published *Worship the Lord* in 1987 and *Liturgy and Confessions* in 1990. In 1988, the Christian Reformed Church in North America (CRCNA) published the *Psalter Hymnal*, which includes not only a directory for worship but also forms for the sacraments and those for excommunication, readmission, ordination, and marriage. It must be acknowledged, however, that the content of *Psalter Hymnal* reveals that the liturgical consensus did not reach as deeply into the CRCNA at this time as it had elsewhere.[22] Outside of the United States, the Presbyterian Church of Canada produced a revised service book in 1991. Finally, the Presbyterian Church (USA), formed by a merger of the United Presbyterian Church in the USA and the (southern) Presbyterian Church in the United States in 1983, published the *Book of Common Worship* in 1993, as already mentioned.[23]

In magnitude and scope, the *BCW* is far more comprehensive than any of its predecessors. Word and sacrament are presupposed as the norm for Lord's Day worship. Its outline is divided into four sections: gathering,

---

[21] Faith and Order Paper No. 111.

[22] The worship life in the CRCNA of course would be influenced by the founding of the Calvin Institute of Christian Worship (CICW) on the campus of Calvin Theological Seminary in 1997. Under the direction of John D. Witvliet, who earned a PhD in liturgical studies at Notre Dame University, the CICW has been active in the study and renewal of worship not only as regards CRCNA congregations, but churches in North America and beyond.

[23] Dorn, "Liturgical Legacy," 31.

word, Eucharist, and sending—the "fourfold shape" of Christian liturgy. Multiple texts for the opening prayer and confession of sins, appropriate to the occasion or season in the liturgical calendar, are provided. It contains eleven options for the prayer for illumination and eight for the prayers of the people. No less than twenty-four Eucharistic Prayers, with a broad variety of complete prayers for each season in the liturgical calendar, appear. Newer and more expansive materials are included for each feast and season of the liturgical calendar, to which is added Christ the King (Reign of Christ), the Baptism of the Lord, and the Transfiguration of the Lord. A liturgy for the Easter Vigil is also provided. Palm Sunday is renamed Palm/Passion Sunday to reflect ecumenical consensus. Extensive resources for morning and evening prayer comprise a separate section. To the three-year lectionary for Sundays and special feast days is added a two-year daily lectionary.[24]

THE DISSOLUTION OF THE LITURGICAL SYNTHESIS

The twentieth-century liturgical and ecumenical movements produced liturgical research and renewal unprecedented and unsurpassed in Christian history. At this point in the twenty-first century, it is at best difficult to believe they succeeded in permanently transforming the worship practices of the North American Reformed and Presbyterian Churches, especially at the level of the local congregation. We return now to the question as slightly rephrased: What *in the world* happened? The observations below are largely anecdotal, drawn largely from direct experience. Nevertheless, the answers we propose to this question will hopefully fit the data well.

First, we must confess that it is misleading to speak of the dissolution of a mode of worship that never existed in many congregations. Some congregations belonged to Reformed denominations that did not participate in these movements. Wary of the threat the liturgical and ecumenical movements posed to the integrity of their traditions, these denominations did not incorporate the movements' contributions into their ecclesial life.

Second, we must take into account the impact of the "worship wars" on Protestant denominations in North America.[25] The publication of the

---

[24] Dorn, "Liturgical Legacy," 32.

[25] For a historical overview, see Terry W. York, *America's Worship Wars* (Peabody, MA: Hendrickson, 2003); for a taxonomy of the worship styles over which church-

BCW coincided roughly with the proliferation of new worship styles associated with "community" churches, which were (and still are) drawing larger numbers than their confessional counterparts. These styles aimed to make churches "contemporary" and "seeker sensitive." The result is worship services led by a praise bands—usually consisting of electric guitars, drummers, and vocalists—and consisting in the singing of praise songs and medleys. Following the singing, there may be dramas or personal testimonies. The service typically concludes with an inspirational message or sermon, often based on a set of biblical "principles."[26] In response to the perceived success many of these community churches were enjoying, many of the "traditional" or confessionally Reformed congregations sought to replicate these strategies in their own contexts. Proponents of such changes argued that the "churchy" language and practices of the tradition were neither relevant nor accessible to the contemporary churchgoer, which they sought to attract. Resistance to this program was inevitable, especially among older generations, shaped as they were by the "traditional" practices and rituals that had sustained them over the decades. The truce in the worship wars was called among many when congregations decided to introduce "split" worship services: the first was usually called "traditional," the second "contemporary." The irony is that, at least in the congregations with which this author is familiar, the only real difference between the two lies in music: the "traditional" service features older hymns, but they are sung within a liturgical framework bearing the unmistakable stamp of the "contemporary" service.

Third, we have to account for the recent reconfessionalization of churches. In the Presbyterian Church in America, the Orthodox Presbyterian Church, and the United Reformed Churches in North America, there has been a movement to retrieve the writings of Calvin, his fellow Reformers, and the Puritan divines for the thought and life of contemporary Reformed churches. This includes a critical retrieval and reappropriation of

es have fought, see Elmer Towns, *Putting an End to Worship Wars* (Nashville, TN: Broadman and Holman, 1997); for a critical assessment from a Presbyterian perspective informed by the liturgical principles enshrined in the liturgical and ecumenical movements surveyed above, see Ronald P. Byars, *The Future of Protestant Worship: Beyond the Worship Wars* (Louisville, KY: Westminster John Knox Press, 2002).

[26] See Frank C. Senn, *Christian Liturgy, Catholic and Evangelical* (Minneapolis, MN: Augsburg Fortress, 1997), 676–83.

their sacramental theology and practices. Far from judging them as defective, the scholars and pastors involved in this movement see them as key to the reinvigoration of the classic Protestant tradition. They argue that this tradition contains rich resources that can be used to address a wide range of problems currently affecting the theology, worship, and ethics of the churches.[27]

WHAT HAS BEEN LOST? DOES IT MAKE A DIFFERENCE?

Because the marks of liturgical catholicity, as defined by the renewal movements of the last century, have not been uniformly incorporated into the worshipping practices of the Reformed churches in North America, we may ask in retrospect what has been lost. In his *Liturgy and Secularism*, Joris Geldhof repeats the concerns voiced more than a century earlier by his compatriot Lambert Beauduin. The liturgy fulfills its true function when it succeeds in uniting people together in corporate acts of praise, petition, and thanksgiving. When the liturgy is neglected, individualism gains in "strength and influence," increasing the probability that individuals will develop themselves in "painful isolation."[28] The disappearance of catholic liturgy destroys community.

But does participation in a catholic liturgy necessarily ensure one's union with fellow worshippers? A document produced by the XV Ordinary General Assembly of the Synod of Bishops reports that Roman Catholic young people (ages sixteen to twenty-nine) desire a liturgy that is "alive and proximate," complaining that liturgy often does not lead to a "sense of community or family as the Body of Christ."[29] Youth also criticize homilies,

---

[27] See, e.g., the annual Philadelphia Conferences on Reformed Theology, sponsored by the Alliance of Confessing Evangelicals; the work of the Davenant Institute, dedicated to retrieving the "riches of classical Protestantism in order to renew and build up the contemporary church" (davenantinstitute.org); and the writings of the church historian Carl Trueman, a high-profile public figure who defends the ongoing relevance of the Reformation and classic Reformed theology for the contemporary church. See especially Trueman's *Grace Alone: Salvation as a Gift of God* (Grand Rapids, MI: Zondervan, 2017).

[28] Joris Geldhof, *Liturgy and Secularism* (Collegeville, MN: Liturgical Press, 2018), 134.

[29] *Synod 2018 on Young People, the Faith and Vocational Discernment*, Vatican City, 2018, para. 69.

which they find to be inadequate in helping them to discern their situation in light of the Gospel. Finally, young people are attracted to the joy of the Christian faith, which many in their parishes seem incapable of exemplifying.[30] Not without reason, then, the offerings of other denominations and even religions are appealing, with their "simpler" and "more direct" language and their "lively" and "high quality" music.[31]

But we may ask an even more basic question: Is the liturgy the only or even the best means by which to foster a sense of "togetherness" among members of the church? In this connection one has only to call to mind the success in many "community" churches of the cell or small-group ministry, through which individuals develop strong relationships with fellow members and thereby come to "plug into" the life of the church. At least at the level of the local congregation, it seems that liturgy is not indispensable for meeting the felt need of community among Christians, a need for which the leaders of the liturgical movement enlisted it.

But perhaps we can raise a more serious concern. In the twentieth century, worship commissions were intent on forging an organic relationship between worship and doctrine, liturgy and confession. Having appealed to the twofold sense of "orthodoxy" as both "correct belief" and "correct worship," they insisted the two mutually express and reinforce one another. We have already noted the classic Eucharistic Prayers express a comprehensive account of the salvific work of Christ. We may also call attention to the inclusion of the Nicene Creed in the revised orders of worship from the last century. The disappearance of a liturgy that bears the marks of catholicity risks the very orthodoxy of the Christian faith itself.

But have the churches most attentive to the preservation of the marks of catholicity in their liturgies succeeded in transmitting orthodox Christianity to their people? It is naïve to assume that the use of "catholic" liturgical texts in an order of worship ensures the appropriation of their content. It is a truism that liberal pastors and priests reject the theological positions articulated in their liturgical texts. In her recent memoir *Why Religion?*, popular historian of religions Elaine Pagels cites the catholic "rituals of the Episcopal church" as one element of her regimen of diverse spiritual practices. She also denies the "list of doctrines called the Nicene Creed."[32]

---

[30] *Synod 2018 on Young People, the Faith and Vocational Discernment*, para. 69.

[31] *Synod 2018 on Young People, the Faith and Vocational Discernment*, para. 162.

[32] Elaine Pagels, *Why Religion?* (New York: HarperCollins, 2018), 34.

The foregoing considerations prompt us, in the final analysis, to ask whether the terms "liturgical" and "catholicity" as we have defined them can be separated. Not all churches that use catholic liturgies stand in the "great tradition" of the one, holy, catholic and apostolic church. Conversely, a strong case can be made that some churches whose worship is not ordered according to these marks do stand firmly in this tradition. To encourage them to remain faithful to it may not necessarily mean recommending to them to incorporate some or all of these marks, even if it may mean affirming the desire to evaluate inadequate worship practices as a sign of spiritual vitality and theological maturity.

CONCLUDING THOUGHTS

Where, then, does the way forward lie? How do the Reformed churches in North America maintain or recover catholicity when many in their contexts are unwilling or unable to repristinate catholic liturgical paradigms?

One direction may lie in the reexamination of the ecclesiological implications of the act of preaching, which is central to traditional Reformed worship. In his "Preaching Makes the Church: Recovering a Missing Ecclesial Mark," Joshua Ralston notes the rediscovery of John Calvin's liturgical thought and sacramental theology in the context of the renewal movements we have just surveyed.[33] For Ralston, the concern to reclaim Calvin in this connection for the purpose of ecumenical dialogue and renewal within the Reformed community of churches is to be applauded. But conspicuous in its absence from these studies is sustained ecclesiological reflection on preaching, which Calvin, following the Augsburg Confession, regards as the first mark of the church.[34]

Significant for Ralston in this regard is the phrase that Calvin appends to the language of the Augsburg Confession: The church is identified not only by the "pure preaching of God's word," but also by its *reception*.[35]

[33] Joshua Ralston, "Preaching Makes the Church: Recovering a Missing Ecclesial Mark," in *John Calvin's Ecclesiology: Ecumenical Perspectives*, ed. Gerard Mannion and Eduardus van der Borght (London: T&T Clark, 2011), 125–42.

[34] The two marks of the church are the "pure preaching of the gospel and the lawful administration of the sacraments." John Calvin, *Institutes of the Christian Religion*, 2 Vols., ed. John T. McNeill, trans. Ford Lewis Battles (Philadelphia: Westminster, 1960), 24–25.

[35] Ralston, "Preaching Makes the Church," 134. Refer also to the relevant state-

Where the Word of God is purely preached and heard, there we find people set apart from the world to form the church. Effective preaching and hearing, however, do not happen apart from the Holy Spirit, who creates faith in the hearers and imparts to them Christ's saving benefits. And these benefits are to be enjoyed in community, since it is Christ's intent to gather the saints into his society "on the principle that whatever benefits God confers upon them, they should in turn share with one another."[36]

The preacher nevertheless is the "symbol of ecclesial unity,"[37] according to Ralston's interpretation of Calvin, insofar as the ordained ministry is the "chief sinew by which believers are held together in one body."[38] It is the preacher's task to build up "the body of Christ, until we all attain the unity of the faith and the knowledge of the Son of God" (Eph. 4:12–13).[39]

Implicit in this brief sketch of Calvin's explication of the first mark of the church is the *unam, sanctam, catholicam et apostolicam Ecclesiam* professed in the creed. Our point in providing it here is to suggest that the loss of the *liturgical* catholicity, reconstructed in the twentieth century, need not entail the loss of catholicity itself in the North American Reformed congregations.

Regardless of the manner in which the church gives it liturgical expression, it remains the case that the "Son of God through his Spirit and Word…gathers, protects, and preserves for himself a community chosen for eternal life and united in true faith."[40] The divine action, of course, does not relieve Reformed and Presbyterian pastors and worship planning committees today of the responsibility to ensure that their orders of worship are rooted in solid liturgical principles. Even if they do not approach the challenges they face in their local contexts with exactly the same concerns, the

---

ment of Calvin: "Wherever we find the word of God purely preached and heard, and the sacraments administered according to the institution of Christ; there, it is not to be doubted, is a Church of God: for His promise can never deceive: 'Where two or three are gathered together in my name, there am I in the midst of them.'" Calvin, *Inst.,* IV.1.9.

[36] Calvin, *Inst.,* IV.1.3.

[37] Ralston, "Preaching Makes the Church," 134.

[38] Calvin, *Inst.* IV.3.1.

[39] See also Calvin, *Inst.* IV.1.5.

[40] Heidelberg Catechism Q&A 54.

same patterns of understanding and interpretation as those of the participants in the liturgical and ecumenical movements of the past century, they must still evaluate whether their current practices serve to embody and express that apostolic faith "once for all delivered to the saints" (Jude 1:3). The diligence with which their predecessors undertook this task, so essential to the life of the church, should inspire them.

BIBLIOGRAPHY

Berger, Theresa. "Lima Liturgy." In *Dictionary of the Ecumenical Movement*, edited by Nicholas Lossky et al., 694–95. Geneva: World Council of Churches, 2002.

Botte, Bernard. *From Silence to Participation: An Insider's View of Liturgical Renewal.* Translated by John Sullivan. Washington, DC: Pastoral Press, 1988.

Byars, Ronald P. *The Future of Protestant Worship: Beyond the Worship Wars.* Louisville, KY: Westminster John Knox Press, 2002.

Calvin, John. *Institutes of the Christian Religion.* 2 Vols. Edited by John T. McNeill. Translated by Ford Lewis Battles. Philadelphia: Westminster, 1960.

Daniels, Harold. "In God's Own Time—The Birthing of the AR&LW." Unpublished paper.

———. "The Making of the *Book of Common Worship* (1993)." In *To Glorify God: Essays on Modern Reformed Liturgy*, edited by Bryan D. Spinks and Ian R. Torrance, 31–53. Edinburgh: T&T Clark, 1999.

Dorn, Christopher. "A Liturgical Legacy from the Presbyterians: Introducing the Association for Reformed & Liturgical Worship." *New Mercersburg Review* 47 (Fall 2012): 16–34.

———. *The Lord's Supper in the Reformed Church in America: Tradition in Transition.* New York: Peter Lang, 2007.

Edwall, Pehr, Eric Hayman, and William D. Maxwell, eds. *Ways of Worship: The Report of a Theological Commission on Faith and Order.* London: SCM, 1951.

Faith and Order Paper No. 111. Geneva: World Council of Churches, 1982.

Geldhof, Joris. *Liturgy and Secularism.* Collegeville, MN: Liturgical Press, 2018.

Guardini, Romano. *The Spirit of the Liturgy.* Translated by Ada Lane. New York: Crossroad, 1998.

Pagels, Elaine. *Why Religion?* New York: HarperCollins, 2018.

Presbyterian Church (USA). *Book of Common Worship.* Louisville, KY: Westminster John Knox Press, 1993.

Ralston, Joshua. "Preaching Makes the Church: Recovering a Missing Ecclesial Mark." In *John Calvin's Ecclesiology: Ecumenical Perspectives*, edited by Gerard Mannion and Eduardus van der Borght, 125–42. London: T&T Clark, 2011.

Roorda, Garrett C. "Worship and Liturgy in the Reformed Church in America." In *A Companion to the Liturgy: A Guide to Worship in the Reformed Church*, edited by Garrett C. Roorda. New York: Half Moon, 1917.

Senn, Frank C. *Christian Liturgy, Catholic and Evangelical.* Minneapolis, MN: Augsburg Fortress, 1997.

Synod 2018 on Young People, the Faith and Vocational Discernment. Vatican City, 2018.

Tatlow, Tissington. "The World Conference on Faith and Order." In *A History of the Ecumenical Movement: 1517–1948.* Vol 1. Edited by Ruth Rouse and Stephen Charles Neill. Geneva: World Council of Churches, 1954.

Thurian, Max. *The Eucharistic Memorial.* Translated by J. G. Davies. Ecumenical Studies in Worship no. 7. London: Lutterworth, 1960.

Towns, Elmer. *Putting an End to Worship Wars.* Nashville, TN: Broadman and Holman, 1997.

Trueman, Carl. *Grace Alone: Salvation as a Gift of God.* Grand Rapids, MI: Zondervan, 2017.

White, James. *Christian Worship in North America: A Retrospective: 1955–1995.* Collegeville, MN: Liturgical Press, 1997.

Wilfong, Marsha M. "Reformed Worship in the United States of America." In *Christian Worship in Reformed Churches Past and Present*, edited by Lukas Vischer, 107–141. Grand Rapids, MI: Eerdmans, 2003.

York, Terry W. *America's Worship Wars.* Peabody, MA: Hendrickson, 2003.

VII:
WEEKLY COMMUNION: A CRITERION OF CATHOLICITY? A SHORT SURVEY OF HISTORICAL CLAIMS IN REFORMED DEBATES

Gregory Soderberg, LAMP Seminary

INTRODUCTION

Learning from the Past

WHEN Reformed churches have nothing better to squabble about, they often focus their polemical energies on the question of worship. In recent years, one of the leading liturgical issues vexing the Reformed is the frequency of communion. More churches are adopting the practice of weekly communion, and many traditionalist congregations have tended to move from quarterly to monthly celebration. Others, however, have resisted such moves in the name of traditional Reformed concerns for due preparation for communion.

This shift (and accompanying debate) in Reformed ranks parallels similar movements across the ecclesial spectrum in recent years.[1] However,

[1] Writing in 1984, Robert Taft remarked on the incredible changes in Catholic communion frequency: "The greatest and most successful liturgical reform in Catholic history is surely the movement for the restoration of frequent communion, sanctioned by Pius X in 1905. There are still pockets of resistance, and there

it raises particularly fundamental questions about the nature of the Reformed tradition. Does the Reformed tradition elevate the Word too far above the sacraments? What does it mean to partake of communion meaningfully? Advocates on both sides of the issue have critiqued and affirmed different aspects of the Reformed tradition. Indeed, perhaps surprisingly, the debate over communion frequency takes us to the heart of questions about religious identity, how to interpret the Bible, and what it means to be part of a religious tradition.

As is often the case in such debates, it can be instructive to see what history has to teach us. Contemporary debates over communion frequency are not as new as we might imagine; indeed, similar conversations have cropped up in the Reformed tradition since the early days of the Reformation. In this essay, I will take the reader on a brief tour through some of these debates, asking what issues and argumentative strategies have been foregrounded in these debates, and what liturgical practices and cultural contexts lurk in the background.[2]

Inasmuch as advocates of increased communion frequency often invoke concerns for "catholicity," I hope this investigation will offer a useful case study on what "Reformed catholicity" might mean in practice. Above all, I hope that these discussions about the past may help us to live and worship wisely in the present.

Overview of Sources

The Scottish liturgical historian William D. Maxwell claimed that, with the exception of Ulrich Zwingli, "it was the Reformers' repeatedly declared aim to restore the eucharist in its entirety and integrity as the principal act of

---

are abuses, but nothing can detract from this great pastoral victory that has turned around fifteen centuries of devotional history in fifty years." Robert Taft, "The Frequency of the Eucharist throughout History," in *Beyond East and West: Problems in Liturgical Understanding* (Washington, DC: Pastoral Press, 1984), 71, quoted in Joseph Dougherty, *From Altar-Throne to Table: The Campaign for Frequent Holy Communion in the Catholic Church*, ATLA Monograph Series, no. 50 (Lanham, MD: Scarecrow Press and American Theological Library Association, 2010), xxiii.

[2] The research for this essay is part of my doctoral research at the Vrije Universiteit of Amsterdam. Special thanks must go to Professors Wim Janse, Gijsbert van den Brink, and for the many fellow doctoral students who commented on this essay and forced me to dig deeper. Special thanks to Kees de Wildt for his analysis and probing questions.

Christian worship on the Lord's day."[3] Although Maxwell was clearly motivated by his desire for liturgical renewal in Reformed churches, there are indications that many sixteenth-century Reformers favored a pattern of frequent communion.[4] There is evidence that Luther advocated weekly communion, and Johannes Oecolampad(ius), Martin Bucer, and John Calvin certainly all valued and tried to implement (with various degrees of success) more frequent communion.[5] Calvin made some of the clearest statements on the desirability of weekly communion. In the *Institutes*, Calvin devotes four sections specifically to the question of communion frequency: "Now, to get rid of this great pile of ceremonies, the Supper could have been administered most becomingly if it were set before the church very often, and at least once a week."[6] In the next section, Calvin argues specifically against the late medieval practice of annual reception of communion, and presents his own construction of how communion patterns developed throughout history.[7]

---

[3] William D. Maxwell, *Concerning Worship* (London: Oxford University Press, 1948), 25.

[4] Of course, since late medieval oral reception of the Eucharist was typically an annual event, the entire Protestant movement could be seen as advocating frequent communion, because they wanted people to participate in communion more than once a year!

[5] I have collected evidence elsewhere on Oecolampadius, Bucer, and Calvin, especially in relation to their views on church discipline and communion frequency. See Gregory Soderberg, "Purity and Polity: Exploring Tensions in the Early Reformed Traditions," in *More Than Luther: The Reformation and the Rise of Pluralism in Europe*, ed. Karla Boersma and Herman J. Selderhuis (Göttingen, Germany: Vandenhoeck & Ruprecht GmbH & Co. KG, 2019), 241–56. Frank Senn helpfully points out that the Reformers "all subscribed to the view that there should be no masses without communicants. So, the frequency of reception of communion in the Reformation became tied to the frequency of celebration of Holy Communion." Frank C. Senn, *A Stewardship of the Mysteries* (New York: Paulist, 1999), 99. For Luther's perspective, see Kenneth W. Wieting, *The Blessings of Weekly Communion* (St. Louis, MO: Concordia, 2006). For more on the historical background of communion frequency in Luther and Lutheranism, see Herman Speelman, *Melanchthon and Calvin on Confession and Communion: Early Modern Protestant Penitential and Eucharistic Piety*, Refo500 Academic Studies, vol. 14 (Göttingen, Germany: Vandenhoeck & Ruprecht, 2016) and Senn, *Stewardship of the Mysteries*, 101–105.

[6] Calvin, *Institutes of the Christian Religion*, ed. John T. McNeill and Ford Lewis Battles, Library of Christian Classics, vols. 20–21 (London: SCM, 1960), IV 17, 43.

[7] Although the main text for the topic of communion frequency is the *Institutes*, as well as some of Calvin's shorter writings, we must remember that Calvin's theology

However, all of these foundational Reformers valued proper participation more than frequent participation; for that reason, they underlined the necessity of teaching their people correct doctrine about the Eucharist and enforcing moral and spiritual purity before communing. They were willing to compromise in frequency for the sake of proper participation.[8] Thus, it can be simplistic for proponents of weekly communion to argue that they are simply trying to fulfill John Calvin's wishes.

In their efforts to "reform" the church, the Reformers made strong claims about the "catholicity" of their efforts and ideals. They viewed the early church as a "norm" of apostolic purity. They appealed to the church fathers whenever they could, including in their arguments for more frequent communion.[9]

---

went through a process of development. Calvin's other writings do not seem to address the topic of communion frequency as much. Sixteenth-century writers were more interested (and angry) about what the Eucharist *was*—not *how often* it should be observed. Wim Janse summarizes the development in Calvin's thought: "Calvin's doctrine of the sacraments shows successively Zwinglianizing (1536–1537), Lutheranizing (1537–1548), spiritualizing (1549–1560), and again Lutheranizing (1561–1562) accents." Wim Janse, *The Calvin Handbook*, ed. Herman J. Selderhuis (Grand Rapids, MI: Eerdmans, 2009), 345. For more details see Wim Janse, "Calvin's Eucharistic Theology: Three Dogma-Historical Observations," in *Calvinus sacrarum literarum interpres: Papers of the International Congress on Calvin Research*, ed. Herman J. Selderhuis (Göttingen, Germany: Vandenhoeck & Ruprecht, 2008), 37–69. For Calvin's early development, and the possible influence of Philip Melanchthon, see Richard A. Muller, "From Zürich or from Wittenberg? An Examination of Calvin's Early Eucharistic Thought," *CTJ* 45 (2010): 243–55.

[8] Late in life, Calvin wrote to another pastor: "We are very pleased that the Supper is being celebrated every month [in your church], provided that this more frequent use does not produce carelessness. When a considerable part of the congregation stays away from communion, the church somehow becomes fragmented." John Calvin, *Calvin's Ecclesiastical Advice*, trans. Mary Beaty and Benjamin W. Farley (Louisville, KY: Westminster John Knox, 1991), 96, and *Consilium*, August 12, 1561, *OC* 10:213. Elsie Anne McKee comments: "Calvin was apparently cautioning this correspondent not to sacrifice unity for the sake of frequency. While he continued to protest against the small number of times the sacrament was offered, the pastor accepted this accommodation as preferable to a conflict which might destroy the church. He chose his battles and determined to take his stand on preparation and unity." Elsie Anne McKee, *The Pastoral Ministry and Worship in Calvin's Geneva* (Geneva: Droz, 2016), 256–57.

[9] For the Reformers' attitudes toward the history of the church, and Calvin's in particular, see Anthony Lane, *John Calvin: Student of the Church Fathers* (Grand Rapids, MI: Baker Books, 1999), Esther Chung-Kim, *Inventing Authority: The Use of the Church*

Movements advocating frequent communion flourished in the English and Scottish Protestant churches in the 1700s and 1800s. The rest of this essay will trace one aspect of the movements in these contexts—claims of "catholicity" within the polemics and pamphlets on both sides of the issue. A few English sources will be surveyed, followed by Scottish sources, and then contemporary voices arguing for frequent communion.

The selection of sources might seem rather arbitrary and limited. Besides the restrictions of space, I have limited my interaction to some of the sources in English that explicitly discuss the topic of communion frequency. I make no claims to present a comprehensive study; rather, I am focusing on the *context* of the communion frequency debate in American Reformed churches where, of course, English has been the main language. Additionally, much of American Protestant practice was framed in terms of the debates that erupted in the English Reformation and the ensuing political and ecclesiastical conflicts between Roman Catholics, Anglicans, Presbyterians, Puritans, Anabaptists, Baptists, and all of the various splinter groups that emerged. The conflicts and tensions between these groups were all transplanted to the Americas as Europeans emigrated.

Many Scottish sources in the 1700s and 1800s deal with communion frequency because of the particular history and circumstances of the Scottish Reformed church. The issue was hotly debated in Scotland, and this debate spilled over into the Americas.[10] I have tried to find sources on both sides of the issue (for and against frequent communion), but advocates for change are more likely to write and, well, advocate. The status quo needs less defending because it is familiar and, in the minds of many, upholds "tradition."

Since this essay focuses on the theme of "catholicity," I have further isolated elements in the source material that make *historical claims*. The question of catholicity is, in part, a question of how a church or a tradition understands itself in relation to the past. For many advocates of liturgical

---

Fathers in Reformation Debates over the Eucharist (Waco, TX: Baylor University Press, 2011), and Gregory Soderberg, "Ancient Discipline and Pristine Doctrine: Appeals to Antiquity in the Developing Reformation" (MA thesis, University of Pretoria, 2006). For some characteristic appeals to "catholicity" in relation to frequent communion, see Calvin, *Institutes* IV.xvii.43–49, which is replete with appeals to the "ancient" church and specific church fathers and councils.

[10] Sadly, the Dutch Reformed tradition must be left out of this essay, simply due to space considerations.

change, the question of catholicity is of fundamental importance. This essay will both focus on specific appeals to church history or historical figures and pay attention to how the authors in question understand their tradition in relation to the larger tradition of the Christian Church.

COMMUNION FREQUENCY IN THE ENGLISH REFORMATION CONTEXT

Scholarly interpretations of the upheavals in sixteenth-century England and beyond are only slightly less contentious than the original events themselves.[11] Although no heretics now burn at the stake, scholars offer conflicting readings of the immense changes in early modern English religion and society.[12] As Peter Marshall observes, "The English Reformation, once an exclusively mid-Tudor business, has become a 'long Reformation,' and a process, not an event."[13] The situation does not improve if we look later in

---

[11] "In a thirty-year period from the latter portion of Henry's reign to the opening of Elizabeth's no less than six varieties of Christian faith and practice successively prevailed in the English Church." William P. Haugaard, "From the Reformation to the Eighteenth Century," in *The Study of Anglicanism*, ed. Stephen Sykes and John Booty (London: SPCK/Fortress, 1988), 6. Euan Cameron comments on the uniquely contentious nature of the reform movements in England and Scotland: "England and Scotland were the most important, if not the only, kingdoms to adopt the south German or Swiss pattern of Reformation as their sole official faith. However, in both these countries the reformed settlement led to decades of controversy: not whether to allow Protestantism or not (as in France), nor yet what 'confession' to choose (as in the Palatinate), nor even (at first) how to keep doctrine pure (as in the intra-Lutheran feuds). The disputes were over how thoroughly 'reformed' the kingdoms were to be; how far the new creed could be enforced; and how the zealots' desire for thoroughness could be reconciled with a monarch's concern to keep the movement under rigid control. In both kingdoms the monarchy faced energetic voluntary Protestants striving to promote the 'confession' at the expense of the monarch's authority." Euan Cameron, *The European Reformation*, 2nd ed. (Oxford: Oxford University Press, 2012), 391.

[12] See Eamon Duffy, *Reformation Divided: Catholics, Protestants and the Conversion of England* (London: Bloomsbury, 2017), 1–15, for a provocative summary of Reformation studies in general, and of perspectives on the English Reformation(s) in particular. The latest landmark study is Peter Marshall, *Heretics and Believers: A History of the English Reformation* (New Haven, CT: Yale University Press, 2017).

[13] Peter Marshall, "England," in *Reformation and Early Modern Europe: A Guide to Research*, ed. David Whitford (Kirksville, MO: Truman State University Press, 2008), 250.

English church history. John Coffey and Paul Lim note that "defining Puritanism has become a favourite parlour game for early modern historians."[14] This section has two very modest and specific goals—to briefly survey the development of communion frequency in the English church as it changed and adapted under the influence of reformists of all stripes, and then to summarize some of the historical claims of authors who wrote specifically about communion frequency.

Whatever the exact nature of the development, and no matter what terms or labels we apply, it is undeniable that various parties and movements were competing for dominance in the English church. To understand some of the context of the debate about communion frequency, it is essential to understand the broad outlines of these parties and movements. What, then, can we know about communion frequency in the English Reformational era?

Like their counterparts on the Continent, the English Reformers were pursuing more frequent communion than was common in the medieval period. For the first generation of English Reformers, however, as on the Continent, the *nature* of the Eucharist was a more pressing issue than the frequency of its reception. Furthermore, Reformers pursued the goal of communion by the *entire church*—only later would weekly communion become a concern.

The English Reformers, like their peers on the Continent, stressed that the laity of the church had to be present to have a biblical communion service.[15] This call for congregational communion was part of their under-

---

[14] John Coffey and Paul C. H. Lim, eds., *The Cambridge Companion to Puritanism* (Cambridge: Cambridge University Press, 2008), 1. Regarding theological labels, Marshall writes: "The tenor of much current work here is to point to the fluidity of religious positions in what was effectively a pre-confessional age. For the first half of the sixteenth century at least, 'Protestant' is an anachronistic term, and 'evangelical' better conveys a sense both of the linkages to pre-Reformation culture and of the nondenominational character of a fissiparous movement for religious renewal." Marshall, "England," 255.

[15] "Here one can discern a common thread uniting the reforms of Luther, Calvin, Zwingli, and Cranmer: all four churchmen believed strongly that the communion of the people is, by dominical institution, absolutely integral to the eucharist—just as they believed that there can be no sacrament without the 'lively preaching' of the Word." Nathan D. Mitchell, "Reforms, Protestant and Catholic," in *The Oxford History of Christian Worship*, ed. Geoffrey Wainwright and Karen Westerfield Tucker (Oxford: Oxford University Press, 2006), 325. As Horton Davies puts it: "They believed that the Mass is essentially a Communion service and that where there is

standing of the "catholicity" of the church. They appealed to the example of the early church, and claimed that their practices accorded with it.[16] This raised the following question: how to educate, train, and teach their congregations about the essential nature of the Lord's Supper and dispel and discredit the teachings and practices of the Roman church? Though the Reformers may have believed in an ideal of weekly communion, they were quickly confronted by the monumental task of changing the minds and hearts of people who had worshipped in particular ways for generations.

The First Book of Common Prayer (1549) is ambiguous on the question of communion frequency.[17] It provides for communion to be observed on Sundays, but also on festivals, special days of devotion, and during the week. In analyzing Thomas Cranmer's Eucharistic theology, Horton Davies states that Cranmer desired weekly communion, but offers no specific proof.[18]

However, there was resistance to this ideal. Peter Newman Brooks summarizes the tumult, known as the "Western Uprising,"or "Prayer Book Rebellion," that followed the imposition of the 1549 Book of Common Prayer through the Act of Uniformity:

> From Devon and Cornwall came demands that the Privy Council reject the very idea of more frequent communion

---

no reception by the faithful there is no Communion." Horton Davies, *Worship and Theology in England*, vol. 1, *From Cranmer to Baxter and Fox, 1534–1690* (Grand Rapids, MI: Eerdmans, 1970, 1975; combined edition 1996), 141.

[16] Mitchell notes that "although in the first Book of Common Prayer (1549) Cranmer retained the traditional form of a eucharistic anaphora for use during 'The Supper of the Lorde, and The Holy Communion, Commonly Called the Masse,' he carefully noted in the rubrics that 'agreeable to the usage of the primitive Church,' the minister 'shall always have some [others] to communicate with him,' and that he 'shall forbeare to celebrate the Communion, except he have some that will communicate with him.'" Mitchell, "Reforms, Protestant and Catholic," 325, quoting *The First and Second Prayer Books of Edward VI*, intro. Douglas Harrison, Everyman's Library (London: Dent, 1910), 212.

[17] According to Senn, *Stewardship of the Mysteries*, 108. He references the Everyman Library version of the First Prayer Book, pg. 32ff.

[18] Comparing Zwingli and Cranmer, he writes: "Both had been Catholic priests, but Cranmer had a higher evaluation of the Eucharist, since he desired a weekly Communion, for the Eucharist was the pledge of the presence of Christ. For Zwingli it was sufficient to have a quarterly communion." Davies, *Worship and Theology in England*, 1:118. He repeats the same basic claim on p. 185.

> and permit the retention of sacramentals such as "holy bread and holy water," oblations for the living and the dead, as well as prayers for the departed.[19]

Despite the vicissitudes of changing monarchs, political upheavals, and outright persecutions, the reforming movement proceeded. James Turrell suggests that "after 1550 there was a broad consensus among English Evangelicals concerning two issues in eucharistic theology: eucharistic presence and the nature of sacrifice."[20] Even though various parties vied for control in the English church, they agreed on some common themes. Davies points out that "Anglicans and Puritans were agreed in much of their understanding of the sacraments. They denied Transubstantiation, Consubstantiation, and a naked Memorialism (the latter is often wrongly attributed to Zwingli). Both Anglicans and Puritans insisted that communion was the commemoration (not the repetition) of Christ's sacrifice, and that it was a means of grace, as also that it must be received in faith. The sacraments, in short, commemorate but also communicate the grace of God."[21] However, differences remained: "There were, of course, differences of emphasis in the understanding of Baptism and Communion. For Anglicans the sacraments were the chief means of grace, whereas for Puritans, in the tradition of Calvin, the sacraments were seals of grace, confirmations of a prevenient grace already fulfilled."[22] Furthermore, although Anglican teaching stressed the Eucharist as the "sacrament of incorporation into the body of Christ," the setting of the Eucharist highlighted individual reception. The Puritans, by receiving the Supper around tables, in a group, could claim to emphasize more clearly the *corporate* nature of the sacrament. Additionally, their "emphasis on the importance of Communion as a testimony or badge of Christian commitment also stressed the corporate aspect of the Communion service."[23]

---

[19] Peter Newman Brooks, "The Theology of Thomas Cranmer," in *The Cambridge Companion to Reformation Theology*, ed. David Bagchi and David C. Steinmetz, (Cambridge: Cambridge University Press, 2004), 157. See also Davies, *Worship and Theology in England*, 1:130–31.

[20] James F. Turrell, "Anglican Theologies of the Eucharist," in *A Companion to the Eucharist in the Reformation*, ed. Lee Palmer Wandel (Leiden: Brill, 2014), 139.

[21] Davies, *Worship and Theology in England*, 1:62.

[22] Davies, *Worship and Theology in England*, 1:62.

[23] Davies, *Worship and Theology in England*, 1:63.

The ideals of theologians and prayer books were just that—ideals. What we can know about the realities of daily parish life suggests that reception of communion continued to be infrequent. *Harrison's Description of England in Shakespeare's Youth* (1557) provides a contemporary description of a typical Sunday Anglican worship service "from the standpoint of a loyal Anglican with some Puritan, but no Separatist, tendencies."[24] He describes a lack of pastors for parishes. Printed homilies were read, with pastors preaching only four of their own sermons a year.[25]

After describing the Scripture readings and prayers, he moves to communion: "This being done, we proceed unto the communion, if any communicants be to receive the eucharist; if not we read the decalogue, epistle and gospel, with the Nicene creed (of some in derision called the dry communion), and then proceed unto an homily or sermon, which hath a psalm before and after it, and finally unto the baptism of such infants as on every Sabbath day (if occasion so require) are brought unto the churches; and thus is the forenoon bestowed."[26]

Based on the rubrics in the 1559 Book of Common Prayer and on the records of episcopal visitations and ecclesiastical directives, Davies suggests some other common features of liturgical life in Elizabethan England in Anglican churches. As on the Continent, the congregants were expected to notify the church authorities if they wished to partake of Holy Communion. The pastors were to warn their people of the dangers of partaking in an unworthy manner.[27] We see here the continuing Reformational concern to

---

[24] Davies, *Worship and Theology in England*, 1:215, quoting *Harrison's Description of England in Shakespeare's Youth*, ed. F. J. Furnivall, 2 vols., I, 32. The context and history of *Harrison's Description* is rather complicated. However, it is primary source material that formed part of *Holinshed's Chronicle*, from which Shakespeare drew much of his material for his historical plays. See https://sourcebooks.fordham.edu/mod/1577harrison-england.asp#Chapter%20I for a brief summary. The text of *Harrison's Description* can be found at https://archive.org/details/harrisonsdescri00harrgoog.

[25] Davies, *Worship and Theology in England*, 1:215.

[26] Davies, *Worship and Theology in England*, 1:215. I have modernized the spelling. Especially interesting here is Harrison's reference to a service without communion being a "dry communion." This is a recurring accusatory phrase in discussions of communion frequency in Protestant churches, but it is not clear to me where this phrase originated.

[27] "Those who intended to communicate at the Lord's Supper or Holy Communion were requested to give their names to the curate, whose duty it was to warn notoriously wicked persons and forbid them to approach the Lord's table until they

teach and enforce "proper" participation in the Eucharist. Also, in keeping with the Reformational principle that communion required the presence of communicants (not just the priest), the rubrics stipulated that there must be at least three other people to commune along with the priest. In cathedrals or churches affiliated with colleges, weekly communion was the prescribed minimum for the deacons and priests.[28] But the rubrics also displayed pastoral wisdom, realizing that both people and priests were wary of communing in an unworthy manner, and so required ordinary parishioners to receive communion just three times a year, with Easter communion being one of the required occasions.[29]

HISTORICAL ARGUMENTS IN ENGLISH COMMUNION POLEMICS IN THE SEVENTEENTH AND EIGHTEENTH CENTURIES

Davies identifies infrequent communion and poor participation in communion as key weaknesses of the Elizabethan church, judging by the complaints from bishops and other clergy.[30] The issue of communion frequency continued to play a role in debates about what healthy English church life should look like. The seventeenth and eighteenth centuries were a time of critical growth, development, and controversy in the English church.[31]

---

had openly declared their repentance and amendment, and to reject those unreconciled in a quarrel until penitent and prepared to return to amity." Davies, *Worship and Theology in England*, 1:216.

[28] Davies, *Worship and Theology in England*, 1:216.

[29] Davies, *Worship and Theology in England*, 1:217.

[30] "If there ever was an ideal of a weekly Communion, it soon lapsed. The second weakness of Anglican worship during this period was infrequent celebration of Communion. The most frequent directive from the bishops is that there must be 'sufficient number of celebrations for the parishioners to receive three times in the year at the last—Easter being one.' In larger city or county town parishes the ideal seems to have been that of a monthly communion. But there was a great abyss between the ideal and the real." Davies, *Worship and Theology in England*, 1:218, referencing W. H. Frere and W. M. Kennedy, *Visitation Articles and Injunctions*, 3 vols. (London: Longmans Green, 1910), 3:275, 307, 337.

[31] For good treatments of this period, see Davies, *Worship and Theology in England*, vol. 1, and Davies, *Worship and Theology in England*, vol. 2, *From Watts and Wesley to Martineau, 1690–1900* (Grand Rapids, MI: Eerdmans, 1961, 1962; combined edition 1996).

Some prominent churchmen argued for more frequent communion, and claims about "catholicity" formed part of their polemical arsenal.

William P. Haugaard summarizes the overall state of worship in the English church in this time period:

> In the established Church, eighteenth-century worship would be judged "dull" by most moderns. A small minority of clerics, known as "High Church," kept up weekly Eucharists and public daily Morning and Evening Prayer, but ceremonial enrichments of like-minded predecessors a century earlier had ceased to distinguish them from other clerics. In most English parishes, the Eucharist was celebrated quarterly, and parishioners attended lengthy Sunday morning services of Morning Prayer, Litany, Antecommunion, and sermon.[32]

However, some historians point out that we must be careful of judging the English church of the seventeenth and early eighteenth century exclusively through the interpretive grids of those who were critical of the church in that time.[33] The clergy in this period are often criticized for their supposed shortcomings. However, as Jeremy Gregory observes, "Part of the problem is knowing what yardstick should be used to view the work of the clergy. Negative judgments have often arisen from this being measured against anachronistic late nineteenth-century standards."[34] Instead, Gregory highlights the various ways in which the struggles of the English church in

---

[32] Haugaard, "From the Reformation to the Eighteenth Century," 23.

[33] Jeremy Gregory notes, "There has indeed been a curious harmony in the way in which High and Low Churchmen have been able to join in condemnation of the Church of the long eighteenth century. The period flanked by the Laudian and Oxford Movements has been castigated by High-Church writers for being a nadir in Church history, whilst evangelically minded historians have bemoaned the supposed lack of zeal within the established Church in the years between the Restoration and the Evangelical Revival." Jeremy Gregory, *Restoration, Reformation, and Reform, 1660–1828: Archbishops of Canterbury and Their Diocese*, Oxford Historical Monographs (Oxford: Clarendon, 2000), 2. So also Bryan D. Spinks: "The older view that the Church of England in the eighteenth century was entirely dreary, Latitudinarian, and in need of reform has been exposed by more recent scholarship as a distorted picture." "Anglicans and Dissenters," in *The Oxford History of Christian Worship*, ed. Geoffrey Wainwright and Karen Westerfield Tucker (Oxford: Oxford University Press, 2006), 517.

[34] Gregory, *Restoration, Reformation, and Reform*, 5.

the 1600s were, in part, the remaining effects of the "long Reformation" in England.[35] The issue of communion frequency was one aspect of the continuing struggle to understand what it meant to be a church following the teachings of both Scripture *and* a faithful Christian.

Communion frequency was a primary concern for many clergy in the Restoration church in England: "Time and again clergy reported that although most of their parishioners attended the usual Sunday services, they were very reluctant to attend communion."[36] Weekly communion was not practiced even in the cathedral at Canterbury until 1683.[37] In the region of Canterbury, "by the early eighteenth century it was also common for the sacrament to be celebrated once a month in the towns in the diocese, with an extra celebration at the major festivals."[38] Tracts arguing for more frequent communion, surveyed below, were part of a larger effort by Anglican leaders to help their parishioners understand the importance of Holy Communion.

Many at the time felt that communion was specially reserved for the wealthy or those with a superior social status. Archbishop Thomas Secker declared: "Some imagine that the sacrament belongs only to persons of advanced years, or great leisure, or high attainment in religion and it is a very

---

[35] Gregory advocates measuring "the clergy's pastoral work in relation to the period more conventionally labelled the Reformation era, for in certain respects the Reformation was seen as unfinished business in the century after 1660." His study presents "a rival interpretation to the usually limited chronological focus (often amounting to less than a century) which has ended consideration of the Reformation in 1559, 1603, or 1640, by emphasizing the long and drawn-out nature of the Reformation in England." He argues that "we will have an improved understanding of what the Reformation implied, and its broad social consequences, if we track its influence and ideology well in to the eighteenth and early nineteenth centuries, for arguably only then were the effects of the Reformation seen in the parishes (such as a professionalized clergy and a religiously educated laity)." Gregory, *Restoration, Reformation, and Reform*, 5.

[36] Gregory, *Restoration, Reformation, and Reform*, 263.

[37] "The Restoration clergy found the resumption of the sacrament one of their hardest tasks. Even at the cathedral it was not until 1683 that the Eucharist was given a regular weekly celebration, in response to pressure from [archbishop] Sancroft who wanted this to be the norm in every cathedral in the land as part of a campaign against the growth of dissent and immorality." Gregory, *Restoration, Reformation, and Reform*, 264.

[38] Gregory, *Restoration, Reformation, and Reform*, 265.

dangerous thing for common people to venture on."[39] Despite his opposition to this notion, however, the clergy may deserve some of the blame for it. Gregory argues that their stress on the importance of communion may have contributed to some people's trepidation and reluctance to participate.[40]

Furthermore, in reaction against James II's Declaration of Indulgence, prominent clergy in the Church of England pushed back, promoting robust pastoral and liturgical life.[41] In 1688, Archbishop Sancroft, although out of favor with his Roman Catholic sovereign, drew up plans for the renewal of Anglican spirituality. This plan included frequent communion, more diligent catechizing, and other essentials of effective pastoral care.[42] In the "Anglican revival" of the late 1600s and early 1700s, more frequent communion formed one part of a plan of resistance to the encroachments of the Roman Catholic Church, which was being encouraged and supported by James II.

---

[39] Gregory, *Restoration, Reformation, and Reform*, 267, quoting Secker, *Eight Charges Delivered to the Clergy of the Dioceses of Oxford and Canterbury* (1769), 60.

[40] "The clergy themselves were, perhaps, in part responsible for this situation. It was their insistence on the importance of the sacrament and their injunctions that parishioners should take it seriously which led sections of the parish to feel that they were unworthy to receive." Gregory, *Restoration, Reformation, and Reform*, 267. Gregory quotes George Berkeley, a longtime dean at Canterbury cathedral, on the dangers of receiving communion unworthily: "It will be equally fatal to you, never to receive the Holy Communion as to come to it unprepared." Gregory, *Restoration, Reformation, and Reform*, 267, quoting Berkeley, *Sermons*, ed. Eliza Berkeley (1709), 89–90.

[41] Brent S. Sirota, *The Christian Monitors: The Church of England and the Age of Benevolence, 1680–1730* (New Haven, CT: Yale University Press, 2014), 54–68.

[42] "Sancroft's notes in the summer of 1688 comprise a sweeping program of ecclesiastical reform. He would see weekly communions instituted throughout London, monthly communions in all market towns, and half that number in all other parishes; daily prayers in all major towns; 'the use of catechizing indispensably in all churches'; and constant residence of all incumbents in their cures. His list of 'things to be endeavored after' included frequent communions, constant catechizing, preparation for confirmation, 'amendment of life,' visitation of the sick, reformation of manners, vigilant warning 'against popery and popish emissaries,' 'charitable visits to Dissenters,' and prayer 'for a general union of all Protestant Churches.'" Sirota, *Christian Monitors*, 62–63. See also Sirota, *Christian Monitors*, 26–32, for a summary of the importance of frequent communion in the overall "Anglican revival" of the late 1600s, and especially in relation to the project of the moral and spiritual renewal of society.

This, then, was part of the context and background against which Edward Wettenhall, William Beveridge, and John Tillotson (among others) argued for the importance of more frequent communion.

John Tillotson (1630–1694)

John Tillotson's eventful life began with a father who was a staunch Puritan, included ongoing associations with the Presbyterian movement, and ended with his appointment as archbishop of Canterbury.[43] As one of the respected circle of London clergy who resisted the pro–Roman Catholic policies of James II, he helped to implement Archbishop Sancroft's overall project of Anglican renewal, which included an emphasis on more frequent communion.[44] His *A Persuasive to Frequent Communion in the Holy Sacrament of the Lord's Supper* (1683) was part of a burgeoning best-selling genre of pamphlets aiming to encourage more regular lay reception of communion.[45]

Expounding on 1 Corinthians 11:26–28, his purpose is to stir up his readers to receive communion more frequently.[46] However, he also reminds

[43] For biographical details see Peter Facer, "John Tillotson: A Reappraisal" (MA thesis, Durham University, 2000), 10–30. Davies has a rather dim overall assessment of Tillotson, especially as a preacher; see Davies, *Worship and Theology in England*, 1:181–84.

[44] See Sirota, *Christian Monitors*, ch. 1.

[45] John Spurr, *The Post-Reformation: Religion, Politics, and Society in Britain, 1603–1714* (London: Routledge, 2014), 283–84. For a short summary of Tillotson's overall Eucharistic theology, see Brian Douglas, *A Companion to Anglican Eucharistic Theology, Vol. 1: The Reformation to the 19th Century* (Leiden: Brill, 2012), 400–401. When Tillotson served as dean of Canterbury cathedral, he was responsible for implementing Archbishop Sancroft's ideals of more frequent communion. He wrote to Sancroft: "As to the Rubrick concerning communion in Cathedral Churches every Sunday, I moved it last week to the Chapter, and we resolved to begin it next month, which was as soon as we could engage a convenient number of our communicants, and I am very glad to see your Grace designs it throughout ye province, because it is plainly required, and will I doubt not be of good example, and of great efficiency to promote piety." Gregory, *Restoration, Reformation, and Reform*, 264.

[46] "My design in this Argument is, from the Consideration of the Nature of this Sacrament of the Lord's Supper, and of the perpetual Use of it to the end of the World, to awaken Men to a sense of their Duty, and the great Obligation which lies upon them to the more frequent receiving of it." John Tillotson, *A Persuasive to Frequent Communion in the Holy Sacrament of the Lord's Supper* (London: H. Hills, 1709), 2. He claims that people are hesitant to receive the Supper because of the "unwary Discourses of some concerning the Nature of this Sacrament, and the danger of

his readers of the danger of partaking of the Supper in an unworthy manner.[47] When he discusses the "Obligation" all Christians have to participate in the observance of the Lord's Supper, he admits that, although the words of 1 Corinthians 11 do not actually prescribe any set pattern of frequency, the practice of the early church seems to exemplify frequent communion. This is one of the few places where Tillotson appeals to the liturgical practices of the early church; nevertheless, he clearly considers it an important precedent worthy of imitation.[48]

Answering objections, Tillotson responds that it is a great danger to deliberately neglect the Lord's Supper. Additionally, it is better to come in an imperfect state, with at least a rudimentary amount of faith and repentance, than to not come at all. Rather than keeping people away from the Supper, an awareness of sinfulness should drive them to more frequent communion.[49] He also appeals again to the example of the "primitive Christians" as believers who received communion frequently and who had (he believes) a keen awareness of their own sinfulness.[50] Note that he appeals to the early church as a norm, although not as a norm on the same level as Scripture. He concludes, "But if we prepare our selves as well as we can, this is all God expects." God has given us a "Cup of salvation," and not a "Cup of deadly Poyson."[51] According to Tillotson, the only reasonable inference we can draw from the warnings about the danger of unworthy par-

---

receiving it unworthily." Tillotson, *Persuasive to Frequent Communion*, 2. My research thus far has not uncovered what these sources were.

[47] "And the same consideration should likewise make us afraid to receive this Sacrament unworthily, without due Preparation for it, and without worthy effects of it upon our Hearts and Lives." Tillotson, *Persuasive to Frequent Communion*, 4.

[48] He writes, "Yet if we compare these words of the Apostle with the usage and practice of Christians at that time, which was to Communicate in this holy Sacrament so often as they solemnly met together to worship God, they plainly suppose and recommend to us the frequent use of this Sacrament, or rather imply an obligation upon Christians to embrace all opportunities of receiving it." Tillotson, *Persuasive to Frequent Communion*, 5.

[49] "But the neglect of the Sacrament is not the way to prevent the sins; but, on the contrary, the constant receiving of it with the best preparation we can, is one of the most effectual means to prevent sin for the future, and to obtain the assistance of God's grace to that end." Tillotson, *Persuasive to Frequent Communion*, 9.

[50] Tillotson, *Persuasive to Frequent Communion*, 10.

[51] Tillotson, *Persuasive to Frequent Communion*, 10.

taking is a recommitment to pursuing repentance and proper preparation.[52]

He refuses to set down legalistic requirements about how much time communicants should devote to preparation. The "end is principally to be regarded," rather than specific rules for time spent and effort.[53] He also appeals again to the "primitive Christians," who appeared to celebrate the Supper weekly (even daily), and do not seem to have devoted much extra time to the business of preparation.[54] As he summarizes: "The great necessity that lies upon Men is to live as becomes Christians; and then they can never be absolutely unprepared."[55]

Edward Wettenhall (1636–1713)

Another prominent English churchman who argued for more frequent communion was Edward Wettenhall (1636–1713), bishop of Kilmore and

---

[52] Tillotson, *Persuasive to Frequent Communion*, 10.

[53] Tillotson, *Persuasive to Frequent Communion*, 15. Tillotson clarifies that he is speaking very carefully in this matter, because some "tender souls" believe that they should refrain from the Lord's Supper if they cannot spend sufficient time preparing for it. He counters, "Whether more or less time be allowed to this work, it matters not so much, as to make sure that the work be throughly [*sic*] done." Tillotson, *Persuasive to Frequent Communion*, 15. He also writes, "For when all is done, the best preparation for the Sacrament, is the general care and endeavour of a good life." Tillotson, *Persuasive to Frequent Communion*, 15.

[54] Tillotson, *Persuasive to Frequent Communion*, 15.

[55] Tillotson, *Persuasive to Frequent Communion*, 15. As he summarizes the matter of preparation: "The sum of what I have said is this, that supposing a person to be habitually prepared by a religious disposition of mind, and the general course of a good life, this most solemn actual preparation is not always necessary: And it is better when there is an opportunity to receive without it, than not to receive at all. But the greater part our actual preparation is, the better. For no man can examine himself too often, and understand the state of his soul too well, and exercise repentance, and renew the resolutions of a good life too frequently. And there is perhaps no fitter opportunity for the doing of all this, than when we approach the Lord's Table, there to commemorate His death, and to renew our covenant with Him, to live as becomes the Gospel." Tillotson, *Persuasive to Frequent Communion*, 16. He also exhorted his servants to frequent communion: "It is the most solemn institution of our religion; and, as we are Christians, we are obliged to the frequent receiving of it, and we cannot neglect it without a great contempt to our blessed Saviour and His religion." John Tillotson, "A Discourse to His Servants Concerning Receiving the Sacrament," in *Several Discourses on the Following Subjects* (London: Chiswell, 1704), 229.

Ardagh in the Kingdom of Ireland.[56] In his *Due Frequency of the Lord's Supper: Stated and Proved from Holy Scripture* (1703), Wettenhall, like many after him, laments the division surrounding the church's sacrament of unity.[57] Wettenhall reveals his ideal for assessing communion frequency when he asks, "How often must they Communicate, who would in some sort live up to the Primitive genuine Christianity?"[58] In section 3 ("The safest Resolution hereof from Scripture") Wettenhall, in a standard Protestant rhetorical trope, defines "primitive" as that which reflects the practice of the early, apostolic church. In eighteenth-century polemics, "primitive" was nearly synonymous with apostolic, so Wettenhall naturally appeals explicitly to Scripture. He claims that "the Rules which are safest ought to be taken from the express word of God (that is from some Text or Texts of Holy Scripture) and that the Holy Scripture alone gives us the true standard and measure of primitive and genuine Christianity."[59] He appeals first to Acts 20:7 and maintains that this verse shows the early Christian practice of gathering together for worship on the "Lord's Day," or the first day of the

[56] Appointing English clergy to posts in Ireland was part of a larger strategy for English dominance in Ireland. According to Cameron: "In 1541 Henry VIII of England converted the Lordship of Ireland into a kingdom, and attempted to bring the country under his control through a succession of Lords Deputy based in Dublin." Cameron, *European Reformation*, 399. William P. Haugaard summarizes the precarious state of the Church of Ireland: "Ireland's subservient Parliaments in the sixteenth century dutifully followed English Reformation precedents, but local struggles against England firmly linked the Reformation 'Church of Ireland' with foreign rule. A Gaelic Bible and Prayer Book were not forthcoming until the seventeenth century. Retaining all the ancient churches and foundations, the Church of Ireland retained only a small minority or Irish people, augmented by Protestant immigrants given land in the wake of the ruthless suppression of Irish support for James II in 1690." William P. Haugaard, "From the Reformation to the Eighteenth Century," in *The Study of Anglicanism*, ed. Stephen Sykes and John Booty (London: SPCK/Fortress, 1988), 21. See Christopher Fauske, *A Political Biography of William King* (London: Routledge, 2016), 67–68, for more on Wettenhall's role in the political tensions between the Church of Ireland and James II.

[57] He notes, "That very Institution, which our Lord designed for the stricktest Outward Bond of Christian Union, is become the great Apple of Contention in the Church of God: And there are, I think, more Controversies risen, touching this single Head of the Lord's Supper, than on any other one Common Place in the whole Body of Divinity." Edward Wettenhall, *Due Frequency of the Lord's Supper: Stated and Proved from Holy Scripture* (London: Benj. Tooke, 1703), 2.

[58] Wettenhall, *Due Frequency of the Lord's Supper*, 4.

[59] Wettenhall, *Due Frequency of the Lord's Supper*, 5.

week.[60] Additionally, it reveals that "breaking bread" was central to the activities of the assembly on that day, in memory of the resurrection of Jesus.[61] He also appeals to the *Apostolic Canons*, which prohibit fasting on the Lord's Day. The implication seems to be that if fasting was prohibited, then feasting (as in the Lord's Supper) was assumed and prescribed.[62]

When Wettenhall responds to the "Grand Objection" brought against frequent communion—lack of preparation—he distinguishes between the "Modern" methods of preparation for communion and "Primitive" preparation. "Modern" preparation takes the form of spending at least one entire day in devotions and prayers. Wettenhall affirms the value of such spiritual preparation, as long as it is done with "sincere intention," "prudence," and with "due understanding" of ourselves and our spiritual duties.[63] Wettenhall labels this pattern of consistent, serious spirituality, as "Primitive Preparation."[64] In "primitive" preparation, Wettenhall envisages a life marked by a "more strict Examination and Knowledge" of ourselves, and a "true Amendment and Change, both of Heart and Life, once for all."[65] If we pursue this, then we will live in a state of constant preparedness to participate in the Lord's Supper.

William Beveridge (1637–1708)

William Beveridge was bishop of St. Asaph and published many popular works.[66] He was greatly concerned to promote and preserve the "catholicity" of the church. His *Prolegomena in Συνοδικὸν sive Pandectae Canonum* (1672), a massive edition of the disciplinary actions taken by the ecumenical coun-

[60] Wettenhall, *Due Frequency of the Lord's Supper*, 19.

[61] Wettenhall, *Due Frequency of the Lord's Supper*, 19–20.

[62] Wettenhall, *Due Frequency of the Lord's Supper*, 20.

[63] Wettenhall, *Due Frequency of the Lord's Supper*, 35–37.

[64] Wettenhall, *Due Frequency of the Lord's Supper*, 41.

[65] Wettenhall, *Due Frequency of the Lord's Supper*, 40.

[66] "Beveridge, William", in *Dictionary of National Biography*, 63 vols. (London: Smith, Elder, 1885–1900), 447–48, https://en.wikisource.org/wiki/Beveridge,_William_(DNB00) , accessed April 4, 2018.

cils, long remained the standard work on the subject.[67] Beveridge had a strong interest in catholicity, as manifested in his monumental *Ecclesia Anglicana Ecclesia Catholica* (1840).[68]

While a priest in St. Peter's, Cornhill, he instituted a daily service and also weekly communion.[69] His work *The Great Necessity and Advantage of Frequent Communion: Designed to Revive Primitive Piety* was published posthumously in 1708.[70] The title demonstrates his desire to call the contemporary church back to a purer, "primitive" era. He makes several significant appeals to the past, which are really claims that frequent communion helps the church to be more *catholic*. Beveridge surveys the Scriptural evidence about the practices of the apostolic church and concludes that the first Christians "usually received this Holy Sacrament every Day in the Week, and constantly upon the Lord's Day."[71]

He then proceeds to a survey of early sources, quoting Tertullian, Pliny's famous letter to Emperor Trajan in which he describes early patterns of Christian worship, Justin Martyr, the Apostolic Canons, demonstrating their support of frequent communion, church discipline, and whole-church participation in the Eucharist.[72] He asserts that the first Christians were bet-

---

[67] See Henry R. Percival, "Bibliographical Introduction" in *NPNF*: *A Select Library of Nicene and Post-Nicene Fathers of the Christian Church*, ed. Philip Schaff and Henry Wace, vol. 14, 2 series (repr., Peabody, MA: Hendrickson, 1999), xvii.

[68] This was published posthumously as *Ecclesia Anglicana Ecclesia Catholica; or, The Doctrine of the Church of England Consonant to Scripture, Reason, and Fathers: in A Discourse Upon the Thirty-Nine Articles Agreed Upon in the Convocation Held at London MDLXII*, 2 vols. (Oxford: University Press, 1847). In this work, Beveridge endeavors to show that each of the Thirty-Nine Articles is supported by Scripture, "right reason," and early church history. As he expresses his appeal to "catholicity," he collected supporting statements from the "Fathers of the primitive church, that so we may see how though in many things we differ from others and from the present church of Rome, yet we recede not in any thing from the primitive and more unspotted church of Christ," x.

[69] "Beveridge, William," in *Dictionary of National Biography*, 447.

[70] It was published along with another tract on public prayer, under the combined title of *The Great Necessity of Publick Prayer, And Frequent Communion: Designed to Revive Primitive Piety* (London: E. P and R. Smith, 1708).

[71] Beveridge, *Great Necessity*, 16.

[72] "It was then, it seems, reckon'd a great Disorder and Confusion for any to go out of the Church, as they now commonly do, till the whole Service, of which the Communion was the principal part, was all over: And if any did so, they were judg'd unfit to come to Church or keep company with Christians any longer. This

ter prepared to face martyrdom by their frequent communion.[73] For Beveridge, the Eucharist was central to the worship of the early church.[74] He sees more frequent communion as a way to attain a greater degree of "catholicity."[75] Later generations felt a kinship with his project, and his works were republished in the Anglo-Catholic Library. Among the three writers surveyed here, Beveridge clearly displayed the greatest concern for "catholicity." Wettenhall and Tillotson show a lesser concern for following the example of the apostolic, or "primitive" church. This concern for continuity with the "primitive" church is also a theme in debates over communion frequency in the Scottish context.

HISTORICAL ARGUMENTS IN SCOTTISH REFORMED FREQUENCY DEBATES (CA. 1700–1800)

The Scottish Reformed church of the eighteenth and nineteenth centuries experienced a minor "pamphlet war" over communion frequency. Partly because of the tradition of infrequent mass communions spanning multiple days, the debate grew hotter and involved more voices than in England.[76]

---

was the Discipline of the Primitive and Apostolick Church. This was the Piety of the first Christians: And it continued in a great measure for some Ages, as might easily be shown." Beveridge, *Great Necessity*, 18–19.

[73] He writes that the Eucharist is "so nourishing, so strengthening, so refreshing to our Souls, that the Primitive Christians by the frequent use of it, were able and ready every Moment not only to do, but to suffer chearfully whatsoever could be laid upon them, even Death itself for the sake of Christ." Beveridge, *Great Necessity*, 41. See also p. 44.

[74] He writes that, "for some Ages" after the coming of Christ, Christians, "ne'er met together upon any Day in the Week, much less upon the Lord's Day, for the Publick Worship of God, but they all receiv'd this Holy Sacrament, as the Principal Business they met about, and the most proper Christian Service they could perform." Beveridge, *Great Necessity*, 43.

[75] "For as in all things else, so particularly in this, Our Church keeps close to the Pattern of the Apostolick and Primitive Church: When, as I have before observ'd, the Lord's Supper administered and receiv'd commonly every Day in the Week, but most constantly upon the Lord's Day." Beveridge, *Great Necessity*, 47.

[76] See William D. Maxwell, *A History of Worship in the Church of Scotland* (London: Oxford University Press, 1955), George B. Burnet, *The Holy Communion in the Reformed Church of Scotland 1560–1960* (Edinburgh: Oliver and Boyd, 1960), Duncan B. Forrester and Douglas M. Murray, eds., *Studies in the History of Worship in Scotland*

Regarding attitudes to church history, we find a clear difference of opinion. Pro-frequency authors appeal often to the early church, to the Reformers, and to other theological authorities. By contrast, what I term "careful" frequency authors dismiss appeals to history, maintaining that the past can prove almost anything. Instead, they seek to rely solely on biblical argumentation.

The controversy over frequent communion in the Scottish Reformed church can only be understood against the background of the unique historical development of the Scottish situation. While the *Scots Confession* (1560) does not prescribe communion frequency, the *First Book of Discipline* (1561) is more specific. It brought order to the emerging Scottish Protestant Church. In the "ninth head," which details matters of "policy" in the church, the authors distinguish between the "utterly necessary" and the "profitable." It is essential for a church to preach the Word, administer the sacraments correctly, pray together, instruct the ignorant, and correct the wayward. But the framers recognize latitude in how often these essentials will be observed. Regarding communion, the *First Book* states: "Four times in the year we think sufficient to the administration of the Lord's Table, which we desire to be distinct, that the superstition of times may be avoided so far as may be."[77] They acknowledge that churches may hold it more or less frequently, but they exhort pastors to "suppress superstition."[78] They also recommend that people be examined beforehand about their basic understanding of Christian orthodoxy.[79] Each "master of household" is ex-

---

(Edinburgh: T&T Clark, 1984), Leigh Eric Schmidt, *Holy Fairs: Scotland and the Making of American Revivalism* (Grand Rapids, MI: Eerdmans, 1989, 2nd ed., 2001).

[77] *The First Book of Discipline*, http://www.swrb.com/newslett/actualNLs/bod_ch03.htm#SEC09, accessed December 21, 2018.

[78] "We do not deny but that any several church, for reasonable causes, may change the time, and may minister ofter; but we study to suppress superstition." *The First Book of Discipline*, http://www.swrb.com/newslett/actualNLs/bod_ch03.htm#SEC09, accessed December 21, 2018.

[79] "All ministers must be admonished to be more careful to instruct the ignorant than ready to satisfy their appetites; and more sharp in examination than indulgent, in admitting to that great mystery such as are ignorant of the use and virtue of the same. And therefore we think that the administration of the Table ought never to be without that examination pass before, especially of those whose knowledge is suspect. We think that none are apt to be admitted to that mystery who cannot formally say the Lord's Prayer, the articles of the belief, and declare the sum of the

horted to diligently instruct his family, children, and servants in true doctrine, so they can participate in the Lord's Supper. The authors of the *First Book* clearly teach that understanding right doctrine is essential to participation in the Lord's Supper, and any head of a household who failed in the duty of instruction was to be disciplined and excommunicated.[80]

Another key text of the Scottish Reformation is the *Book of Common Order* (1562). John Knox brought the original text of what became known as the *Book of Common Order* from Geneva to Scotland. It had been the service book of the English congregation he pastored in Geneva, and it was a slightly modified English translation of Calvin's liturgy.[81] The preface to the *Book of Common Order* provides part of the interpretive grid that many subsequent authors would follow as they argued for frequent communion. Discussing the practice of singing psalms in worship, the preface states: "Seeing, therefore, God's Word does approve it, antiquity bears witness of it, and best Reformed churches have received the same, no man can reprove it, except he will condemn God's Word, despise antiquity, and utterly condemn the godly reformed churches."[82] This threefold rubric of Scripture, antiquity, and the "best" Reformed churches reappeared often in Scottish Protestant frequency polemics.

The section on the Lord's Supper notes the contemporary practice of monthly communion in the Scottish Reformed church, but it leaves the matter to the discretion of the churches.[83] Like the *First Book of Discipline*, it

---

law." *The First Book of Discipline*, http://www.swrb.com/newslett/actualNLs/bod_ch03.htm#SEC09, accessed December 21, 2018.

[80] *The First Book of Discipline*, http://www.swrb.com/newslett/actualNLs/bod_ch03.htm#SEC09, accessed December 21, 2018.

[81] Maxwell, *History of Worship*, 48.

[82] Jonathan Gibson and Mark Earngey, eds., *Reformation Worship: Liturgies from the Past for the Present* (Greensboro, NC: New Growth, 2018), 564–65. It states further: "For the end of our coming here is not to make protestation that we are upright or just in our lives, but on the contrary, we come to seek our life and perfection in Jesus Christ, acknowledging in the meantime, that we of ourselves are the children of wrath and damnation." Gibson and Earngey, *Reformation Worship*, 595.

[83] Introducing the words that were said before communion, it states: "The day when the Lord's Supper is ministered, which commonly is used once a month, or so often as the congregation shall think expedient, the minister says as follows …" Gibson and Earngey, *Reformation Worship*, 593, quoting from John Knox, *The forme of prayers and ministration of the Sacraments, &c. vsed in the Englishe Congregation at Geneua:*

stresses the importance of participating properly in communion. The minister's words introducing the Lord's Supper warn all flagrant sinners against the danger of "profaning" the "most holy table." However, the *Book of Common Order* quickly comforts anyone who thinks perfection is required: "And yet this I pronounce not to exclude any penitent person however grievous his sins have been before, so that he feels in his heart sincere repentance for the same; but only those who continue in sin without repentance."[84] At the end of the *Book of Common Order* a final note to the reader reiterates the importance of spiritual examination and preparation before partaking of the Lord's Supper.[85]

The Scottish Reformed church took seriously its mandate to teach and enforce moral discipline and theological orthodoxy in the church. This emphasis, however, discouraged more frequent communion because of the time needed to evaluate the doctrine and life of prospective communicants. Only those who understood communion correctly were allowed to partake.[86] The *First Book of Discipline* laid out a minimum standard of being able to recite the Lord's Prayer, the articles of the "Beleiff," and the Ten Commandments.[87] The standard rose subsequently—in 1570 the assembly mandated that children be examined by their ministers at ages nine, twelve, and fourteen. Other sessions passed similar injunctions, culminating in the general expectation that youths should come for their first communion around the ages of fifteen and sixteen.[88] Along with a regimen of catechizing for the youth, all the congregants were expected to participate in a "diet of examination" before communing.[89]

---

and approued, by the famous and godly learned man, Iohn Caluyn (Geneva: John Crespin, 1556).

[84] Gibson and Earngey, *Reformation Worship*, 594.

[85] "We, firstly, therefore, examine ourselves, according to St. Paul's rule, and prepare our minds, that we may be worthy partakers of such high mysteries." Gibson and Earngey, *Reformation Worship*, 600.

[86] Burnet, *Holy Communion*, 44–45.

[87] Burnet, *Holy Communion*, 45.

[88] Burnet, *Holy Communion*, 46.

[89] "But catechising alone was not held to be sufficient. There was a public and special examination of old and young in the church, usually a week or more before the Communion. This 'diet of examination' took the place of confession and absolution before Easter in the Old Church. It was an understood preliminary to every celebration for 'such as are to be admitted to the table of the Lord Jesus.' If it was

The corollary to teaching correct doctrine was enforcing correct moral behavior. The Scots Reformed transformed the medieval system of penance into a mechanism for dealing with individual and social sins. They did this through the establishment of elders in "sessions." The elders were responsible for the oversight of the community. As Margo Todd explains: "Traditional histories of the Scottish Reformation have too quickly claimed that the Reformers altogether discarded penance and the rites associated with it; in fact, the public confession of sin and demonstration of repentance not only remained in practice a rite of the kirk, it actually expanded to become arguably the central act of protestant worship in Scotland."[90] Ministers and elders visited their parishioners throughout the year, often testing their knowledge of various catechisms.[91] Before communions, which were usually biannual, the sessions would typically divide a parish into "quarters," and elders would be assigned to "examine" the people in different quarters. This examination period could take several weeks.[92]

The foundational documents of the Scottish Reformed church, and its ecclesial practices of catechesis and church discipline, clearly emphasize *intelligent participation* and *proper participation* in the Eucharist. If one could not say the Lord's Prayer and the "articles of the belief," they could not be admitted to the Supper. Pastors and church sessions routinely delayed the Lord's Supper so that people could be adequately catechized.[93] A key pattern emerges here: *in the Scots Reformed context, "intelligent reception" or "catechetical aptitude" seems to have institutionalized infrequent communion.* Although the Reformed churches of Scotland led their people to the communion table more frequently than the Roman Catholics, the emphasis on catechesis would preclude weekly communion, simply because of the requirements of the catechetical process.

As in England, the 1700s saw the birth of a movement in Scotland advocating for more frequent communion. Local synods recommended

---

found impossible to complete the examination of all the people before the appointed date, the Sacrament was delayed." Burnet, *Holy Communion*, 48.

[90] Margo Todd, *The Culture of Protestantism in Early Modern Scotland* (New Haven, CT: Yale University Press, 2002), 128–29. See also Burnet, *Holy Communion*, 52–63, for a description of the Scottish Reformed system of catechesis and penance.

[91] Todd, *Culture of Protestantism*, 74–75.

[92] Todd, *Culture of Protestantism*, 76–77.

[93] Burnet, *Holy Communion*, 48, 184–85.

more frequent communion, primarily to discourage the extended, and sometimes chaotic, mass communions or "communion fairs." They also encouraged "Winter Communions," since the colder weather would put a damper on the "sacramental fairs." However, these recommendations were largely ignored.[94] Many ministers wrote pamphlets criticizing traditional Scots Reformed communion practices and advocating more frequent communion. Many of these authors appealed to church history to buttress their arguments. In essence, they were making claims about "catholicity." They argued that the historical church, or the church in its more "pure" form, observed the Lord's Supper more frequently. The Scottish church did not celebrate communion frequently and so lacked catholicity. Of course, much of the debate turned on the exact nature of this norm, and some authors were not entirely consistent in their claims. But nevertheless, as used in their polemical pamphlets, many Scots Reformed authors made claims about the "catholic" practices of communion frequency and urged their churches to embrace frequent communion as a step toward being more faithful to the teachings of Scripture and to the practice of the Catholic (universal) Church.

BRIEF SURVEY OF SCOTTISH REFORMED AUTHORS AND THEIR USE OF HISTORICAL CLAIMS

John Willison (1680–1750) was one of the most popular and influential Scots Presbyterian writers of the 1700s. His *Sacramental Directory* (1716), *Sacramental Catechism* (1720), *Young Communicant's Catechism* (1734) and *Sacramental Meditations* (1747) were immensely popular on both sides of the Atlantic and helped shape the sacramental imagination of an entire generation of Scots Reformed communicants.[95] In his *Sacramental Catechism*, Willison recounts the spiritual fervor that many Scots experienced during communion seasons and exhorts his readers to reject "formalism" in their communion observance:

> Sacrament days in Scotland have been solemn and sealing days, yea of heaven to many; at such occasions many have had their trysts, and Bethel meetings with God, which they

[94] Schmidt, *Holy Fairs*, 185.

[95] Schmidt, *Holy Fairs*, 46.

> will never forget. O let us all then beware of formality creeping in among us in our preparations for, and partaking of this solemn ordinance; for then God will withdraw himself from our assemblies, and our solemn feasts will be melancholy and heartless.[96]

Although Willison advocates frequent communion, he reminds his readers of the necessity to participate in an *intentional* way: "O communicants, however frequently you approach the Lord's table, yet still make conscience of secret, serious, and solemn preparation for it; press always for a token of Christ's love at his table."[97] He gives various reasons for writing his catechism, and one of them stresses due preparation: "I aim to reprove and reform those who rush upon this ordinance in an ignorant or careless manner, without due preparation; by shewing who only have a right to this table, what is the nature and importance of the work of communicating, with the sin and danger of doing it unworthily."[98] Willison exemplifies both arguing for more frequent communion *and* stressing spiritual preparation.

Willison appeals to the early church: the "primitive" church celebrated communion weekly without a lessening of their devotion.[99] When Willison turns to history, he appeals to the Westminster Directory and to various Scottish ecclesial statements, which he claims express the "mind" of the Scots Reformed church in regard to frequency.[100] He does not make any further claims about the "catholicity" of frequent communion.[101]

---

[96] John Willison, *A Sacramental Catechism: Or, A Familiar Instructor for Young Communicants* (Glasgow, Scotland: David Niven, 1794), v–vi.

[97] Willison, *Sacramental Catechism*, vi.

[98] Willison, *Sacramental Catechism*, vii.

[99] "Let none think, that the frequency of the administration would expose to contempt; for I am sure no worthy communicant will undervalue this ordinance, because of a frequent repetition, but rather prize it the more. Did the primitive Christians bring it to contempt by partaking every Lord's day? Nay, was not their esteem of it much higher than those who dispense, or receive it only once in two years? I wish, the words of our dying Savior, and the acts of our General Assembly, relative to this matter, were more adverted to, by one and all of us." Willison, *Sacramental Catechism*, viii.

[100] Willison, *Sacramental Catechism*, vii–ix.

[101] "The mind of our church, with respect to this point, is well known; for our Directory for public worship declares 'that the Lord's supper is frequently to be celebrated.'" Willison, *Sacramental Catechism*, viii–ix.

Another important source is John Erskine's *An Attempt to Promote the Frequent Dispensing of the Lord's Supper.* Originally published in 1749, Erskine (1721–1803) sought to present a biblical, theological, and practical case for more frequent communion in the Scottish Reformed church. Erskine deals with historical claims much more than Willison. Like many Protestants, Erskine regarded the early church as a model to follow.[102] He appeals to various church fathers as well, no doubt reflecting his wide reading.[103] Based on this evidence, he claims that the church "of the first four centuries" observed frequent communion. In fact, the church in those times did not just celebrate communion every Sunday, but sometimes more often than that.[104] Erskine argues that the church declined from the early church's more "primitive purity," which was a standard Protestant polemic refrain.[105] As part of this polemic, he blames the "church of Rome" for introducing and establishing infrequent communion.[106] So the Roman Catholic practices that encouraged infrequent communion were, in essence, practices that detracted from the "catholicity" of the church.[107] For Erskine, and for other

---

[102] As he argues for the normative example of the early church: "The practice of those, who lived in the very infancy of the church, must deserve peculiar regard. … And as many of them sealed their doctrine with their blood, we cannot reasonably entertain the least suspicion, that they would dare knowingly to alter the least circumstance in the last, the dying command of their dear Master." John Erskine, *An Attempt to Promote the Frequent Dispensing of the Lord's Supper* (Kilmarnock, Scotland: J. Wilson, 1803), 24–25.

[103] Erskine, *Attempt to Promote*, 25–27. He draws evidence from Pliny's letter to Trajan, Justin Martyr, Tertullian, Minutius Felix, Cyprian, Victorinus of Petau, Basil of Caesarea, Ambrose, Jerome, and Augustine. On Erskine's reading habits and efforts to distribute sound theological literature, especially in the Americas and to his friend Jonathan Edwards, see Jonathan M. Yeager, *Enlightened Evangelicalism: The Life and Thought of John Erskine* (Oxford: Oxford University Press, 2011), ch. 8.

[104] "These passages are more than sufficient to prove, that during the first four centuries, the sacrament of the Lord's supper was dispensed even oftener than once a-week, and that it was a constant branch of the sanctification of the Sabbath." Erskine, *Attempt to Promote*, 27.

[105] Erskine, *Attempt to Promote*, 27–33.

[106] Erskine, *Attempt to Promote*, 32–33.

[107] The point is not to defend every detail of Erskine's historical analysis, or to extend his attacks against the Roman Catholic Church. The point is to summarize and categorize typical polemical strategies in regard to communion frequency. In the Protestant polemical writings of the 1700s, it was a standard tactic to blame Roman Catholic "corruption" or "degeneration" for the decline of communion frequency. It is ironic that similar debates about communion frequency would soon unfold in

Protestant polemical authors, the apostolic/early/primitive church was a normative standard, and they saw their efforts as attempts to return their church communities to this ideal.

But ideals were not just archeological relics. Erskine, and many other English Protestants, looked abroad for their inspiration about what it meant for a church to be fully "reformed," or "conformed" to the teachings of Scripture. Erskine ends his section dealing with historical claims by appealing to the example of the "purest Reformed churches" for additional support.[108] Apparently, some Scots worried that greater communion frequency would bring them closer to the Church of England (and of "Episcopacy"), but Erskine turns the question around—if the Church of England is obeying Christ more faithfully in this matter, is that a reason to disobey?[109] He maintains that "progress in reformation can never be expected, when the best things are rejected that other churches practice, under pretense of guarding against their corruptions."[110]

Thomas Randall (1710–1780) wrote *A Letter to a Minister from His Friend, Concerning Frequent Communion* at roughly the same time as John Erskine published his treatise arguing for weekly communion.[111] Randall argues that, since the Lord's Supper is a divinely appointed means of grace, it should be celebrated more frequently.[112]

---

the Roman Catholic communion. See Dougherty, *From Altar-Throne to Table*, for examples of the debate in the Catholic Church. There are significant opportunities here for truly ecumenical discussions.

[108] Erskine, *Attempt to Promote*, 33–37. He surveys the practices of the "Bohemian" churches (four times a year); the French Reformed (a national synod met in 1664—although their practice was currently quarterly communion, the synod desired greater frequency); the Lutherans (every Sunday); the Anglicans (obligated to commune at least three times a year); Calvin's Geneva; and the New England Congregational churches.

[109] He asks: "Is her observing an institution of Christ any reason for our neglecting it? The purest church on earth may learn something from churches less pure." Erskine, *Attempt to Promote*, 34.

[110] Erskine, *Attempt to Promote*, 35.

[111] Erskine, *Attempt to Promote*, 71–72. In fact, Erskine states that he has seen draft pages of Randall's work, quotes liberally from it, and commends it to his readers as well worth their examination. He notes that Randall provides "many new and ingenious proofs, that communicating as often as the primitive church did, is our duty," again highlighting the normative authority of the "primitive" church.

[112] The key point of Randall's essay is found in the "Advertisement" at the very end, in which he attempts to correct several mistakes and errors in the original

Randall begins his essay with a quote from the preface to the *Book of Common Order*, which previews his main points of argumentation. As noted above, the Preface refers to the Word of God, the witness of "antiquity," and the example of the "best reformed Churches." Like Erskine, Randall adopts the rhetorical structure of this preface, and so his treatise follows the same general pattern as Erskine's. Randall maintains that frequent communion prevailed for the first "four or five hundred Years after Christ" and blames the corruptions of the Roman Catholic Church for disrupting this ancient norm.[113] Erskine and Randall set the template for the Scottish pro-frequency authors who followed them, and when we compare a representative sample of these writers, a consistent pattern emerges:

> 1. Appeal to the first four or five hundred years of the early church as a time of purity, including citations of church fathers[114]
>
> 2. Description of the medieval (Roman Catholic) degeneration and corruption of the church[115]
>
> 3. Appeal to John Calvin and other Reformers on the issue of communion frequency[116]

---

printing. As he summarizes his key argument: "The Principle which all along is gone upon, is, That in using Means for Promoting Christ's Religion, the greatest Success and Blessing is to be expected upon such as are of Christ's Appointment; and the Right or Wrong of what is said in this Letter turns intirely on this Hinge." Thomas Randall, *A Letter to a Minister from His Friend, Concerning Frequent Communicating, Occasioned by the late Overture of the Synod of Glasgow and Air upon that Subject* (Glasgow, 1749), 89.

[113] Thomas Randall, *Letter to a Minister*, 17–27.

[114] Erskine, *Attempt to Promote*, 24–31; Randall, *Letter to a Minister*, 17–22; John Mason, *Letters on Frequent Communion, Addressed Particularly to the Members of the Associate-Reformed Church in North-America* (New York: T. & J. Swords, 1798), 37–38; John Brown, *An Apology for the More Frequent Administration of the Lord's Supper; with Answers to the Objections Urged against It* (Edinburgh: J. Ritchie, 1804), 6–7, 14; A Presbyterian, *View of the Mode of Celebrating the Lord's Supper, in the Presbyterian Churches in Scotland; in Reference to the Fast and Other Days—Infrequency of Celebration—and Accommodation and Addresses at the Tables. With an Appendix* (Edinburgh: John Wardlaw, 1830), 6–7.

[115] Erskine, *Attempt to Promote*, 31–33; Randall, *Letter to a Minister*, 22–28; Mason, *Letters on Frequent Communion*, 38–41; Brown, *Apology*, 9–12; A Presbyterian, *View of the Mode*, 6–7.

4. Appeal to the "purest Reformed churches" and their communion practices[117]

5. Appeal to the early Scots Reformed church and its ecclesial standards[118]

In response to this, "careful frequency" authors largely chose *not* to respond to historical claims, viewing them as dangerous territory. For John Thomson and John Anderson, appeals to church history are spurious and possibly dangerous.[119] Thomson's acerbic response to John Mason's *Letters on Frequent Communion* (1798) undercuts Mason's appeals to church history by claiming that the early church quickly fell away from apostolic purity (interpreting the seven letters to the churches in Revelation as describing periods of church history).[120] Additionally, he notes that Roman Catholic apologists also argue from antiquity, so Thomson remains skeptical of any appeals to church history.[121] Thomson's reply to Mason's appeal to the "best Reformed churches" ignores Mason's examples, focusing instead on

---

[116] Erskine, *Attempt to Promote*, 36, 56–59; Randall, *Letter to a Minister*, 29–31; Mason, *Letters on Frequent Communion*, 41–43; Brown, *Apology*, 7, 14; A Presbyterian, *View of the Mode*, 33–36.

[117] Erskine, *Attempt to Promote*, 33–37; Randall, *Letter to a Minister*, 28–33; Mason, *Letters on Frequent Communion*, 44; Brown, *Apology*, 7–9; A Presbyterian, *View of the Mode*, 7. The "best (or purest) Reformed churches" are a somewhat nebulous grouping. Not every author refers to all of the same churches, but the following is a collective grouping of the churches that are appealed to under the heading of "best," or "purest" Reformed churches: the Bohemian churches, French Protestants, Lutherans, the Church of England, churches in New England, Calvin's Geneva, Zwinglian churches, English Dissenters, Dutch church, English Puritans, and Presbyterians.

[118] Erskine, *Attempt to Promote*, 37–42; Randall, *Letter to a Minister*, 33–35; Mason, *Letters on Frequent Communion*, 44–46; Brown, *Apology*, 18–19; A Presbyterian, *View of the Mode*, 8–10.

[119] John Thomson wrote, contra John Mason's appeals to early church history: "I will not follow you, Sir, into the thorny copse of antiquity, and therefore shall not examine your cloud of witnesses. You and I have both appealed our cause to our blessed Lord and his apostles; and by these let us stand or fall." John Thomson, *Letters Addressed to Rev. John Mason, M.A. of New-York, in Answer to his Letters on Frequent Communion* (Glasgow: William Paton, 1799), 22–23.

[120] Thomson, *Letters Addressed to Rev. John Mason*, 22–24.

[121] "The church of Rome, Sir, lays mighty stress in many particulars upon your celebrated antiquity." Thomson, *Letters Addressed to Rev. John Mason*, 23.

Mason's use of the Belgic Confession. Thomson rightly notes Mason quotes the Belgic Confession out of context to condemn current Scots Reformed practice.[122] Thomson also chides Mason for appealing to antiquity when Mason himself elsewhere stated that antiquity is a "wretched" standard for truth.[123] Thomson states that he will only appeal to "scriptural antiquity."[124] He also dismisses Mason's appeal to various authors who support more frequent communion with his own appeal to current opinion. Thomson maintains that the "greater number of respectable ministers" are content to follow the current Scots Reformed communion practices.[125]

John Anderson also responded to Mason's *Letters on Frequent Communion* and, like John Thomson, focuses on biblical argumentation rather than history.[126] He does quote noted Protestant authorities (such as Herman Witsius, James Durham, John Owen, and Thomas Boston), but the core of his case for "careful" frequency centers on principles and application from the Old Testament. As with Thomson, Anderson warns against appealing to the early church because "corruptions" crept in so quickly. Anderson

---

122 Thomson, *Letters Addressed to Rev. John Mason*, 33–34. Thomson reacts to Mason quoting the Belgic Confession's condemnation of extrabiblical rites and ceremonies (ch. 35). Thomson asks if Mason seriously believes that the Reformers and the confessional documents he appeals to would condemn the "precious exercise of spiritual fasting" in preparation for the Lord's Supper. Mason is using anti–Roman Catholic polemics to condemn something totally outside their purview.

123 "Your plea from antiquity, I have already noticed; and you, Sir, have formally given it up, by saying, in page 106, 'Antiquity is a wretched standard of truth; the abominations of Popery are more ancient than they by several centuries'; meaning sacramental fasts &c." Thomson, *Letters Addressed to Rev. John Mason*, 38.

124 "Let us then, Sir, be restricted to scriptural antiquity, in the frequency of communion, and then your principal objections to fasts and thanksgivings will be removed." Thomson, *Letters Addressed to Rev. John Mason*, 39.

125 Thomson, *Letters Addressed to Rev. John Mason*, 40.

126 John Anderson, *Communion Seasons Defended: A Scriptural Response to John M. Mason's "Letters on Frequent Communion,"* ed. Sean McDonald (Grand Rapids, MI: Torwood, 2013). Originally published as "Of Humiliation-days before, and Thanksgiving-days after, the Administration of the Lord's Supper," in John Anderson, *Vindicae Cantus Dominici. In two parts: I. A discourse of the duty of singing the book of Psalms? in solemn worship. II. A vindication of the doctrine taught in the preceding discourse. With an appendix: containing essays and observations on various subjects* (Philadelphia: David Hogan, 1800), 301–21. The larger work was a defense of singing only biblical psalms in worship, and the appendix contains miscellaneous essays on themes related to worship in Reformed churches. The original text can be viewed at https://archive.org/details/vcantusd00ande/page/n17.

maintains that Scripture should be the only norm.[127] He recognizes Calvin desired more frequent communion but cautions against pursuing frequency at the expense of solemnity.[128] In fact, Anderson claims he does not want to dissuade anyone from pursuing more frequent "Scriptural" communion—communion preceded by fasting and thorough spiritual preparation. In essence, he claims to be a realist and reminds his readers how hard it is to commune both frequently and with the correct spiritual attitude.[129]

Appeals to church history also figure prominently when pro-frequency authors respond to objections. John Brown of Haddington (1722–1787) anticipates and answers the objection that the early church and Reformation were times of greater spiritual vitality, and, therefore, of more frequent communion. However, in times of spiritual decay (nearly all the writers on both sides of the issue agree that they are living in such a time), communion should be less frequent. In reply, Brown asks whether a garden should be watered less when it is dry or when it is wet?[130] Thomson employs a similar tactic, attempting to relativize the early church's communion practices. For Thomson, it is apparent that the early church lived in a state of fervent expectation for the second coming of Christ and were suffering persecution. Both of these historical circumstances justified frequent communion; however, Thomson contends the church no longer lives in such circumstances.[131] Additionally, he believes that Matthew 9:15 suggests that the church would later live in a time of "fasting."

---

[127] "With regard to the example of Christians after the apostolic age, recorded in human writings; the early corruptions that seem to have obtained, especially in the administration of the sacraments, admonish us to be cautious of imitating them in any one thing in which we cannot see that they had Scriptural warrant." Anderson, *Communion Seasons Defended*, 24.

[128] "It is hoped, that the candid reader will not view the considerations now offered, as intended to discourage any attempt towards bringing about a greater frequency of the Scriptural practice of communicating. With what ardor does the great author just now mentioned speak on this subject in his *Institutes*? The lukewarmness of church members in this matter can never be sufficiently lamented." Anderson, *Communion Seasons Defended*, 23.

[129] "Such a frequency of communicating, as some plead for, seems to be inconsistent with our preserving due impressions of the solemnity of this ordinance." Anderson, *Communion Seasons Defended*, 22.

[130] Brown, *Apology*, 21–22. Erskine deals with the same objection in *Attempt to Promote*, 48–49.

[131] Thomson, *Letters Addressed to Rev. John Mason*, 22.

The Scottish Reformed church tradition exemplifies some of the most intense debates about communion frequency in Protestantism. Thus, their polemics can help navigate this issue in the present. Authors on both sides of the issue tend to argue in certain ways, favoring particular texts and traditions. "Careful" frequency authors tended to favor the Old Testament, and they valued the tradition of mass communions that had developed in Scotland. These mass communions were preceded by days of sermons and serious soul-searching. Because of this buildup, and because of the infrequency of the events, many Scottish Protestants had almost mystical experiences at these extended "communion seasons."[132] These authors steered away from interacting with church history, viewing "antiquity" as the provenance of Rome and as too entangled with corrupt teachings and practices to prove anything with certainty.

In contrast, Scots Reformed authors who argued for more frequent communion focused on New Testament imperatives and the witness of the first "five centuries" of the undivided "primitive" church, before the corruptions of the Roman church crept in. They also appealed to the examples of the "best reformed" churches and theological heavyweights like John Calvin. Although they may not have used the term "catholicity," something like it was clearly in their minds. They argued for more frequent communion because they believed it accorded with the normative tradition of Scripture as exemplified in early church history. The trajectories of the communion frequency debates in both the English and Scottish Protestant churches continue to shape discussions in the present.

SURVEYING THE CONTEMPORARY LANDSCAPE

Recent decades have witnessed a growing interest in and practice of weekly communion in American Reformed churches. This applies not only to mainline churches, such as the Presbyterian Church USA, but also to more conservative denominations like the Presbyterian Church in America and some Baptist congregations. Both theologically mainstream and conserva-

---

132 See Schmidt, *Holy Fairs*, especially ch. 3, for numerous firsthand accounts of heightened spiritual experiences at the mass communions. See also J. Todd Billings, *Remembrance, Communion, and Hope: Rediscovering the Gospel at the Lord's Table* (Grand Rapids, MI: Eerdmans, 2018), 45–56, for astute theological and psychological commentary on the Scottish Reformed "communion fairs."

tive authors argue for the implementation of more frequent communion.[133] Some sources of this contemporary movement are found in the international liturgical renewal movement of the early twentieth century.[134] Among others, William Maxwell's liturgical scholarship energized this movement early in the twentieth century (at least in historically Reformed circles). He claimed, "The eucharist perfectly expresses the essential Christian belief. No other act of Christian worship can so completely show forth the fullness of the Faith."[135] Additionally, in 1965, the Swiss liturgist and ecumenist J. J. von Allmen agreed with Karl Barth that "worship without the Eucharist is a theological impossibility," going on to compare removing the Eucharist from worship to an amputation.[136] Clearly, for writers at the height of the ecumenical and liturgical movement, Reformed worship without the Eucharist was crippled.

More recent writers concur. Nicholas Wolterstorff maintains that this is the most "fundamental" issue in Reformed liturgics today. He asks, "Does it serve the health of the church to celebrate the Lord's Supper infrequently?" and then proceeds to pit Calvin against Zwingli on this mat-

---

[133] Two quotations, from both sides of the spectrum, illustrate the shared emphasis. First, a conservative author: "Worship is incomplete, thus, if it does not lead to the Lord's Supper ... Otherwise, worship becomes nothing more than songs plus a lecture, degenerating into Pelagian praise and legalistic instruction." James B. Jordan, *Theses on Worship: Notes toward the Reformation of Worship* (Niceville, FL: Transfiguration Press, 1994; 2nd ed. 1998), 87. Secondly, authors from a mainline denominational perspective: "Our infrequent celebration of the Lord's Supper suggests that we do not believe it is essential for the Christian life and is, perhaps, an 'add-on' to worship. The integrity of the relationship between Word and sacrament has dissolved into an emphasis upon the Word over against the sacrament." Howard L. Rice and James C. Huffstutler, *Reformed Worship* (Louisville, KY: Geneva, 2001), 76.

[134] See "Liturgical Movement, The," in *The New Westminster Dictionary of Liturgy & Worship*, ed. Paul Bradshaw (Louisville, KY: Westminster John Knox, 2002), 283–89. Although the liturgical movement began in Roman Catholic circles, there does seem to have been a broader movement to return to the "sources" of each respective tradition, whether Catholic, various types of Protestant, or even Orthodox. Advocacy for more frequent communion appears to have been a common concern in many of the scholars, theologians, and pastors in this broader movement.

[135] William D. Maxwell, *Concerning Worship* (London: Oxford University Press, 1948) 3–4.

[136] J. J. von Allmen, *Worship: Its Theology and Practice* (New York: Oxford University Press, 1965), 155–56. Von Allmen quotes from Barth, but only gives the attribution, "Dogmatics," without further specification.

ter.[137] Leonard Vander Zee adds, "We need every nourishment that God provides, and to miss the meal not only snubs his gracious hospitality but creates spiritual anorexics."[138] Michael Horton has argued cogently that "one's view of the efficacy of Communion largely determines one's views concerning frequency. It is not surprising that a more Zwinglian approach, which emphasizes the subjectivity of the believer and the community, will yield a more introspective Eucharistic practice. To the extent that the Supper is considered a divine gift, its frequent celebration is likely to be affirmed."[139]

One of the most articulate and original proponents of weekly communion is Peter J. Leithart.[140] In *The End of Protestantism*, Leithart argues that churches must, if they are to obey Jesus' prayer in John 17, repent of their denominationalism and tribalism, and seek to grow past the confessional boundaries of Protestant, Roman Catholic, and Orthodox. His ideal of "reformational Catholicism" includes a vision of the future church as "sacramental and liturgical," and one key facet of this is the restoration of weekly communion:

> In the churches of the future, the Lord's Supper will be a weekly event, the climax of every worship service. It will become so habitual that a worship service without the Supper will feel unfinished and worshippers will feel cheated.[141]

---

[137] Nicholas Wolterstorff, "The Reformed Liturgy," in *Major Themes in the Reformed Tradition*, ed. Donald McKim (Grand Rapids, MI: Eerdmans, 1992), 295, quoted in Leonard J. Vander Zee, *Christ, Baptism, and the Lord's Supper: Recovering the Sacraments for Evangelical Worship* (Downers Grove, IL: InterVarsity, 2004), 232.

[138] Vander Zee, *Christ, Baptism, and the Lord's Supper*, 232.

[139] Michael Horton, *People and Place: A Covenant Ecclesiology* (Louisville, KY: Westminster John Knox, 2008), 137.

[140] At this point, I should acknowledge my profound intellectual and personal debt to Leithart, whose courses in theology and literature I took as an undergraduate exemplified a rare combination of erudition and humility. His works continue to influence me in countless ways.

[141] Peter Leithart, *The End of Protestantism* (Grand Rapids, MI: Brazos, 2016), 31. He continues: "Every member of the church will be allowed to come to the table, no matter how old, young, or mentally infirm. Christians in the future church will develop a eucharistic form of piety. They will recognize that they commune most deeply with Jesus through the Spirit at the Lord's table, and they will come to see the table as the center of their communion with one another as well Eucharistic

Leithart makes it clear that weekly communion should be at the center of a healthy, biblical church.[142] He acknowledges that this will be a dramatic and disruptive change for many Protestant churches that are "deeply, un-Protestantly anti-sacramental and anti-liturgical." However, he cautions against pastors rushing into instituting weekly communion without patient teaching and instruction. If they force liturgical changes, however healthy or biblical, they are "abusing their office."[143]

Leithart also acknowledges weekly communion will have profound effects on a church. This stems from his belief that the Eucharist is an efficacious means of grace. Just as the preached Word of God is powerful and affects its hearers, so the Lord's Supper affects those who commune:

> In the Supper, we commune in the body and blood of Jesus. Those who do so unworthily get sick and some die, Paul says (1 Cor. 11). When Jesus comes to dinner every week, things happen. Strange things: Hidden sin gets exposed. Smoldering marriages explode. The church may split. All hell breaks loose, and the pastor and other leaders have to pick up the pieces and try to reassemble them. This is not a mistake or an accident. It is the effect of Jesus coming near every week to inspect and judge, as well as to feed.[144]

Writers like James Jordan, Leithart, and those influenced by them seem to see weekly communion as one of God's ordained ways to deal with sin. They do not stress preparation for communion (which is especially ob-

---

piety will spread out in daily eucharistic practice, in lives of joy and thanksgiving, in lives of hospitality and sharing."

[142] "Liturgically, at a minimum, the pastor or pastors should strive to institute a weekly celebration of the Lord's Supper in the church. They need to convince the members that this is a good and right thing to do, but it is less important to understand the Supper than to obey Jesus's command to 'do this.'" Leithart, *End of Protestantism*, 180.

[143] Leithart, *End of Protestantism*, 180.

[144] Leithart, *End of Protestantism*, 180–81. He explains: "When we set the table each week as a memorial of Jesus, we are calling on God to remember his covenant, his covenant jealousy as well as his covenant faithfulness. In the love feast of the Eucharist, we call on God to come near in all his jealous faithfulness, his faithful jealousy, which are but two sides of the passion that is the inner life of the Triune God."

vious in their advocacy for infant communion). Rather, they urge us to simply "do this," like Jesus commanded His disciples, and then expect God to work through His appointed means. Frequent partaking of communion tends to eclipse faithful preparation for communion.

However, this does not mean that Leithart and other contemporary advocates of frequent communion want to relax all restrictions surrounding the Eucharist. Although he believes that the "table is at the center of Christian worship" and "must be open to all his disciples," Leithart also argues that "flagrant, impenitent sinners must be rebuked and if necessary cut off from the Lord's table."[145] Furthermore, pastors should not allow excommunicates from another church to partake at their own church. They must respect the discipline of other churches.[146] This is one practical outworking of Leithart's stress on churches in a locality forming relationships and working together, seeking a *localized catholicity*. Leithart's emphasis on "catholicity" also extends to the issue of interecclesiastical communion. He states that, although various Christian traditions understand the Eucharist in divergent ways, "differences of theological formulation should not separate members of the corporate body from a common share in Christ's eucharistic body."[147] He applies the warnings of 1 Corinthians 11:29 to this issue—"Those who exclude other believers because of different beliefs about the Supper *fail* to discern the body."[148]

CONCLUSION

To return to our initial research questions, we can conclude that the writers from the past surveyed here did not make frequent communion a "mark" of the church or equate it with "catholicity." They did, however, point to the pattern of frequent communion in the apostolic and patristic eras as a standard. By that standard, they judged their own times deficient. However, writers like Edward Wettenhall, who argued stridently for frequent communion, also devoted many pages to warning people to prepare themselves thoroughly and to approach the Lord's Supper with a serious and earnest

---

[145] Leithart, *End of Protestantism*, 181.

[146] Leithart, *End of Protestantism*, 181.

[147] Leithart, *End of Protestantism*, 181.

[148] Leithart, *End of Protestantism*, 181.

sense of the magnitude of what they were doing. This aspect of preparation is missing in some current discussions of frequent communion. Contemporary advocates risk departing from what we might tentatively call a "catholic consensus" of the church regarding the necessity of spiritual preparation for the Eucharist. Although there are undoubtedly many salutary aspects of how some contemporary Reformed churches and theologians are pursuing, practicing, or advocating weekly communion, it would be nearsighted to ignore the wisdom of the past regarding proper observance of the Lord's Supper. What might it mean for us to prepare more fully for this rite—the sign of union and communion broken by schism?

In the pendulum swing of history, most branches of the Christian Church (Reformed, Orthodox, and Roman Catholic) have neglected frequency and stressed preparation for communion. As various branches of the church move toward more frequent communion, would a more integrated and balanced pattern of frequency and preparation help the church at large to attain a great degree of catholicity? This preliminary study suggests that it might, and that there are rich resources to continue to mine in our shared theological and historical heritage.

BIBLIOGRAPHY

Primary Sources

The First Book of Discipline (1560). Still Waters Revival Books. http://www.swrb.com/newslett/actualNLs/bod_ch03.htm#SEC09, accessed December 21, 2018.

A Presbyterian, View of the Mode of Celebrating the Lord's Supper, in the Presbyterian Churches in Scotland; in Reference to the Fast and Other Days—Infrequency of Celebration—and Accommodation and Addresses at the Tables. With an Appendix. Edinburgh: John Wardlaw, 1830.

Anderson, John. *Vindicae Cantus Dominici. In two parts: I. A discourse of the duty of singing the book of Psalms? in solemn worship. II. A vindication of the doctrine taught in the preceding discourse. With an appendix: containing essays and observations on various subjects*. Philadelphia: David Hogan, 1800.

———. *Communion Seasons Defended: A Scriptural Response to John M. Mason's "Letters on Frequent Communion."* Edited by Sean McDonald. Grand Rapids, MI: Torwood, 2013.

Berkeley, George. *Sermons*. Edited by Eliza Berkeley. 1709.

Beveridge, William. *The Great Necessity of Publick Prayer, And Frequent Communion: Designed to Revive Primitive Piety*. London: E. P and R. Smith, 1708.

———. *Ecclesia Anglicana Ecclesia Catholica; or, The Doctrine of the Church of England Consonant to Scripture, Reason, and Fathers: in A Discourse Upon the Thirty-Nine Articles Agreed Upon in the Convocation Held at London MDLXII*. 2 vols. Oxford: OUP, 1847.

Brown, John. *An Apology for the More Frequent Administration of the Lord's Supper; with Answers to the Objections Urged against It*. Edinburgh: J. Ritchie, 1804.

Calvin, John. *Institutes of the Christian Religion*. Edited and translated by John T. McNeill and Ford Lewis Battles. Library of Christian Classics. Vols. 20–21. London: SCM, 1960.

——. *Calvin's Ecclesiastical Advice.* Edited and translated by Mary Beaty and Benjamin W. Farley. Louisville, KY: Westminster John Knox, 1991.

Erskine, John. *An Attempt to Promote the Frequent Dispensing of the Lord's Supper.* Kilmarnock, Scotland: J. Wilson, 1803.

Harrison, William. *Harrison's Description of England in Shakespeare's Youth.* Edited by F. J. Furnivall. London: N. Trubner, 1877-81.

Knox, John. *The forme of prayers and ministration of the Sacraments, &c. vsed in the Englishe Congregation at Geneua: and approued, by the famous and godly learned man, Iohn Caluyn.* Geneva: John Crespin, 1556.

Mason, John. *Letters on Frequent Communion, Addressed Particularly to the Members of the Associate-Reformed Church in North-America.* New York: T. & J. Swords, 1798.

Randall, Thomas. *A Letter to a Minister from His Friend, Concerning Frequent Communicating, Occasioned by the late Overture of the Synod of Glasgow and Air upon that Subject.* Glasgow: Booksellers in Glasgow and Edinburgh, 1749.

Secker, Thomas. *Eight Charges Delivered to the Clergy of the Dioceses of Oxford and Canterbury.* London, J. and F. Rivington, 1769.

Thomson, John. *Letters Addressed to Rev. John Mason, M.A. of New-York, in Answer to his Letters on Frequent Communion.* Glasgow, Scotland: William Paton, 1799.

Tillotson, John. *A Persuasive to Frequent Communion in the Holy Sacrament of the Lord's Supper.* London: H. Hills, 1709.

——. "A Discourse to His Servants Concerning Receiving the Sacrament." In *Several Discourses on the Following Subjects.* London: Chiswell, 1704.

Wettenhall, Edward. *Due Frequency of the Lord's Supper: Stated and Proved from Holy Scripture.* London: Benj. Tooke, 1703.

Willison, John. *A Sacramental Catechism: Or, A Familiar Instructor for Young Communicants.* Glasgow: David Niven, 1794.

Secondary Sources

"Beveridge, William." In *Dictionary of National Biography*, 63 vols. London: Smith, Elder, 1885–1900, 447–48.

Billings, J. Todd. *Remembrance, Communion, and Hope: Rediscovering the Gospel at the Lord's Table.* Grand Rapids, MI: Eerdmans, 2018.

Bradshaw, Paul, ed. *The New Westminster Dictionary of Liturgy & Worship.* Louisville, KY: Westminster John Knox, 2002.

Bagchi, David and David C. Steinmetz, eds. *The Cambridge Companion to Reformation Theology.* Cambridge: Cambridge University Press, 2004.

Burnet, George B. *The Holy Communion in the Reformed Church of Scotland 1560–1960.* Edinburgh: Oliver and Boyd, 1960.

Cameron, Euan. *The European Reformation.* 2nd ed. Oxford: Oxford University Press, 2012.

Chung-Kim, Esther. *Inventing Authority: The Use of the Church Fathers in Reformation Debates over the Eucharist.* Waco, TX: Baylor University Press, 2011.

Coffey, John and Paul C. H. Lim, eds. *The Cambridge Companion to Puritanism.* Cambridge: Cambridge University Press, 2008.

Davies, Horton. *Worship and Theology in England.* Vol. 1, *From Cranmer to Baxter and Fox, 1534–1690.* 1970. Combined Edition, Grand Rapids, MI: Eerdmans, 1996.

——. *Worship and Theology in England.* Vol. 2, *From Watts and Wesley to Martineau, 1690–1900.* 1961. Combined edition, Grand Rapids, MI: Eerdmans, 1996.

Duffy, Eamon. *Reformation Divided: Catholics, Protestants and the Conversion of England.* London: Bloomsbury, 2017.

Dougherty, Joseph. *From Altar-Throne to Table: The Campaign for Frequent Holy Communion in the Catholic Church.* ATLA Monograph Series. No. 50. Lanham, MD: Scarecrow Press and American Theological Library Association, 2010.

Douglas, Brian. *A Companion to Anglican Eucharistic Theology.* Vol. 1, *The Reformation to the 19th Century.* Leiden: Brill, 2012.

Facer, Peter. "John Tillotson: A Reappraisal." MA thesis, Durham University, 2000.

Fauske, Christopher. *A Political Biography of William King.* London: Routledge, 2016.

Forrester, Duncan B. and Douglas M. Murray, eds. *Studies in the History of Worship in Scotland.* Edinburgh: T&T Clark, 1984.

Frere, W.H., and W. M. Kennedy. *Visitation Articles and Injunctions.* 3 vols. London: Longmans Green, 1910.

Gibson, Jonathan and Mark Earngey, eds. *Reformation Worship: Liturgies from the Past for the Present.* Greensboro, NC: New Growth, 2018.

Gregory, James. *Restoration, Reformation, and Reform, 1660–1828: Archbishops of Canterbury and Their Diocese.* Oxford Historical Monographs. Oxford: Clarendon, 2000.

Haugaard, William P. "From the Reformation to the Eighteenth Century." In *The Study of Anglicanism*, edited by Stephen Sykes and John Booty, 3-29. London: SPCK/Fortress, 1988.

Horton, Michael. *People and Place: A Covenant Ecclesiology.* Louisville, KY: Westminster John Knox, 2008.

Janse, Wim. "Calvin's Eucharistic Theology: Three Dogma-Historical Observations." In *Calvinus sacrarum literarum interpres: Papers of the International Congress on Calvin Research.* Edited by Herman J. Selderhuis. Göttingen, Germany: Vandenhoeck & Ruprecht, 2008.

——. *The Calvin Handbook.* Edited by Herman J. Selderhuis. Grand Rapids, MI: Eerdmans, 2009.

Jordan, James B. *Theses on Worship: Notes toward the Reformation of Worship.* 1994. 2nd ed. Niceville, FL: Transfiguration Press, 1998.

Lane, Anthony. *John Calvin: Student of the Church Fathers.* Grand Rapids, MI: Baker Books, 1999.

Leithart, Peter. *The End of Protestantism.* Grand Rapids, MI: Brazos, 2016.

Marshall, Peter. *Heretics and Believers: A History of the English Reformation.* New Haven, CT: Yale University Press, 2017.

———. "England." In *Reformation and Early Modern Europe: A Guide to Research*, edited by David Whitford. Kirksville, MO: Truman State University Press, 2008.

Maxwell, William D. *A History of Worship in the Church of Scotland.* London: Oxford University Press, 1955.

———. *Concerning Worship.* London: Oxford University Press, 1948.

McKee, Elsie Anne. *The Pastoral Ministry and Worship in Calvin's Geneva.* Geneva: Droz, 2016.

McKim, Donald, ed. *Major Themes in the Reformed Tradition.* Grand Rapids, MI: Eerdmans, 1992.

Muller, Richard A. "From Zürich or from Wittenberg? An Examination of Calvin's Early Eucharistic Thought." *Calvin Theological Journal* 45 (2010): 243–55.

Percival, Henry R. "Bibliographical Introduction." In *NPNF: A Select Library of Nicene and Post-Nicene Fathers of the Christian Church,* edited by Philip Schaff and Henry Wace. Vol. 14, 2 series. Reprinted, Peabody, MA: Hendrickson, 1999.

Rice, Howard L. and James C. Huffstutler. *Reformed Worship.* Louisville, KY: Geneva, 2001.

Schmidt, Leigh Eric. *Holy Fairs: Scotland and the Making of American Revivalism.* 2nd ed. Grand Rapids, MI: Eerdmans, 2001.

Senn, Frank C. *A Stewardship of the Mysteries.* New York: Paulist, 1999.

Sirota, Brent S. *The Christian Monitors: The Church of England and the Age of Benevolence, 1680–1730.* New Haven, CT: Yale University Press, 2014.

Soderberg, Gregory. "Ancient Discipline and Pristine Doctrine: Appeals to Antiquity in the Developing Reformation." MA thesis, University of Pretoria, 2006.

———. "Purity and Polity: Exploring Tensions in the Early Reformed Traditions." In *More Than Luther: The Reformation and the Rise of Pluralism in Europe*, edited by Karla Boersma and Herman J. Selderhuis, 241-56. Göttingen, Germany: Vandenhoeck & Ruprecht, 2019.

Speelman, Herman. *Melanchthon and Calvin on Confession and Communion: Early*

Modern Protestant Penitential and Eucharistic Piety. Vol. 14 of *Reformation 500 Academic Studies*. Göttingen, Germany: Vandenhoeck & Ruprecht, 2016.

Spurr, John. *The Post-Reformation: Religion, Politics, and Society in Britain, 1603–1714*. London: Routledge, 2014.

Taft, Robert. "The Frequency of the Eucharist throughout History." In *Beyond East and West: Problems in Liturgical Understanding*, 87-110. Washington, DC: Pastoral Press, 1984.

Von Allmen, J.J. *Worship: Its Theology and Practice*. New York: Oxford University Press, 1965.

Wainwright, Geoffrey and Karen Westerfield Tucker, ed. *The Oxford History of Christian Worship*. Oxford: Oxford University Press, 2006.

Wieting, Kenneth W. *The Blessings of Weekly Communion*. St. Louis, MO: Concordia, 2006.

Todd, Margo. *The Culture of Protestantism in Early Modern Scotland*. New Haven, CT: Yale University Press, 2002.

Yeager, Jonathan M. *Enlightened Evangelicalism: The Life and Thought of John Erskine*. Oxford: Oxford University Press, 2011.

Wandel, Lee Palmer, ed. *A Companion to the Eucharist in the Reformation*. Leiden: Brill, 2014.

Vander Zee, Leonard J. *Christ, Baptism, and the Lord's Supper: Recovering the Sacraments for Evangelical Worship*. Downers Grove, IL: InterVarsity, 2004.

ABOUT THE DAVENANT INSTITUTE

The Davenant Institute aims to retrieve the riches of classical Protestantism in order to renew and build up the contemporary church: building networks of friendship and collaboration among evangelical scholars committed to Protestant resourcement, publishing resources old and new, and offering training and discipleship for Christians thirsting after wisdom.

We are a nonprofit organization supported by your tax-deductible gifts. Learn more about us, and donate, at www.davenantinstitute.org.

Made in the USA
Monee, IL
19 April 2023

32089444R00125